INTERPRETING AMERICAN JEWISH HISTORY AT MUSEUMS AND HISTORIC SITES

INTERPRETING HISTORY

About the Series

The American Association for State and Local History publishes the *Interpreting History* series in order to provide expert, in-depth guidance in interpretation for history professionals at museums and historic sites. The books are intended to help practitioners expand their interpretation to be more inclusive of the range of American history.

Books in this series help readers quickly learn about the questions surrounding a specific topic, introduce them to the challenges of interpreting this part of history, and highlight best practice examples of how interpretation has been done by different organizations.

They enable institutions to place their interpretative efforts into a larger context, despite each having a specific and often localized mission. These books serve as quick references to practical considerations, further research, and historical information.

Titles in the Series

INTERPRETING AMERICAN JEWISH HISTORY AT MUSEUMS AND HISTORIC SITES

AVI Y. DECTER

ROWMAN & LITTLEFIELD
Lanham • Boulder • New York • London

Published by Rowman & Littlefield
A wholly owned subsidary of The Rowman & Littlefield Publishing Group, Inc.
4501 Forbes Boulevard, Suite 200, Lanham, Maryland 20706
www.rowman.com

Unit A, Whitacre Mews, 26-34 Stannary Street, London SE11 4AB

British Library Cataloguing in Publication Information Available

Library of Congress Cataloging-in-Publication Data
Names: Decter, Avi Y., author.
Title: Interpreting American Jewish history at museums and historic sites / Avi Y. Decter.
Description: Lanham ; Boulder ; New York ; London : Rowman & Littlefield, [2016] | Series: Interpreting history ; no. 11 | Includes bibliographical references and index.
Identifiers: LCCN 2016037464 (print) | LCCN 2016038218 (ebook) | ISBN 9781442264342 (cloth : alk. paper) | ISBN 9781442264359 (pbk. : alk. paper) | ISBN 9781442264366 (Electronic)
Subjects: LCSH: Jews—United States—Museums. | Jews—United States—Historiography. | Jews—United States—Material culture. | Museums—Social aspects—United States. | Public history—United States. | United States—Ethnic relations.
Classification: LCC E184.33 .D43 2016 (print) | LCC E184.33 (ebook) | DDC 973/.04924—dc23
LC record available at https://lccn.loc.gov/2016037464

♾️™ The paper used in this publication meets the minimum requirements of American National Standard for Information Sciences—Permanence of Paper for Printed Library Materials, ANSI/NISO Z39.48-1992.

Printed in the United States of America

DEDICATION

This book is dedicated to the memory of three friends, public history leaders and superb interpreters all:

Adina Back
Kim Louagie
Gail Stern

Lovely and pleasant in their lives,
even in their death they were not divided;
They were swifter than eagles,
They were stronger than lions.

2 SAMUEL 1:23

CONTENTS

LIST OF ILLUSTRATIONS

ACKNOWLEDGMENTS

THIS BOOK began with an inquiry from Bob Beatty on behalf of the American Association for State and Local History; his subsequent encouragement and good counsel have been instrumental in realizing our shared intentions. Two leaders of the Council of American Jewish Museums, Melissa Martens Yaverbaum and Gabe Goldstein, also encouraged me to take on the project and commented on the work in progress. I am also indebted to my co-authors, Zev Eleff, Josh Furman, and Grace Cohen Grossman, who picked up the challenge, wrote three of the chapters, and commented on various drafts.

My wife, Naomi, is my first reader and best critic. I offer her my gratitude and love. I also want to thank a number of friends who were kind enough to read one or more chapters and offer editorial comment: Rick Beard, David M. Cohen, Juliana Ochs Dweck, Benjamin Filene, Barbara Franco, Anita Kassof, Herb Levine, Richard Rabinowitz, Laura Schiavo, Steve Whitfield, and Ken Yellis. Thanks, also, to my editors at Rowman & Littlefield, Charles Harmon, Kathleen O'Brien, and Karen Ackermann for their guidance and editorial advice. Of course, none of these colleagues is responsible for any errors or deficiencies in the final text.

Many people were helpful in providing background information for the case studies and in reviewing them for accuracy: Barry Kessler, Independent Curator; Annie Polland, Lower East Side Tenement Museum; Jerome Thompson, The State Historical Society of Iowa; Sandi Yoder, Iowa Jewish Historical Society; Stacy Lieberman, Autry National Center; Karen S. Wilson, University of California, Los Angeles; Timothy Wroten and Marilyn Kushner, New-York Historical Society; Linda Levin, Joint Distribution Committee; David Gradwohl, Iowa State University; Sara Ann Elk and Sean Kelley, Eastern State Penitentiary; Selina Rojas, Philadelphia Folklore Project; Laura Weber, Minnesota Historical Society; Allison Termine and Alex Mann, Chrysler Museum of Art; Stace Treat, Diane Carroll, Mindy Besaw, and Valerie Sallis, Crystal Bridges Museum of American Art; John Coffey, North Carolina Museum of Art; Elizabeth Farish and Madeline J. Beihl, Strawbery Banke Museum; Eric Goldstein, Emory University; Therese Feicht, Lori Weber, Brigid Novak, and Donna Fried, Geauga County Public Library; Paul Needham, Princeton University Library; Edna Nahshon, Jewish Theological Seminary; Rabbi David Ross Senter, Elissa Kaplan Senter, and state senator Elaine Krasker, Portsmouth,

New Hampshire; Olivia Mahoney, Chicago History Museum; Sarah Henry and Lauren Robinson, Museum of the City of New York; David Lehman, The New School; Robin Waites, Historic Columbia; Jan Longone and Avery Robinson, University of Michigan; and Stacy Lieberman and Maren Dougherty, Autry Museum of the American West.

Thanks also to the individuals and institutions who provided images and releases for the book: Bruce Nielsen and Arthur Kiron, Katz Center for Advanced Jewish Studies, University of Pennsylvania; Judy Margles and Anne LeVant Prahl, Oregon Jewish Museum and Center for Holocaust Education; Claire Pingel and Sasha Makuka, National Museum of American Jewish History; David Kraemer and Sharon Liberman-Mintz, Jewish Theological Seminary; Lawrence Bell, Arizona Jewish Historical Society; Maria A. Day, Maryland State Archives; Morris Vogel and Jon Pace, Lower East Side Tenement Museum; Holi Levish, Oviatt Library, California State University, Northridge; Becky Laughner, Museum of the City of New York; Jeremy Munro, Crystal Bridges Museum of American Art; Marvin Pinkert, Deborah Cardin, and Rachel Kassman, Jewish Museum of Maryland; John Coffey and Karen Malinofski, North Carolina Museum of Art; Carole Counihan, Millersville University; Sean Kelley, Eastern State Penitentiary; Madeline J. Biehl, Strawbery Banke Museum; and Olivia Mahoney, Chicago History Museum.

Avi Decter, Philadelphia

CHAPTER 1

APPROACHING AMERICAN
JEWISH HISTORY

An Introduction

The history of the Jews must forever be interesting. The modern part
of it is at the same time so little generally known that any ray of light
on the subject has its value. —James Madison

[American Jewish history] is the story of how people *shaped* events:
establishing and maintaining communities, responding to challenges,
working for change. —Jonathan Sarna

JEWS ARE part and parcel of American history. They are present throughout four
centuries of American life and they are found everywhere, from colonial port cities
to frontier outposts, from commercial and manufacturing centers to rural villages,
and from metropolitan regions to intentional communities. From the early seventeenth
century to the present, the story of American Jews has been one of immigration, adjustment, and accomplishment, sometimes in the face of prejudice and discrimination. This
story embraces minority-majority relations, evolving norms and traditions, and ongoing
conversations about community and culture, identity, and meaning. And because Jews
have long been America's most persistent and most prominent non-Christian minority,
the narrative of Jewish participation in the nation's history helps to illuminate what it
means to be an American, as will be seen in the five thematic chapters that follow this
introduction. Indeed, American Jews have been defined by their American experiences
and, in turn, have helped to define them as well.[1]

Figure 1.1 Portrait of Abigaill Levy Franks (1696-1756), c. 1735, attributed to Gerardus Duyckinck I. She was the wife of New York merchant and community leader Jacob Franks. Her letters to their son Naphtali in London provide a unique picture of Jewish family life in early America.

Photography by Dwight Primiano. Courtesy of Crystal Bridges Museum of American Art, Bentonville, Arkansas. 2005.8.

A Challenging History

Despite their presence in communities both large and small across the continent, especially in the most recent 150 years, Jews and their histories are frequently unknown or misunderstood, even in their own locales. Gaps in knowledge among public history professionals lead all too frequently to the unfortunate omission of the American Jewish experience in projects undertaken by history museums and historic sites. There are exceptions. Several leading museums of art and culture devote significant attention to American Jewish history, especially as it pertains to literature, music, theater, film, and the fine arts. Jewish museums, of course, place Jewish history and culture at the top of their agendas, as do many Holocaust centers and museums (though mainly focused on European Jewry). But of the thousands of history institutions in the United States and Canada, relatively few have essayed substantial interpretive projects on the culture and experience of American Jews.

Why is this so? One obvious explanation is that Jewish history is complicated. American Jewry ranges over a wide variety of ethnic, cultural, and religious identities, practices, and experiences, reflecting American diversity and pluralism. Another reason for neglecting the history of American Jews is lack of familiarity. The overwhelming majority of staff and volunteers at history museums and other historical organizations know little or nothing about Judaism or Jewish history, and what may be known is often anecdotal, inaccurate, or stereotypical. (The same, by the way, might be said of some American Jews!) Another factor is that the documents, objects, images, and oral histories of American Jewry are concentrated in relatively few collections—many under Jewish auspices—or remain in private possession. Since most historical organizations have their hands full dealing with subjects with which they are familiar and in which their own collections are deeply invested, it is little wonder that engaging American Jewish history in all its variety and complexity falls pretty far down the list of institutional priorities.

Even in those organizations with an interest in doing Jewish history, risk can be an inhibiting factor. Tackling the history of any unfamiliar ethnic, religious, or cultural group is fraught with challenges and pitfalls. As more than one practitioner put it, "We're afraid to get it wrong." Interpreters of African American history are familiar with this trope; so are those who want to see and hear more stories about gays and lesbians, the poor, and other disenfranchised or marginalized populations. This leads directly to suppression. Not necessarily suppression by intent, but suppression in practice. If history organizations balk at dealing with historical topics for fear of "getting it wrong," then they end up erasing that topic from the historical record—and taking whole populations and communities out of our shared history.

Neglect of American Jewish history by so many history organizations also plays into the dubious notion that America was and is (or should be) "a Christian nation." That the overwhelming majority of the American people have been and remain self-identified as Christian is certainly true. But the idea that the nation's founders were Christian and that Christianity is embedded in our national character—if not actually in the U.S. Constitution—persists among many Americans. In this construct, American Jews have been the most obvious and most enduring exception. For those individuals, communities, and institutions who view Jews as "the Other," there is little rationale for devoting time and attention to fellow citizens whose presence from the colonial period to the present undercuts the logic of "a Christian nation," and even less so given Jews' long-time advocacy for equal rights and religious liberty under the Constitution. Addressing Jewish history directly can provide a valuable corrective to attitudes uninflected by historical understanding.[2]

The principal theme of this book is that doing American Jewish history is no less and no more challenging than tackling the history of any other ethnic, religious, or cultural group (although it must be said that American Jewish history involves all three strands—ethnicity, religion, and culture). It is the object of this book to make this seemingly daunting task easier and more productive. We begin by looking at some of the many factors that make Jewish life and culture complicated—and fascinating.

Dispersed and Diverse

One of the critical factors that make American Jewish history complex is the sheer diversity of American Jews. In one sense, Jews are an ethnos, a people. But they are also a nation whose people trace their origins to a wide variety of Old World countries. In fact, the Hebrews, the people of ancient Israel, were themselves something of a mixed multitude: the Hebrew Bible emphasizes their tribal character and distinctive characteristics, and also speak of "the strangers who reside in your midst." Even in ancient times, intermarriages and conversions leavened the mix: in the eponymous Book of Ruth, a Moabite woman declares to her mother-in-law Naomi, "Your people will be my people and your God shall be my God."

Then came exile and diaspora. The conquest of the Kingdom of Israel in 722 BCE and the dispersion of its people, the fabled Ten Lost Tribes, foreshadowed the collapse of the Kingdom of Judah 125 years later, when many Judeans were exiled to Babylonia and others fled into exile in Egypt. Even with the later restoration of autonomy in the Israelite homeland, diaspora—literally, scattering—became a condition of Jewish life that has persisted for two thousand years. Jews have found homes and carried on their lives in communities throughout the Middle East, the Mediterranean world, and Europe. By 1654, when the first Jewish community came into being in North America, Jewish communities were scattered from England to India, North Africa to the Baltic. Despite the establishment of the State of Israel in 1948, diaspora remains a condition of Jewish life to the present day.[3]

In each diaspora setting, Jews have adapted as minorities to the surrounding majority culture, borrowing languages, foodways, costume, and folk traditions from the host population and blending them into their own culture. As a result, by the modern era Jews varied greatly in appearance, speech, and culture. Numerous dialects and languages reflect the diversity of Jewish life in the Old World, among them Judeo-German (Yiddish) in much of central and eastern Europe, Judeo-Spanish (Ladino) along the northern Mediterranean and into the Balkans, Judeo-Arabic in North Africa and the Arab Middle East, and Judeo-Persian in what is now Iran.[4] Even religious life—a unifying factor—fell into distinct traditions. Sephardi Jews, descendants of Jews from Spain, banished from Iberia, found new homes in Italy, France, and the Netherlands. Ashkenazi traditions predominated in central and eastern Europe, especially Poland, the German states, and Russia. And Mizrahi traditions developed in Muslim countries of the Middle East.[5]

Many of these distinctive traditions arrived in America over three centuries of immigration. Some of the early colonial Jews brought with them Sephardi rituals. They were quickly outnumbered by Ashkenazi Jews: by 1820, even when congregations followed the Sephardi *minhag* (ritual tradition), most worshippers were of Ashkenazi descent. Then came the "century of migration," the period from the 1820s to the 1920s when war, revolution, nationalism, industrialization, and modern secular culture transformed political boundaries, disrupting traditional patterns of thought and established ways of life. As a people dispersed among the nations, enjoying limited political autonomy and subject to burdensome restrictions, European Jews were particularly vulnerable to the swirling currents of change. As a result, Jews across Europe migrated to new homes in other countries, most especially in the Americas.[6]

In 1820, after nearly two hundred years of immigration, American Jewry numbered only three thousand. But over the next sixty years, 250,000 Jews came to the United States, and from 1880 to 1924 were joined by more than 2,500,000 new Jewish immigrants. The stream of Jewish migration to America continued even after restrictive legislation was enacted in the 1920s, and migration remains a factor in American Jewish life. Chain migration—the process by which people from a particular place or family migrate to the same destination—coupled with specific local economic and occupational opportunities, created a variety of Jewish ethnic communities across North America: a Syrian Jewish community in New York City, a Persian (Iranian) Jewish community in Los Angeles, a community of Holocaust survivors and displaced persons in Vineland, New Jersey.

Successive streams of Jewish immigrants have produced multicultural communities in major cities and even in smaller cities and towns across the continent. In the early and mid-nineteenth century, Jews from central Europe predominated (though Jews trickled in from other places as well). The last decades of the nineteenth century brought a vast influx of Jews from eastern Europe—Russia, Ukraine, Austria-Hungary, the Baltic, and the Balkans. Following World War I, Jews came from the former Ottoman Empire—Syria, Turkey, and Greece. In the 1930s, as Jews fled the Nazi regime and the Nazi occupation of much of western Europe, Jewish refugees made their way into America. After World War II, displaced persons arrived from Europe, followed by an influx of Persian Jews in the 1980s and a large migration of Jews from the former Soviet Union, particularly since 1990. Among the recent immigrants are five hundred thousand Israelis. Today, American Jewry is a mosaic composed of multiple ethnic and cultural traditions.[7]

And Yet One People

Despite exile, diaspora, geographic distance, and a variety of distinct traditions, for two thousand years Jews have thought of themselves as belonging to a single people. The glue that held this scattered community together was a shared religious culture, grounded

Figure 1.2 Historically, Jews living all over the world have been multicultural and multiracial. In recent generations, American Jews are becoming more multiracial and multicultural. Here, the rabbi and children of Temple Or Olam in Concord, North Carolina.

Photo courtesy of Kate Lord.

in the Hebrew Bible and the teachings of the ancient rabbis. Rabbinic Judaism, which touched on almost every aspect of daily life, constituted a portable culture that could be carried from place to place, providing a sense of continuity and connection. The core of this religious culture could be found in the Bible, the Talmud (a vast compendium of rabbinic discourse), in codes and commentaries, and in the practices of lived religion.[8]

Over the centuries, of course, Jewish religious life continued to evolve. Even in its earliest manifestations two thousand years ago, the rabbis disputed the meaning of sacred texts, the forms of religious worship and ritual, and the application of religious and ethical principles in daily life—a discourse that persists to the present day. Leon Wieseltier, the literary critic, has termed this "the Jewish conversation," an unending dialogue about what is meaningful and relevant in Jewish tradition and culture. During two millennia, numerous schools of thought and religious movements have emerged within the Jewish tradition. Yet the idea of peoplehood has endured: it remains a fundamental value of Jewish life that every Jew is responsible for the good and welfare of other Jews.[9]

The commitment to Jewish peoplehood has made Judaism a transnational culture. Throughout the modern era, Jews living in North America have marshaled their resources and their communities on behalf of Jews in other countries. In the colonial era, this effort mostly took the form of philanthropy in support of the small population of impoverished Jews living in the Holy Land. In the nineteenth century, American

Jews mobilized in support of Jewish causes in Europe, protesting forced conversion and violence against Jews. In the early twentieth century, American Jews advocated against restrictive immigration policies that would cut off Jewish arrivals in America. During World War I, American Jews organized the Joint Distribution Committee to assist those suffering from displacement and deprivation. Between the World Wars, American Jews protested the rise of Nazism and assisted refugees from the Nazi regime to flee Europe and to find new homes. And, after World War II, Jewish organizations aided survivors of the Holocaust, working to resettle displaced persons and helping them to re-start their lives. In more recent decades, American Jews have demonstrated and lobbied on behalf of Jews in Ethiopia and the Soviet Union. And throughout the century, various Zionist organizations advocated for the creation of a Jewish state in the land of Israel and, since its establishment in 1948, for its security and the welfare of its citizens.[10]

The transnational commitment to Jewish people and culture has coexisted with an overwhelming commitment to America. Among the European immigrant communities of the nineteenth and twentieth centuries, Jews were fervent in their embrace of America. During the "century of migration," many Jews came to America with kinfolk or to join earlier-arriving family members. Their rate of return to the Old World was among the lowest among the streams of new arrivals. To be sure, Jewish newcomers maintained communication with those who remained behind, and before the Second World War some American Jews traveled to Europe to visit relatives and friends. But when Jews left the Old World to come to America, they came to stay, establishing families, homes, businesses, congregations and communal institutions, and a variety of social and fraternal organizations.[11]

Across the Continent

When we think of Jewish communities, we think of cities—New York, Los Angeles (Hollywood), and Miami among the most prominent. Certainly, American Jews have been for the most part an urban people from the colonial period to the present day. But Jews have also been a presence in the hinterland, along the frontiers, and as residents and stakeholders in small towns and villages across the continent. As the nation moved westward in the nineteenth century, Jews settled in the midwest, the southwest, and the far west. By 1919, Jews living in small communities ranging from fifty to one thousand (not to speak of scattered individuals and families) could be counted in more than seven hundred locales in every region and virtually every state in the country. A 1927 survey found Jews living in more than three thousand places across the United States.[12]

Moreover, in many places, Jews—despite their distinctive religion and traditions—were tightly woven into the fabric of their communities. In 1954, Bernard Postal and Lionel Koppman published *A Jewish Tourist's Guide to the U.S.*, a seven-hundred-page compendium of Jewish sites and landmarks in the then-forty-eight states.[13] Organized state by state and town by town, the *Guide* calls out people and places that range from Simon Fishman, "one of the country's largest landholders and the wheat baron of western

Figure 1.3 Studio photograph of Seligmann Heilner (r) and friend, nineteenth century. Heilner was a blacksmith who settled in Oregon.

Courtesy of the Oregon Jewish Museum and Holocaust Education Center. OJM 01532.

Kansas" (an 1890 immigrant from Russia whose base was in Tribune, Kansas, and who defeated a Ku Klux Klan candidate to take a seat in the state legislature in 1926), to the Sons of Israel Cemetery six miles from the North Dakota town of Garske, the sole remnant of a failed Jewish agricultural colony sponsored by the Baron de Hirsch Fund in 1884.[14] Contemporary online compendia such as the *Encyclopedia of Southern Jewish Life* developed by the Goldring/Woldenberg Institute in Jackson, Mississippi, presents a "history of every congregation and significant Jewish community" in twelve southern states from Virginia to Texas.[15] These readily available resources offer a trove of telling instances on the roles of Jews in every aspect of local life, such as Seligman Heilner, a pioneer blacksmith in nineteenth-century Oregon.

Local histories reveal a remarkable range of Jewish occupations in America. Familiar types such as the peddler, the sweatshop worker, the small-town storekeeper, the doctor, the Hollywood mogul, and—often in a pejorative way—the financier tend to dominate popular imagination. And, like many stereotypes, they are grounded in historical reality—peddling and retailing, the garment industry and the professions, the entertainment industries and finance are studded with Jewish names. Indeed, clothing manufacture, wholesaling, and retailing were a backbone of the Jewish economy for several generations. And Jews were in fact among the leading pioneers of movie-making in the first half of the twentieth century. But many immigrants were working class and some were simply poor, so it is instructive to consider a full panoply of Jewish occupations—manual laborers and craftspeople, educators and religious functionaries, miners, cowboys, and Indian traders, journalists, politicos, and gangsters, all-star athletes and beauty queens, scholars and intellectuals.[16]

Adjusting to America

By the 1950s, American Jews were being described as a "model minority." The sobriquet suggested that Jews had made a successful adjustment to America, gaining high socioeconomic status and enjoying stable families, above-average educational levels and income, and low rates of poverty and crime. While commercial activity was a key feature of Jewish life during the colonial and early national periods, the century of migration (1820 to 1924) brought thousands of European Jews into the growing manufacturing sector. By 1900, just under 60 percent of American Jewish workers were engaged in manufacture as proprietors, managers, and workers; just over 20 percent were in trade; and fewer than 3 percent were in the professions. By 1934, many had moved out of manufacturing work and into commerce: 51 percent were now in trade, fewer than 14 percent worked in manufacturing, and 13 percent were professionals. And by 1980, 48 percent of American Jews in the workforce were professionals, 25 percent were managerial, and only 9 percent were working in crafts, transport, and services, or as operators and laborers.[17]

Though often seen as a distinct minority, American Jews quickly blended in. As soon as they could, new immigrants adopted American dress and adjusted many aspects of their traditional foodways to the abundance of America.[18] The process of what has been termed Americanization proceeded rapidly in the twentieth century, so that by the century's end, American Jewish families were fully integrated into middle-class life. By 1920, the second-generation Jews of eastern European descent outnumbered their immigrant parents. And these American-born Jews "underwent a remarkable social metamorphosis."[19] Despite antisemitism, discrimination in housing and employment, and quotas in colleges, Jews achieved high levels of education. By 1957, 29 percent of Jews had completed four years of college, by 1970, 36 percent, and by 1980, an astonishing 65 percent.[20] As their means expanded, masses of Jewish families moved from areas of first settlement into newer neighborhoods and then, in the postwar decades, into the suburbs.[21] And as they acculturated, second-generation Jews increasingly practiced family planning and emphasized the nuclear family, loosening the ties of extended kinship. As Arden J. Geldman and Rela Mintz Geffen put it, "One important consequence of these changes was the virtual full acceptance and social integration of the Jewish family into American society."[22]

Adaptation and acceptance came with costs. The openness of America produced an array of theologies and religious movements (Orthodox, Reform, Conservative, and Reconstructionist) unknown in the Old Country. The shift from dense ethnic neighborhoods to the more dispersed suburban settings required structural changes in Jewish institutional life. Many among the second generation moved from affiliation with the

Orthodox congregations of their parents to the burgeoning Conservative movement. The synagogue center (sometimes characterized as "a shul with a pool and a school") and the Jewish community center came into their own, supplemented by a growing number of Jewish day schools and Jewish summer camps. By the 1970s, reactions against conventional congregational life and worship produced an efflorescence of counter-cultural activity—the publication of *The Jewish Catalog*, a populist shift from rabbinically led traditional observance; the *havurah* (fellowship) movement, a turn away from the arid anonymity of suburban synagogue life; the rise of Jewish feminism; and a new emphasis on Jewish spirituality in myriad forms ranging from ecstatic prayer to explorations in Buddhism. In 1968, the Reconstructionist movement established its own seminary, while in recent decades the number of ultra-observant Orthodox Jews has increased rapidly.[23]

Some of these trends reflected larger cultural currents, but others were responses to distinctively Jewish concerns. Chief among these were increasing rates of intermarriage and declining rates of institutional affiliation among younger generations of American Jews outside the Orthodox community. As a result, the twenty-first century has seen new efforts to embrace the unaffiliated, the intermarried, and the lesbian, gay, bisexual, and transgender community. The liberal Jewish seminaries (Reform, Conservative, and Reconstructionist) now ordain women as rabbis and cantors, while openly gay and lesbian clergy officiate in many congregations. Jewish philanthropy has shifted its giving to a variety of outreach and in-reach projects, to the support of inclusive programs such as the Lab/Shul and The Mash-Up Americans, and to the seeding of new Jewish culture. The Orthodox, too, via movements such as CHABAD, are committed to engaging the unaffiliated.

These recent efforts at adapting to novelty through Jewish renewal have precedents in earlier generations, as Jonathan Sarna has shown: the Reform movement, the Jewish literary societies, and the Young Men's Hebrew Association movement of the mid-nineteenth century; the establishment in 1886 of the Modern Orthodox Yeshiva College and the Conservative Jewish Theological Seminary; and the founding of new nationwide organizations such as the Jewish Publication Society (1888), the American Jewish Historical Society (1892), Gratz College (1893), the National Council of Jewish Women (1893), and the Jewish Chautauqua Society (1893), as well as the start of the *Jewish Encyclopedia* (1898).[24] Repeated efforts to renew and transform American Jewish life are a key factor in its current diversity and complexity.

Making History

As Jews adapted to life in America, they in turn changed the society around them. "From their very first steps on American soil, back in 1654, Jews extended the boundaries of American pluralism, serving as a model for other religious minorities and, in time, expanding the definition of American religious liberty so that they (and other minorities) might be included as equals," writes Jonathan Sarna. Jews changed "in less than two hundred years, from a curiosity into America's 'third faith.' No longer were they grouped with exotic religions and nonbelievers, as in the well-known colonial-era phrase 'Jews, Turks, and infidels.' Instead, by the late twentieth century, they emerged as religious insiders."[25]

Jewish influences on American culture, high and low, are pervasive. To take but one example, Yiddish—the language of most Jewish immigrants from the colonial period through the 1920s—has added new flavor to American English. We Americans *kvetch* (gripe or complain) about *gonifs* (scoundrels and thieves), *pishers* (nobodies), *yentas* (gossips or scolds), *nudniks* (pests), and *schlemiels* (bunglers); *dreck* (worthless, distasteful, or nonsensical stuff), *mishegaas* (craziness), and *schlock* (something cheap, shoddy, or inferior). We *kvell* (express pleasure and pride) over a *mensch* (an upright person), a decent *bagel* and *schmear* (cream cheese), a satisfying *nosh* (snack), and our *shul* (synagogue), which is *haimish* (home-like and friendly). We admire *chutzpah* (daring or audacity) and deplore *schmutz* (dirt); we enjoy a *tummler*'s (entertainer) *shtick* (comic theme) or *spiel* (sales pitch); and we indulge a *maven* (expert or know-it-all) even when he or she is going on about *tchotchkes* (knickknacks). And, like all interpreters, we gain *naches* (a feeling of pride or gratification) in having a chance to *kibitz* (offer unwanted advice).

Names like Albert Einstein, Jonas Salk, Mark Rothko, and Leonard Bernstein conjure up the realms of science, art, and music in which American Jews have helped to shape American intellectual life and the visual and performing arts. The merest listing of literary greats could go on for pages—among many others, Emma Lazarus, Gertrude Stein, Lillian Hellman, Tillie Olsen, Norman Mailer, J.D. Salinger, Bernard Malamud, Arthur Miller, Adrienne Rich, Joseph Heller, E.L. Doctorow, and Philip Roth; the Nobelists Isaac Bashevis Singer, Saul Bellow, and Joseph Brodsky; and also such notable contemporary writers as Michael Chabon, Paul Auster, Cynthia Ozick, Tony Kushner, Rebecca Goldstein, and Jonathan Lethem; children's authors Judy Blume, Shel Silverstein, and Maurice Sendak; and luminaries of the graphic novel such as Will Eisner and Art Spiegelman. Jews have been equally prominent in the American entertainment industry, ranging from song writers to network executives.[26]

Mass culture, in particular, has been pioneered by Jews. From Billy Bronco (Max Aronson) through the Warner Brothers to Steven Spielberg, Jews have shaped Hollywood and the American movie industry. Likewise, American radio and television: at one point, all three national television networks were headed by Jews. Especially at the local level, Jews have had a distinctive role as proprietors and managers of local movie theaters and vaudeville halls. From the mid-nineteenth century, Jews also played a parallel role in disseminating ideas about fashion and taste, both as heads of national mail-order houses like Sears Roebuck and wholesalers such as the Baltimore Bargain House and as owners of the nation's leading department stores. Solomon Lazard, for example, re-named his Los Angeles store "City of Paris" in the nineteenth century, setting local taste for generations of Angelenos.[27]

Although less well known, Jews have had important roles in shaping American historical consciousness and practice. In the 1870s, for example, Frank Marx Etting (1833–1890), a descendant of the prominent Gratz family, led the effort to restore the Pennsylvania State House (Independence Hall) in anticipation of the Centennial celebration of 1876. Etting envisioned a public display of objects associated with the Founding Fathers as "a system of object instruction in history for the masses." Although Etting's

Figure 1.4 Portrait of Emma Lazarus (1849–1887) from her book, *The Poems of Emma Lazarus,* 1888. Her poem, "The New Colossus"—"Give me your tired, your poor, / Your huddled masses yearning to breathe free, / The wretched refuse of your teeming shore. / Send these, the homeless, tempest-tost to me. / I lift my lamp beside the golden door."— provided a new identity for the Statue of Liberty: "Mother of Exiles."

Courtesy of the Library of the Jewish Theological Seminary (Abraham and Deborah Karp Collection). JTS PS2233.A1 1888 v.1c.1, JTS catalog number 101a.

role was terminated on the eve of the Centennial Exposition, "his project transformed the interior and function of the building for years to come," according to Charlene Mires.[28] Another landmark of American history, Jefferson's Monticello, was saved (twice) by members of the Levy family: Commodore Uriah Phillips Levy acquired and restored Jefferson's home in 1833; after his death, Monticello passed out of the family, but was reacquired by the Commodore's nephew, Jefferson Monroe Levy, in 1879 and restored for a second time. And then of course, there is the Statue of Liberty, re-framed as the "Mother of Exiles" by poet Emma Lazarus in her sonnet, "The New Colossus."[29]

A more subtle but even more influential role in shaping historical consciousness was that of Jewish antique dealers in New England and New York who, in the first half of the twentieth century, helped to create the market for American antiques. According to historian Briann G. Greenfield, Jewish dealers were "adaptable to the new language of aesthetics, [and] they located many important pieces, separated commonplace examples from the extraordinary, and packaged and marketed them for sale. Finding, classifying, and distributing historic objects, Jewish dealers were important collaborators in the invention of the antique."[30] Jewish dealers brought antiques to market, repaired damaged pieces and detected forgeries, and made reproductions that popularized the antique aesthetic. For newly arrived Jews, the antique business offered a livelihood and cultural cachet: "associating with antiques provided an intimate knowledge of their adopted nation's artistic heritage and a claim on American citizenship."[31]

As this overview suggests, American Jewish history embodies many of the themes of American history in general and, for that matter, of Atlantic history and Atlantic studies. For Jews, America has been an important sphere of cultural encounter and exchange. The thematic chapters that follow argue that Jews have, in the words of Jonathan Sarna, "*shaped* events: establishing and maintaining communities, responding to challenges, working for change."[32] In so doing, they have helped to define some of our most important historical concepts and tropes—migration and mobility, openness and inclusion, economic opportunity, and the acceptance of diversity, within and between ethnic, religious, and cultural groups.

Notes

1. For reflections on the larger meanings of American Jewish history, see Steven T. Katz, ed., *Why Is America Different? American Jewry on its 350th Anniversary* (Lanham, MD: University Press of America, 2010); and *The Meaning of the American Jewish Experience* (Waltham, MA: Brandeis University, 2004). For an overview of American Jewish historiography, see Jonathan D. Sarna. "Historiography - United States." In *Encyclopaedia Judaica*, 2nd ed. (Detroit: Macmillan Reference USA, 2007), vol. 9, 161–63; and Hasia R. Diner, "American Jewish History," in Martin Goodman, ed., *Oxford Handbook of Jewish Studies* (Oxford: Oxford University Press, 2003), 471–90.

2. This despite President Washington's unequivocal statement (1790) that all American citizens possess "alike liberty of conscience and immunities of citizenship," and that the Federal government "gives to bigotry no sanction, to persecution no assistance, requires only that they who live under its protection should demean themselves as good citizens in giving it on all occasions their effectual support." See also, Steven K. Green, *Inventing a Christian America: The Myth of the Religious Founding* (New York: Oxford University Press, 2015); and Kevin M. Kruse, *One Nation Under God: How Corporate America Invented Christian America* (New York: Basic Books, 2015). We do need to bear in mind that some of the states maintained established churches or required officials to take Christian oaths as a requirement for taking office; see Naomi W. Cohen, *Jews in Christian America: The Pursuit of Religious Equality* (New York: Oxford University Press, 1992).

3. Menahem Stern. "Diaspora." *Encyclopaedia Judaica*, 2nd ed., Vol. 5, 637–43. See also Howard M. Sachar, *Diaspora: An Inquiry into the Contemporary Jewish World* (New York: Harper & Row, 1985).

4. *Encyclopaedia Judaica*, 2nd ed., s.v., "Yiddish Language," "Ladino," "Judeo-Arabic," and "Judeo-Persian."

5. *Encyclopaedia Judaica*, 2nd ed., s.v., "Minhag," "Liturgy," "Ashkenaz," and "Sephardim."

6. Hasia R. Diner, *The Jews of the United States, 1654 to 2000* (Berkeley: University of California Press, 2004); Howard M. Sachar, *A History of the Jews in America* (New York: Vintage Books, 1993); and Marc Lee Raphael, ed., *The Columbia History of Jews & Judaism in America* (New York: Columbia University Press, 2008).

7. Diner, *Jews of the United States*, 73–77.

8. Michael L. Satlow, *Creating Judaism: History, Tradition, Practice* (New York: Columbia University Press, 2008).

9. My Jewish Learning website, "All of Israel Are Responsible for One Another," accessed April 4, 2016, http://www.myjewishlearning.com/article/all-of-israel-are-responsible -for-one-another/.

10. Reena Sigmund Friedman, *These Are Our Children: Jewish Orphanages in the United States, 1880-1925* (Hanover, NH: University Press of New England, 1994); Naomi Cohen, *Not Free to Desist: The American Jewish Committee, 1906-1966* (Philadelphia: Jewish Publication Society of America, 1972); Oscar Handlin, *A Continuing Task: The American Joint Distribution Committee, 1914-1964* (New York: Random House, 1964); Henry Feingold, *Bearing Witness: How America and Its Jews Responded to the Holocaust* (Syracuse: Syracuse University Press, 1995); Leonard Dinnerstein, *America and the Survivors of the Holocaust* (New York: Columbia University Press, 1982); Naomi Cohen, *American Jews and the Zionist Idea* (Hoboken, NJ: KTAV, 1975).

11. Jonathan Sarna challenges the view that Jewish rates of return to Russia were extremely low (in the 5 to 7 percent range), but his rich and varied evidence still points to a return rate of about 15 percent, comparable to the rate of return of immigrants from Germany, a much closer and more industrially advanced nation. Jonathan Sarna, "The Myth of No Return: Jewish Return Migration to Eastern Europe, 1882-1924," *American Jewish History* 71, no. 2 (December 1981), 256–68.

12. Lee Shai Weissbach, *Jewish Life in Small-Town America* (New Haven: Yale University Press, 2005), 21, 27–29. See also Lee Shai Weissbach, "The Jewish Communities of the United States on the Eve of Mass Migration: Some Comments on Geography and Bibliography," *American Jewish History* 78, no. 1 (September 1988), 79–108.

13. Bernard Postal and Lionel Koppman, *A Jewish Tourist's Guide to the U.S.* (Philadelphia: Jewish Publication Society of America, 1954).

14. Postal and Koppman, *Jewish Tourist's Guide*, 187–88, 488.

15. Institute of Southern Jewish Life website, "Encyclopedia of Southern Jewish Communities," accessed April 4, 2016, http://www.isjl.org/encyclopedia-of-southern-jewish-communities .html.

16. See, for example, Beth S. Wenger, *The Jewish Americans: Three Centuries of Jewish Voices in America* (New York: Doubleday, 2007).

17. Nathan Goldberg, "Occupational Patterns of American Jews," in Jeffrey S. Gurock, ed., *American Jewish History* (New York: Routledge, 1998), 4:198; Barry R. Chiswick, "The Postwar Economy of American Jews," in Gurock, ed., *American Jewish History*, 4:223.

18. Barbara A. Schrier, *Becoming American Women: Clothing and the Jewish Immigrant Experience, 1880-1920* (Chicago: Chicago Historical Society, 1994); Hasia R. Diner, "'Our Parents Were Hungry and We Are Sated': The Immigrant World of American Jewish Food," in Avi Y. Decter and Julian Ochs Dweck, eds., *Chosen Food: Cuisine, Culture, and American Jewish Identity* (Baltimore: Jewish Museum of Maryland, 2011), 8–19. See also Hasia R. Diner, *Hungering for America: Italian, Irish, and Jewish Foodways in the Age of Migration* (Cambridge, MA: Harvard University Press, 2001); and Jenna Weissman Joselit, *A Perfect Fit: Clothes, Character, and the Promise of America* (New York: Metropolitan Books, 2001).

19. Henry L. Feingold, *A Time for Searching: Entering the Mainstream, 1920-1945* (Baltimore: Johns Hopkins University Press, 1992), 125–32.

20. Chiswick, "The Postwar Economy of American Jews," 217–18. Wikipedia website, "Model Minority," accessed October 14, 2015, https://en.wikipedia.org/wiki/Model_minority#Model_minority_stereotype.

21. Edward S. Shapiro, *A Time for Healing: American Jewry since World War II* (Baltimore: Johns Hopkins University Press, 1992), 143–58.

22. Arden J. Geldman and Rela Mintz Geffen, "Family, American Jewish," in *Encyclopaedia Judaica*, 2nd ed., 16:700.

23. Marc Lee Raphael, *Profiles in American Judaism: The Reform, Conservative, Orthodox, and Reconstructionist Traditions in Historical Perspectives* (New York: Harper & Row, 1988); Jeffrey S. Gurock, *From Fluidity to Rigidity: The Religious Worlds of Conservative and Orthodox Jews in Twentieth Century America* (Ann Arbor, MI: Frankel Center for Jewish Studies, 1998); David Kaufman, *Shul with a Pool: The "Synagogue-Center" in American Jewish History* (Hanover, NH: University Press of New England, 1999); Edward S. Shapiro, *A Time for Healing*, 159–94.

24. Jonathan D. Sarna, *A Great Awakening: The Transformation That Shaped Twentieth Century American Judaism And Its implications For Today* (New York: Council for Initiatives in Jewish Education, 1995), 4 and *passim*. See also, Jonathan D. Sarna, *JPS: The Americanization of Jewish Culture, 1888-1988* (Philadelphia: Jewish Publication Society, 1989).

25. Jonathan D. Sarna, *American Judaism: A History* (New Haven: Yale University Press, 2004), xv.

26. For an introduction to novels by American Jewish authors, see Joshua M. Lambert, *American Jewish Fiction* (Philadelphia: Jewish Publication Society, 2009).

27. Neal Gabler, *An Empire of Their Own: How the Jews Invented Hollywood* (New York: Crown, 1988). See also, Sachar, *Jews in America*, 357–66.

28. Charlene Mires, *Independence Hall in American Memory* (Philadelphia: University of Pennsylvania Press, 2002), 123–33.

29. Mark Leepson, *Saving Monticello: The Levy Family's Epic Quest to Rescue the House that Jefferson Built* (New York: The Free Press, 2001). Even less well-known is the role of James Myers, who purchased and restored Lincoln's law offices in Springfield, now the Lincoln-Herndon Museum. See Sachar, *Jews in America*, 5.

30. Briann G. Greenfield, *Out of the Attic: Inventing Antiques in Twentieth-Century New England* (Amherst, MA: University of Massachusetts Press, 2009), 57–89.

31. Ibid., 89.

32. Sarna, *American Judaism*, xx.

Select Bibliography

Diner, Hasia R. *The Jews of the United States, 1654 to 2000*. Berkeley: University of California Press, 2004.

Diner, Hasia R. *A Time for Gathering: The Second Migration, 1820-1880*. Baltimore: Johns Hopkins University Press, 1992.

Dreams of Freedom. Philadelphia: National Museum of American Jewish History, 2011.

Encyclopaedia Judaica, 2nd. ed. (22 vols.). Detroit: Macmillan Reference USA, 2007.

Faber, Eli. *A Time for Planting: The First Migration, 1654-1820*. Baltimore: Johns Hopkins University Press, 1992.

Farber, Roberta Rosenberg, and Chaim I. Waxman, eds. *Jews in America: A Contemporary Reader*. Hanover, NH: University Press of New England, 1999.

Feingold, Henry L. *A Time for Searching: Entering the Mainstream, 1920-1945*. Baltimore: Johns Hopkins University Press, 1992.

Grunberger, Michael W., ed. *From Haven to Home: 350 Years of Jewish Life in America*. Washington, DC: Library of Congress, 2004.

Gurock, Jeffrey S., ed. *American Jewish History* (8 vols.). New York: Routledge, 1998.

Hyman, Paula E., and Deborah Dash Moore, eds. *Jewish Women in America: An Historical Encyclopedia*. (2 vols.). New York: Routledge, 1998.

Pew Research Center, "A Portrait of Jewish Americans," October 1, 2013.

Raphael, Marc Lee, ed. *The Columbia History of Jews and Judaism in America*. New York: Columbia University Press, 2008.

Sachar, Howard M. *A History of the Jews in America*. New York: Random House, 1992.

Sarna, Jonathan D. *American Judaism: A History*. New Haven: Yale University Press, 2004.

Shapiro, Edward S. *A Time for Healing: American Jewry Since World War II*. Baltimore: Johns Hopkins University Press, 1992.

Sorin, Gerald. *A Time for Building: The Third Migration*. Baltimore: Johns Hopkins University Press, 1992.

Wenger, Beth S. *History Lessons: The Creation of American Jewish Heritage*. Princeton: Princeton University Press, 2010.

Wenger, Beth S. *The Jewish Americans: Three Centuries of Jewish Voices in America*. New York: Doubleday, 2007.

Wertheimer, Jack. *A People Divided: Judaism in Contemporary America*. New York: Basic Books, 1993.

CHAPTER 2

GETTING STARTED

There is a magical omnipotent dispeller of the mystery; it is *contact*.
—Howard Zinn

Museums should expend their political and cultural capital and take risks to help their visitors find a useful, usable, inclusive, and meaningful history that engages us all. —Lonnie Bunch

PLUNGING INTO American Jewish history may seem to many like the proverbial leap in the dark. But this book is designed and organized to help you advance methodically through the subject, moving from the general to the particular. The introduction called out some key themes and cited a number of telling instances. The five thematic chapters that follow develop these ideas in greater detail and specificity. Each chapter offers an interpretation of one broad aspect of Jewish life in America—migration, movement, and social mobility; family and domestic life; community life and communal organizations; cultural expressions; and prejudice, discrimination, and tolerance. While these chapters are suggestive rather than comprehensive, and sometimes overlap, they offer avenues into the broader subject. And, since many interpretations are thematic, the chapters constitute a first step on the road to conceptualizing an interpretive project.

The five chapters diverge somewhat from conventional historical scholarship and narratives. Jewish life in America was, like the Jewish population, concentrated in a dozen large urban areas. These essays deliberately skew the storyline by foregrounding and privileging Jewish experiences in smaller cities and towns. Even stories like those of national movements and national organizations are tied to local communities. The American Jewish Congress, for example, had chapters in dozens of communities; likewise the National Council of Jewish Women; and, of course, all the major religious movements comprised local congregations. Jewish cultural expressions transcended categories such as popular music or literature: for many communities, the Jewish-owned or managed department store, or vaudeville hall, or movie theater, were instrumental in shaping local fashion and taste.

Following the thematic chapters are a series of case studies—projects mounted by local history museums and historic sites on their own or in collaboration with Jewish groups. Here, too, I have highlighted cases in which secular organizations have taken the lead, eschewing projects mounted by Jewish museums and historical organizations. The Shady Side Rural Heritage Society, a small, mostly volunteer organization on the Chesapeake Bay, produced a large-scale, multidimensioned oral history research effort, a major exhibition, and a book on a local Jewish club by hiring a curator with Jewish history expertise to spearhead the project. Historic Columbia (South Carolina) is carrying out a large-scale oral history project and incorporating Jewish history into its neighborhood tours without Jewish staff or Jewish history expertise in part by partnering with the Jewish Historical Society of South Carolina and the College of Charleston, which is the repository of the Jewish Heritage Collection.

Like the historical chapters, the case studies are organized thematically, constituting a parallel narrative that is concrete and detailed. The case studies function very much as interpretive commentaries on the historical chapters, demonstrating how concepts and themes can be made salient and meaningful to a variety of stakeholders and constituents. This chapter calls out some of the key characteristics that successful interpretive projects have in common: collaboration, new research, inclusiveness, appropriate formats, and, above all, strong stories. The case studies are not intended to be models of "best practice," but rather effective efforts to tackle difficult or little-known subjects. In effect, the case studies suggest guidelines for thinking about challenges and process as you embark on a new interpretive project.

The case studies suggest the range and variety of interpretive projects that can be mounted by history organizations. These include publications, gallery exhibitions, living history, curricula, online resources, videos, markers, historic sites and historic house museums, tours, and public programs. The levels of cost and institutional investment vary greatly from one project to another. Interestingly, the scale of the sponsoring organization need not correlate with the scale of the project. The Shady Side Rural Heritage Society, for example, successfully mounted a multiyear research, preservation, and interpretive project. In contrast, some large state historical societies have limited their efforts to creating one or two historical markers or a couple of entries in online compendia. In any case, the case studies are presented as instances of effective interpretation in museums and historic sites, rather than templates or ideal types.

Like the preceding historical chapters, the case studies are organized thematically: the historical chapters and case studies, therefore, complement each other. Our focus on a handful of broad themes embraces a rich variety of instances that are available to those interested in Jewish history in North America. Also, since most interpretive projects and historical narratives are organized around a central or overarching theme—what we often term the Big Idea—the case studies, like the chapters, can serve as springboards for comparable projects in the reader's own community. In addition, some specific projects are described as possible models in the chapter on "Next Practice."

Common Ground

Amid the welter of case studies that follow, we can find some common ground. Each project, of course, has its particular character and its specific nuances. But, broadly speaking, we can find some threads that weave through most of the case studies and are worth calling out in general terms here. It is useful to note up front that historical interpretation has been evolving quite rapidly over the past fifty years, and in the past decade has speeded up, leading at least one astute observer to call out a revolution in interpretation.[1] This means that the methods employed in the case studies are likely to be changing even as this book goes to press. Still, it is worth looking at some of the commonalities they share.

Collaboration: Most public interpretive programming is done collaboratively. Exhibitions, tours, media, educational curricula, public programs, and online resources typically involve a team of people to complete. Usually, these teams begin with an institution's staff and volunteers and then move on to consultants and contractors. Team process can vary from institution to institution and project to project and still work effectively. A number of typical models are described by Kathleen McLean in her now-classic book on exhibition development, *Planning for People in Museum Exhibitions*.[2] Another more recent book along the same lines is *Creating Exhibitions: Collaboration in the Planning, Development, and Design of Innovative Experiences* by Polly McKenna-Cress and Janet Kamien.[3] Many of the same principles of team process can be applied to educational and public programs, publications, media, and online resources.

Many public history projects also involve collaboration with other organizations. Because the number of Jewish museums and history organizations is limited and the opportunities for interpreting American Jewish history are manifold, it follows that many secular museums and historic sites will need or want to partner with a Jewish counterpart that can bring resources (collections, contacts, and context) and expertise to the project. A good number of the case studies described here are based on collaborations between secular and Jewish organizations, each bringing specific strengths to the interpretive project. This kind of partnership often brings with it a strategic benefit in fundraising: many donors and funders recognize the advantages of funding multiple agencies through a single gift or grant.

Collaborations with communities are also a common part of the interpretive process. Oral history projects and projects designed to identify historical resources held by families and individuals frequently provide a critical mass of information, ideas, and instances for a public history project. Workshops, reunions, appraisal events, and online outreach can garner a wealth of previously inaccessible material, and many of these resources can be added to the sponsoring institution's collections and data banks. Working with community leaders and community historians can also provide a multiplicity of viewpoints, enriching the interpretive narrative. And while none of these tried-and-tested modes of community collaboration extends quite so far as community curating, they are steps that can lead toward a sharing of authority between the institution and the community it seeks to interpret.[4]

Figure 2.1 Collaboration is essential. Two Jewish children help to prepare Thanksgiving dinner in Baltimore, Maryland, 1978.

Courtesy of the Jewish Museum of Maryland (Gift of the Jewish Community Center). JMM 2006.13.2188.

Research: The interpretive projects described below began in many different ways. A few started as scholarly publications that were later translated into public history programs. Some came about because a community or organization was looking for a way to celebrate an anniversary or to commemorate a recent achievement. Some projects were conceived and implemented to engage a new or underserved constituency. And still others were developed more serendipitously—research on a site or subject may have unexpectedly turned up an unknown Jewish role or angle, opening the way for a Jewish history project.

In all these cases, significant projects tend to involve some degree of original research. Close study of historical documents by Professor Jonathan Sarna of Brandeis University and Benjamin Shapell, founder of the Shapell Manuscript Foundation, confirmed and documented President Lincoln's many involvements with Jews before and during his presidency; this led to a book, which in turn led to a major exhibition. The Philadelphia Folkore Project, which preserves traditional folk culture, became involved with a distinguished klezmer musician, which led to a documentary video that revised accepted scholarship on the history of klezmer music in America. And when the State Historical Society of Iowa borrowed a traveling exhibition on Jews in the Upper Midwest and decided to supplement it with an exhibition on Iowa Jews, it produced a wealth of material culture and historical anecdotes that had mostly resided in private hands.

One interpretive project can even lead to another. In 2002, the Autry National Center in Los Angeles opened a major exhibition on Jews in the American West. The exhibition proved to be very popular, but many Los Angeleno visitors wondered why the history of the Los Angeles Jewish community was treated so sketchily. The Autry responded by organizing a second research effort led by a local scholar, mounting a second major exhibition, *Jews in the LA Mosaic*, accompanied by a book of essays and a number of public programs that was widely acclaimed as the most searching public interpretive project on the Los Angeles Jewish community. Original research in social history and material culture made both projects possible and also made them significant, to both the Autry and to one of its key constituencies.

Inclusiveness: Original research in the history of Jewish life often turns up a multiplicity of family traditions, institutional and communal narratives, and historical perspectives, especially if the idea or issue or incident under consideration is meaningful to its community. Having to deal with a plethora of views complicates matters. But it also offers opportunities to highlight incidents, trends, individuals, and institutions that have been previously neglected, denied, or suppressed. Presenting a multiplicity of views can also help to convey the complexity and nuances of a particular subject.

Inclusiveness also offers opportunities to interpret the interactions of various groups. Since neither minorities nor the majority in any given locale live in isolation from one another but rather interact continuously, it is important to incorporate the interplay of various groups into our narratives. On the other hand, as Historic Columbia (South Carolina) reminds us, we may need to first pull out the narratives of each group separately before plaiting them with the narratives of other groups.

Appropriate Formats: All too often, history organizations try to turn every good idea into an exhibition, our conventional stock-in-trade. But it is critical to select the right format for the topic or theme being interpreted. Just because we are holding a hammer does not make a nail the most appropriate or effective solution! We have a whole kit bag of tools at our disposal, and before we start planning for another exhibition we should ask ourselves what format is most likely to communicate our projected story to a given audience.

The pervasiveness of digital media makes this exercise imperative. These days, visitors can (and do) dial into the World Wide Web for information, games, and stories in real time. If they are touring a gallery or site, walking, biking, or driving around a neighborhood—or even a whole community—they have a world of resources readily available at their fingertips. As a result, more and more history organizations are creating online resources to complement or to carry their interpretive messages to diverse audiences and users.

The museums and historic sites represented in the case studies that follow have made a wide range of decisions about the formats they employ to tell their stories. The Philadelphia Folklore Project, for example, tells the story of a local klezmer musician in a DVD. At the Shapiro House in Strawbery Banke (Portsmouth, New Hampshire) the story is told by a re-enactor speaking in first-person voice. For *Lincoln and the Jews*, the New-York Historical Society, in collaboration with the Shapell Manuscript Foundation, developed an exhibition of historical documents. And Historic Columbia (South Carolina) is creating a walking tour based on oral histories.

Strong Stories: "We live by stories," wrote Nobelist Elie Wiesel. And so do history organizations and the communities they serve. If there is one thing that the disparate case studies included here have in common, it is that they tell compelling stories. Some are intriguing because they are unfamiliar or unexpected, others because they offer a new insight or slant on a well-known story. Some stories confirm, others challenge; some amuse, and others bend the arc of justice or expand our moral universe. As the American Association for State and Local History (AASLH) puts it, "Stories explain how things are, why they are, and their role and purpose." In other words, stories "help communities to tell their shared history, explore their lived experiences, and heal divisive pasts."[5]

But what, exactly, makes a story strong? While there are no universal rules for effective storytelling, there are a few fundamental considerations to bear in mind. One is the old-fashioned idea that good stories usually have a beginning, middle, and end. Missing one of these key components can lead to confusion and disappointment in the audience. Good history tales also tend to be authentic to the most informed historical understanding we possess, in spirit if not in every detail. And compelling stories are meaningful— they matter to the audience viscerally and existentially, not just intellectually. As AASLH puts is: "Stories live in the heart, not the head."

Telling strong stories requires tools, none more important than voice and vocabulary. We can tell good stories in first-person, second-person, or third-person voice, as long as our story is vivid, concrete, and engaging. But we need to be aware that each voice implies certain perspectives and comes with its distinctive set of constraints. Too frequently, our institutions fall into the same choice of voice, even though the subjects of our narratives vary tremendously. If we want to invoke memory and meaning, we will need to think hard about which voice (or combination of voices) will lend itself best to the complexity of a situation and the multitude of its possible interpretations.

And this brings us to vocabulary. The language in which we couch our stories can make or break them. Some word choices are like sludge—clogging up the works and stemming the flow. Some words are anachronistic, others are clichés, and still others are dead metaphors. There is little or no excuse for poor word choices or murky phrasings.

English is the richest and most vibrant language on Earth, full of life both past and present. When the New-York Historical Society and the American Jewish Joint Distribution Committee chose the title for their collaborative exhibition—"I Live. Send Help."—they caught the spirit of the Joint Distribution Committee and delivered the story line in just four punchy words. The felicitous word is almost always ready at hand—real, lively, concrete, and vivid. But we have to make conscious decisions about every word we use.[6]

Communication, Engagement, and Trust

Obviously, if we want to interpret Jewish history, we are going to need to bring Jews into our research, planning, and program development. In hundreds of communities across North America, there are organized Jewish communities represented by congregations, Jewish community centers, federations, local chapters of national organizations, and so on. Even where there is no Jewish organization, there are likely to be useful resources in a nearby town, city, or university. And there is always opportunity to engage with surrogates—rabbis, communal professionals, professors—who can speak for those communities that once were here and are now vanished.

The first order of business, then, is to communicate. In a recent AASLH Technical Leaflet, Mark Sundlov writes, "The first and most critical link in demonstrating relevance is the initiation of communication," and he goes on to say, "History organizations must be sincerely involved with their communities."[7] Engagement with the community whose story we propose to tell is a commonsensical idea. It is also empowering. Without talking to their local communities, the Chicago History Museum could not have organized its first major effort to interpret the history of Chicago Jewry. With the help of its neighbors, the Chicago History Museum rose to the challenge—and won the 2016 Institute of Museum and Library Services National Medal for Museum Service.

The next step is engagement. This is no longer as simple as it was once thought to be nor as engagement has been practiced. Right into the last decade of the twentieth century, the mantra for history institutions was "education." History organizations were seen, by both themselves and their communities, as repositories of historical "truth," which was shared—often in a highly didactic manner—with the community. For a time, history museums and like institutions shared an unchallenged reputation for accuracy and authenticity, as evidenced in *The Presence of the Past* by Roy Rosenzweig and David Thelen.[8] Concern for historical accuracy and authentic content remains a hallmark of our institutions today.

However, times and standards are changing. By the beginning of this century, calls were being issued by the American Association of Museums (now the American Alliance of Museums) for museums to become more engaged with their communities. While retaining a traditional concern for education, agencies like the Institute of Museum and Library Services were now talking about transforming the "role of museums . . . from educational destinations to full-fledged community partners and anchors" and encouraging museums and like institutions to seek "new opportunities for active local involvement."

Americans, of course, were not just waiting for institutions to invite their participation. Enthusiastic adapters, many Americans were using the Internet, online resources,

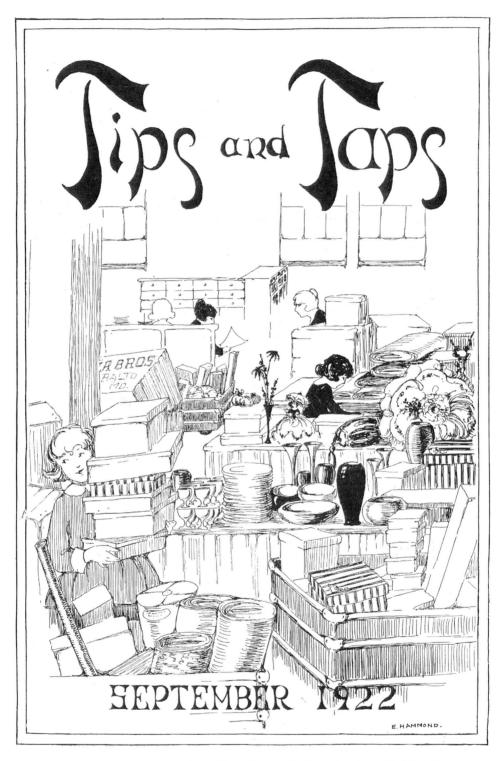

Figure 2.2 Inclusivity means a lot of hands—and a lot of voices. Behind the scenes at Hutzler's Department Store, Baltimore, Maryland, as seen in the company newsletter, *Tips and Taps.*

Courtesy of the Jewish Museum of Maryland. JMM 1989.207.007.

and social media to transform their participation in shaping historical narratives. Today, history organizations of all types, sizes, and locations have to deal with users who are no longer mere auditors, but participants who want their voices and their stories to play more prominent roles in our storytelling. New terms of art have emerged—inclusivity, sharing authority, radical trust, and civic engagement are now on our agendas.

As suggested in the conclusion to this book, we are all going to have to find ways to adapt our practice to new realities, to make our history organizations more participatory, and to create more space for our users to share in the privilege and challenge of creating historical narratives. Quite aside from demonstrating our relevance and drawing in visitors (thus ensuring our futures), new expectations and new orientations make it possible for history organizations to participate in the ongoing challenge of "animating democracy." This is an opportunity worth seizing. And the place to start is with a neighborly conversation.[9]

Notes

1. Rick Beard, "Is It Time for Another Revolution?" *History News* (Spring 2015), 22–27.
2. (Washington, DC: Association of Science-Technology Centers, 1993).
3. (Hoboken, NJ: Wiley, 2013).
4. See John H. Falk and Lynne D. Dierking, *Learning from Museums: Visitor Experiences and the Making of Meanings* (Nashville: Altamira Press, 2000); Nina Simon, *The Participatory Museum* (Santa Cruz, CA: Museum 2.0, 2010); and Bill Adair, Benjamin Filene, and Laura Koloski, eds., *Letting Go? Sharing Historical Authority in a User-Generated World* (Philadelphia: Pew Center for Arts and Heritage, 2011).
5. American Association for State and Local History Workshop, *Can You Hear Me Now? Connecting Visitors through Real Stories of Artifacts and Place* (A STEPS Resource), developed by Sarah Pharaon, accessed April 28, 2016, http://resource.aaslh.org/view/course-curriculum-can-you-hear-me-now-connecting-to-visitors-through-real-stories-of-artifacts-and-place/.
6. Another favorite title is a children's book by Aminah Robinson titled *A Street Called Home*.
7. Mark Sundlov, "Demonstrating Relevance," American Association for State and Local History Technical Leaflet #273 (Nashville: American Association for State and Local History, 2016), 2 and 4.
8. Roy Rosenzweig and David Thelen, *The Presence of the Past: Popular Uses of History in American Life* (New York: Columbia University Press, 2000).
9. Pam Korza and Barbara Schaffer Bacon, *History as Catalyst for Civic Dialogue: Case Studies from Animating Democracy* (Washington, DC: Americans for the Arts, 2005); and Pam Korza and Barbara Schaffer Bacon, *Museums and Civic Dialogue: Case Studies from Animating Democracy* (Washington, DC: Americans for the Arts, 2005).

CHAPTER 3

ACROSS THE OCEAN
AND ACROSS TOWN

Migration and Mobility in
American Jewish History

Joshua J. Furman

I N MAY 1942, the YIVO Institute for Jewish Research in New York City sponsored an autobiographical essay contest on the theme, "Why I left Europe and what I have accomplished in America." The contest winner, Ben Reisman, described his journey from orphanhood in poverty-stricken Galicia, a region of eastern Europe between modern-day Poland and Ukraine, to New York City in 1896. From there, Reisman narrated his challenging but upward path of socioeconomic mobility from a tinsmith laborer in New York to a metal shop owner in Pittsburgh with a vacation home in Florida and successful children. At the same time, his story of progress is tinged with sadness and nostalgia for the life he left behind in Europe, a life of piety and simplicity, and ambivalence toward the materialism and hypocrisy he detected in some of his fellow Americans.[1]

In multiple ways, Reisman's prize-winning story encapsulates many of the experiences of generations of American Jews. From the 1650s to the present, Jews have come to North America seeking relief from poverty and persecution. Once they arrived, their quest for a livelihood or for a better quality of life took them to new regions and new neighborhoods, and required them to negotiate the complex and often difficult process of adaptation to life in a new country. In the colonial period, Jews concentrated primarily in a handful of eastern port cities. In the nineteenth century, while most Jewish immigrants settled in urban centers, many were drawn to rural areas and small towns, where they filled an important commercial role in the retail and trade sectors of new and developing communities. In the first half of the twentieth century, American Jews were primarily drawn to cities, which suited their economic niche in such fields as commerce, manufacturing, and the professions. Following World War II, many Jewish families left the urban neighborhoods of first and second settlement for suburban settings. Their geographic mobility has been closely connected to their social and occupational mobility.

The American Jewish community has grown from a population of 2,500 in the year 1800 to more than 6.5 million in 2013. Though a small proportion of the American population (3.6 percent at its peak in the 1940s) from the end of World War II until recently, America's Jewish community was undisputedly the largest in the world.[2] Why was America such an attractive destination for Jewish immigrants, and why have Jews enjoyed such remarkable socioeconomic mobility in the United States?

While American Jews have had to confront antisemitic prejudice throughout their history, such as occasional restrictions on their rights of political and religious expression, quotas on immigration and academic admissions, and discrimination in the workplace, these experiences paled in comparison to the hostility and violence they encountered in other lands. As historian Hasia Diner has argued, American Jews, accepted as a white ethnic group, "never functioned as their nation's most stigmatized group" in a country where race, not religion, has proved the most enduring and intractable barrier to equality.[3]

Jews have also benefited from living in a country where their right to assemble and worship as Jews is enshrined in the Constitution. Despite periodic efforts to define America as a Christian nation, Jews have been able to build a vibrant religious, cultural, and social life in the United States, free from the interference of state authorities. In Europe, by contrast, the process of granting Jews civic and political equality from the eighteenth to the twentieth century was complex and uneven, and both the state and Jewish communal authorities often tightly controlled the religious lives of the Jews in their domain.[4]

As significant as religious freedom and social acceptance have been for American Jewry, however, the most important "pull" factor enticing Jewish immigrants to American shores has been economic opportunity. Though the means by which American Jews, as a group, have managed to climb the socioeconomic ladder have changed somewhat over time, Jews have continued to enjoy a remarkable degree of success in the United States. Barred from owning land and farming—the principal means of earning a living in agrarian societies—for much of their history in the Diaspora, Jews concentrated heavily in finance and trade. Their networks, capital, and commercial experience served Jews well in America's free market economy. In the twentieth century, access to free public education and the professions furthered the ascent of most American Jews into the middle class.[5]

Examining American Jewish narratives of migration, mobility, and adaptation illuminates both the blessings that the United States has bestowed on those who came to its borders seeking a better life, as well as the many obstacles faced and costs incurred by American Jews along the way.

From Colonists to American Citizens, 1654–1820

The founding of a Jewish community in America was the result of colonial expansion, wars between western European powers, and religious persecution. The group of twenty-three Jewish men, women, and children who left Brazil and docked on Manhattan

Island in 1654 were primarily Sephardic Jews, who traced their family origins back to the Iberian Peninsula. Their ancestors were New Christians—Spanish and Portuguese Jews who were forced to convert to Christianity at the end of the fifteenth century. Many New Christians continued to practice Judaism in secret, an act of heresy with potentially fatal consequences in the eyes of the Inquisition. Seeking a more tolerant place to live, some *conversos* migrated to Holland in the late sixteenth and early seventeenth centuries, where a vibrant Jewish community developed. From Amsterdam, many Jews elected to participate in the Dutch project of colonization in the New World. By 1645, about 1,450 of them had settled in Brazil (then ruled by the Dutch), where they earned a living as artisans and merchants in the sugar trade.[6]

In 1654, Portugal successfully recaptured Brazil and expelled all those inhabitants affiliated with the Dutch West India Company. While most Jewish refugees returned to Amsterdam, others headed to new destinations in the New World—Barbados, Martinique, and Curaçao. The twenty-three Jews who arrived in New Amsterdam were not the first to make landfall there, as two Jewish individuals had recently preceded them, but they were the first to remain there with the intent of establishing a community. Difficult economic and political conditions in New Amsterdam ultimately led to the attenuation of this first community prior to Britain's conquest of the colony in 1664, when it was renamed New York. A new and permanent Jewish settlement took hold there in the 1680s, however, and by the mid-eighteenth century, Jewish communities had also been formed in Savannah, Georgia; Newport, Rhode Island; Charleston, South Carolina; and Philadelphia.[7]

The establishment and concentration of Jewish communities in major American port cities from the colonial period into the early nineteenth century reflected the economic profile of American Jewry and the migration patterns that brought Jews to American shores. Whereas most European immigrants to America during this era settled in rural areas and engaged in agriculture, most Jewish colonists earned a living in artisanry and trade. Many of them came to the American colonies from London and Amsterdam, sent as representatives from successful Jewish merchant families seeking to extend their commercial networks throughout the Atlantic. In this manner, Jacob Franks came to New York from a family of merchants in London in the early 1700s, and he later sent two of his own sons on to Philadelphia and another back to his extended family in London. These business connections, and their potential to enrich the coffers of colonial treasuries and nurture economic growth, made Jews attractive settlers in the eyes of most local authorities in the New World, though their way of life took its toll on immigrant families. Jacob's wife Abigail despaired to her son Naphtali back in London that "the Cares of giting a Liveing" had scattered her children "Up and down the world and the Only pleasure wee injoy (and that's intermixt with Anxiety) is to hear they doe well."[8]

American Jews often bought and sold goods with each other, as was the case in September 1760, when Isaac Delyon of Savannah shipped four barrels of rice and more than a hundred deer skins to his co-religionist Barnard Gratz of Philadelphia in exchange for a list of groceries that included chocolate, herrings, linseed oil, and apples.[9] Like many other colonial Americans, Jews also owned and sold African slaves along with other lucrative commodities. In October 1762, Isaac Elizer and Samuel Moses, a pair of Jewish merchants based in Newport, wrote to the captain of the ship *Prince George*, whom they hired to transport and sell their goods in Africa. With the proceeds from the sale of their merchandise, Elizer and Moses directed the captain to purchase "as many good merchantable young slaves as you can," and to sell them in the Bahamas. Jews did not play a prominent role in the international or domestic slave trade, but they did participate in the market, and until the Civil War those who lived in areas where slavery was legal owned slaves if they could afford to do so.[10]

While some Jews arrived in the colonies with mercantile connections and capital, poverty and oppression also motivated migration. These dire circumstances drove Jews from central and eastern Europe, along with exiles from Spain and Portugal, to London and Amsterdam, where communal resources to alleviate their condition were quickly overwhelmed. The first group of Jews to land in Savannah, Georgia, in 1733 were from among the less fortunate recent arrivals to London. A trio of wealthy leaders of the London Jewish community, who were engaged in financing and supporting the settlement of the new colony in Georgia, arranged for them to be part of the initial group of colonizers, in hopes that their co-religionists would find better opportunity abroad. Indeed, fourteen of the Jews in this group arrived with enough resources to purchase land in Georgia upon their arrival.[11]

While many Jews did not arrive in the colonies with wealth, some managed to prosper and elevate their status from small-scale shop owner to international trader. Though Joseph Tobias of Charleston advertised himself as a "shopkeeper" to local residents in the 1730s, by 1743 he gave himself the title of "merchant." Isaac Da Costa, also of Charleston, followed this same trajectory in the 1750s. Women also managed stores and businesses. In Philadelphia, Hannah Moses owned a general store where she sold jewelry, knives, and other household items; she also took in boarders as a source of income, as did Hetty Hays and Charity Cohen in New York City. In some cases, women took over their husbands' businesses and ran their estates when their spouses became ill or died. In this manner, Abigail Minis of Savannah assumed control of her husband's mercantile business around the year 1757, while overseeing a plantation and seventeen slaves. She succeeded in expanding the family estate by more than a thousand acres.[12]

As early as 1720, a majority of Jews in the colonies were of Ashkenazi descent, with family origins in central and eastern Europe. As of 1790, the Jewish population in the United States numbered approximately 1,500, a miniscule number in comparison to the total population of the country, then around four million. By 1820, the American Jewish community had grown moderately to about 2,750, or about 0.03 percent of all those living in the United States. In part, these low numbers reflect the fact that, into the nineteenth century, America was not an obviously attractive destination for Jewish immigrants, as success was far from guaranteed. "Only if you are satisfied to live in the country and keep a shop—if you are at all able to do that— . . . would I advise you to come here," wrote Barnard Gratz from Philadelphia to his brother Michael, who was weighing immigration to America in 1758. Difficulties in finding a marriage partner in a small Jewish community, as well as mercantile occupations requiring a considerable amount of travel, also inhibited immigration and population growth.[13] Over the course of the ensuing century, however, successive waves of Jewish immigration from Europe would completely transform the demographics and geography of the fledgling community.

The "Century of Migration," 1820–1924

In 1846, Max Lilienthal, a rabbi who was born in Munich and had arrived in America a year earlier, wrote a series of letters describing the conditions of life for immigrants in the United States that were published in the *Allgemeine Zeitung des Judentums*, a German Jewish newspaper. Lilienthal painted a stark contrast for his readers in Europe between America, "the God-blessed country of freedom," and "[t]he old Europe with its restrictions," which resembled nothing but "a bad dream." He encouraged all those "willing and able to work, ready to overcome the first hardships that meet everyone coming to a strange country" to make the journey to America, where Jews would no longer be restrained by oppressive laws that limited where they could live, whether they could marry, and how they could earn a living.[14] Lilienthal's endorsement of America as a land of opportunity, echoed in hundreds of other newspapers, books, poems, and letters home to European Jews from relatives and friends, helped inspire a mass migration.[15]

Between 1820 and 1924, economic and political developments, as well as technological advancements in transportation and industry, dramatically reshaped American life and the American Jewish community. Over the course of one hundred years, about 25 percent of European Jewry left the continent for destinations in the Americas, primarily the United States. From 1880 to 1924, a third of the Jews from eastern European lands migrated to other countries, with almost 80 percent entering America.[16]

Hasia Diner, who has termed this era in American Jewish history the "century of migration," argues that migration was a central feature of the global Jewish experience during the nineteenth and early twentieth centuries. In these years, she observes, "[t]he migration went almost always from east to west, from places of limited Jewish rights and restricted opportunities to places of expanded rights and greater opportunities."[17] From a population of fewer than three thousand in 1820, the American Jewish community grew by more than 250,000 by 1880. Between 1880 and 1924, when the Johnson-Reed Act severely curtailed Jewish immigration to the United States, more than 2.5 million Jews came to America.[18] Once an insignificant and transitory community, American Jewry by 1920 constituted one of the largest and most important Jewish communities in the world.

The mass migration of Jews is part of a larger chapter in European history, as a series of social, political, and economic upheavals contributed to significant population shifts across the continent. European immigration to America, from roughly 1820 to 1880, consisted primarily of individuals from northern and western Europe. After 1880, while migrants continued to emigrate from those regions, immigrants from southern and eastern Europe considerably outnumbered them. Wars and failed revolutions, declining agrarian economies, and the twin phenomena of industrialization and urbanization drove Europeans from their countries of origin. While European Jews also faced many of these same pressures, discrimination, oppression, and outbreaks of violence intensified their inclination to emigrate. Jews from central and eastern Europe may have journeyed across the Atlantic for similar reasons, but their experiences as new immigrants were not identical, due to rapid social and economic changes in American life from the mid-nineteenth century to the early twentieth. As historian Eric Goldstein explains, Jewish immigrants who came to America in the decades before the Civil War entered a country in the early

Figure 3.1 Immigrants and their belongings, 1912. Photograph by Underwood & Underwood.

Courtesy of the Library of Congress.

phase of industrialization and territorial expansion. In these circumstances, many of them found success as artisans and retailers providing needed goods and important resources to developing towns and cities across the country. After 1880, however, the United States was well on its way to becoming a global industrial force and an urbanized country. Economic opportunity for most immigrants now entailed factory jobs in America's largest cities, which offered a slower path to socioeconomic mobility.[19]

Jewish Immigration from Central Europe

Though the era from 1820 to 1880 is sometimes described as the "German" period in American Jewish history, this is a problematic term. Until 1871, there was no unified German nation: most Jewish immigrants to the United States during these years came from German-speaking lands, such as Bavaria, Baden, and Württemburg, or territories where German culture predominated among the urban middle and upper classes, such as Bohemia, Moravia, and Posen. They were therefore a diverse group linguistically, religiously, and socioeconomically. Additionally, during the middle decades of the nineteenth century, Jews from Lithuania, Galicia, and other parts of eastern Europe made their way to the United States as well, further complicating the profile of the American Jewish immigrant of this epoch.[20]

Most Jews who immigrated to America in the mid-nineteenth century were neither poor nor wealthy. Primarily, they were young single men from lower-middle-class families whose ambitions to marry and earn a living were thwarted by legal restrictions that limited the numbers of Jews who could reside and marry in certain parts of central Europe. Many of them had completed apprenticeships in crafts but were unable to turn these into a stable livelihood. In some cases, they emigrated to avoid conscription. The new immigrants came over with some formal education and some start-up capital, which both aided in their transition in America and made the trip across the ocean affordable. Women emigrated as well, sometimes together with their marriage partners, or once their tickets abroad had been paid for by their future spouses.[21]

This practice was one facet of the chain migration by which many Jews came to America, having been sent for or encouraged to come over by a husband, sibling, relative, or fellow townsman. In 1847, Menasses Hirsch of New York City sent his sister Babette back in Europe a letter in which he enclosed seventy-five dollars, "sufficient funds for the journey" to America for herself and their brother. Three years earlier, in 1844, at the age of nineteen, Julius Weis made up his mind to leave for America upon hearing from a cousin whose return to Europe to visit family "created quite a stir among our people." His relative lived in Natchez, Mississippi, and worked in a dry goods business. As Weis, who later settled in New Orleans, recalled in his memoirs, "I listened to his accounts of [America] and made up my mind to come here."[22]

For some Jewish immigrants of this era, especially those of higher socioeconomic standing, participation in German cultural and political clubs and activities in the United States eased their transition into their new surroundings. These Jews patronized German theaters and opera halls, sang in German musical societies, and celebrated some German festivals. At the same time, as Hasia Diner indicates, the vast majority of Jewish immigrants came over from central Europe with little formal education, did not necessarily speak German, and found little to identify with in German American associational life. Vivid memories of antisemitism back in Germany may also have kept Jews and Germans from mingling in the United States.[23]

Many new American Jews began their climb up the socioeconomic ladder as peddlers, bringing manufactured goods to both urban and rural customers in the era before department stores and mass transit. Abraham Kohn came to the United States from Bavaria in 1842 when he was twenty-three years old. Though he was successful enough as a peddler to open his own dry goods store in Chicago two years later—a pattern of mobility followed by many of his immigrant contemporaries—his diary describes the trials and tribulations he and his fellow peddlers faced in adjusting to America and the challenges of an itinerant lifestyle:

> Thousands of peddlers wander about America; young, strong men, they waste their strength by carrying heavy loads in the summer's heat; they lose their health in the icy cold of winter. And thus they forget completely their Creator. They no longer put on the phylacteries; they pray neither on working day nor on the Sabbath. In truth, they have given up their religion for the pack which is on their backs.[24]

Jewish peddlers in America played a critical role in an expanding nineteenth-century economy in the early stages of industrialization. They served markets that lacked easy access to goods, and they facilitated the growth and settlement of cities and small towns across the United States. In the process, Jewish immigrants adapted to American culture, learned the geography and language of their new home country, and in many cases were able to save enough money after a short time to open a store, work in wholesale distribution, or venture into manufacturing. In Boston in 1860, almost a third of the Jewish workforce engaged in peddling, while more than half of the Jews of Syracuse, New York, and Easton, Pennsylvania, earned their livelihood this way. Many of the most famous names in American retail—Strauss, Gimbel, Rosenwald, Bloomingdale—belonged to German-Jewish immigrant families who followed the trajectory from peddler to shop-keeper to commercial elites in the course of only one or two generations. A small number of other families, including the Lehmans and Seligmans, made their fortunes in finance.[25]

The vast majority of Jewish immigrants did not become so wealthy, but many were able to rise into the ranks of the middle class in a relatively short period of time. Those who began earning a livelihood as craftsmen—tailors, cigar makers, watch makers—later opened stores that sold those goods. A number of Jews also made a living in garment manufacturing and distribution, an industry that was revolutionized by the invention of the sewing machine in the 1850s and the introduction of standard sizes during the Civil War. The sewing machine made it possible for garment shops to meet the unprecedented demand for uniforms during the war, as well as a rise in the demand for ready-made civilian clothing. Both before and after 1880, Jews found the garment industry to be amenable to economic mobility, despite low profit margins and unpleasant working conditions, since little capital was required to advance from sweatshop employee to contractor. Many young Jewish women as well as men earned a living through the garment trade, in which Jews soon predominated at all levels from laborer to manufacturer. Nearly a quarter of Philadelphia Jewry was active in the garment business in 1860.[26]

As they fanned out across America, selling goods and opening retail stores, this generation of immigrants established Jewish communities from coast to coast. Some of them settled in small towns such as Marion, Indiana, and Greeley, Colorado, where they predominated in dry goods retailing. "Jew stores," as they were commonly known across the South, provided towns and rural communities with clothing and household goods.[27] While New York, Philadelphia, and Charleston remained the most important centers of American Jewish life into the mid-nineteenth century, new communities in the Midwest, along the Gulf Coast, and in California became significant as well.[28] Cincinnati, strategically located on the Ohio River, became an important commercial gateway during westward expansion. Goods from the East Coast made their way to merchants and manufacturers in Cincinnati, who then provided Midwestern peddlers and retailers with wares to sell. As Jewish immigrants played an integral role in this economy at multiple levels, the community grew from a population of one thousand in 1840 to 7,600 by 1860. In a sign of its prominence on the American Jewish landscape, Isaac Mayer Wise established Hebrew Union College, the first successful Jewish seminary in the United States, in the "Queen City" in 1875.[29]

Following the discovery of gold in California in 1848, a quarter of a million people made the arduous journey by boat, horse, and wagon to the West Coast in search of riches. San Francisco, a tiny town of less than a thousand people, rapidly became one of the most vibrant, diverse, and attractive cities in the country. Its Jewish community grew quickly as well. As of 1860, about ten thousand Jews were living in the western United States; half of them chose to make their home in San Francisco. In 1849, Louis Sloss set out from Kentucky for California at the age of twenty-five, surviving cholera and hunger on his way to Sacramento. Five years later, in 1854, Fanny and Julius Bruck left New York, having only arrived there five months earlier from Hamburg. Their trek to California took them to Illinois, then to Nebraska, where they joined company with a wagon train that traversed the Oregon Trail. Fanny remembered that "[t]he dust was terrific in the hot summer and after a rain or a thunderstorm the roads were impassable, and the poor animals could barely pull their load." Their first child died along the way, but they survived the trek to the West, eventually choosing to settle in Salt Lake City.[30]

The American Jewish community in 1880 numbered more than a quarter of a million people, with a rich institutional infrastructure of synagogues, benevolent societies, and cultural organizations. While New York and the port cities of the East Coast remained the most important centers of American Jewish life, substantial communities had developed in the Midwest, along the West Coast, and in New Orleans. As of 1878, about 30 percent of Jews lived in small cities and towns in every region and almost every state in the Union, in Jewish communities with populations numbering in the tens and hundreds in places such as Mobile, Alabama, and Wheeling, West Virginia. On the western frontier, Jews faced fewer barriers to social and political advancement; by 1900, they had

Figure 3.2 The Nudelman family at home in Wellington, Nevada, 1895. The Nudelmans tried repeatedly to farm in South Dakota, California, and Nevada before settling in Portland, Oregon.

Courtesy of the Oregon Jewish Museum and Holocaust Education Center. OJM 00643.

been elected to mayoral offices in cities such as Los Angeles, San Francisco, Portland, and Tucson.[31] Over the next forty years, about 2.5 million Jews from eastern Europe would make their way to the United States, transforming the contours of American Jewish life yet again.

Jewish Immigration from Eastern Europe

Rose Silverman was born in Berdichev, a city in modern-day Ukraine, in 1892. Her father manufactured saddles and struggled to earn a living for the family, and her mother died before she turned four years old. She remembered her childhood as "pieces of torn, crumbled days . . . of nakedness, going barefoot and hungry—and obviously unhappy." Rose taught herself how to read and write in Yiddish, and she absorbed modern literature and political tracts. By the time she was nineteen, she supported her father and younger brother with a modest income as a dressmaker, but she felt intellectually and emotionally stifled. Two of her sisters had already left for the United States, but her father resisted letting her emigrate. She told him, "My future is in America. Whether you like it or not." With sixty rubles and her meager possessions, Rose arrived "onto the free ground of the Golden Land" in August of 1913.[32]

From 1881 to 1924, more than 2.5 million Jews immigrated to the United States along with Rose, ten times the number of Jews who had arrived over the preceding sixty years. Not all came from eastern Europe—thirty thousand Sephardic Jews from Greece, Turkey, and the Balkans made their way to America in the first decades of the twentieth century, and many of them settled together in a section of the Lower East Side in New York City. Primarily, however, new immigrants from the Russian Pale of Settlement, Galicia, and the Kingdom of Poland came to America as a result of poverty and limited economic prospects, as well as stifling regulations on their civil rights—conditions similar to those that drove Jews from central Europe in earlier decades. A devastating series of *pogroms*, or outbursts of peasant mob violence directed at Jews and tolerated by Russian authorities, certainly encouraged migration. However, Jews also left eastern Europe in large numbers from regions that experienced little mob violence, such as Galicia, where difficult economic conditions were the primary "push" factor.[33]

Whereas previous generations of Jewish immigrants consisted primarily of single Jewish men, during the late nineteenth and early twentieth centuries, women emigrated in equal numbers, often as part of multigenerational family units. As before, the absolute poorest among European Jewry remained behind. The majority of those who left eastern Europe were not merchants or retailers, but skilled workers with experience in manufacturing who struggled to earn a living in an economy without enough factory jobs to support them. When they arrived in America, they discovered a country that was well into the process of urbanization and industrialization. While some among this larger, later wave of migration followed their predecessors into peddling and settlement in small towns, the vast majority chose to remain in New York City and other large industrial centers, including Boston, Philadelphia, and Chicago. There, they found work in garment factories and other manufacturing sectors, such as cigar making, diamond cutting, and book-binding.[34]

Immigrant Jews of this generation tended to settle in urban neighborhoods near the ports where they embarked and the factories where many of them worked. Living conditions in these communities were generally poor, due to overcrowding and lack of effective sanitation and ventilation in the tenement buildings that many called home. Rose Cohen, who arrived in New York City in 1892 at the age of twelve to join her father, worked for a time alongside him sewing men's coats in a shop on Monroe Street on the Lower East Side. In a memoir, she described how her workday began at six in the morning, and her "fingers often stiffened with pain" from the labor. But she took great pride in being able to learn and complete her tasks. They lived in a nearby tenement apartment on Cherry Street, "a dingy place where the sun never came in."[35]

A pattern of neighborhood turnover tied to socioeconomic progress, with new Jewish immigrants moving into areas abandoned by their upwardly mobile predecessors, took hold in major cities.[36] In Boston, for example, eastern European Jewish immigrants in the 1880s first settled in the South End neighborhood, which already had a small but established presence of German and Polish Jews. Over the next fifteen years, however, the North End became the hub of the eastern European Jewish immigrant community, thanks to its proximity to the waterfront and to factories, while the wealthier community of Central European Jews migrated out to Roxbury and the Back Bay. Between 1892 and 1917, when eastern European Jews earned enough to move, they went to the West End and then to Roxbury and Dorchester to the south.[37]

Like Boston, Chicago's Jewish community also dates to the early 1840s, when a number of peddlers, mostly from Bavaria, settled in the city's commercial district along Lake and Clark. There were about four thousand Jews in Chicago as of 1871, with the most well-off among them now living at the southern end of downtown, and newer immigrants moving into the original Jewish neighborhood. That year, the Great Chicago Fire of 1871 ravaged the downtown area, displacing hundreds of Jewish families and prompting many of them to relocate to the South Side of the city, where a vibrant and affluent German Jewish community took root.

Immigrants arriving from eastern Europe in the second wave of migration after 1880 settled southwest of downtown, near the railroad tracks where they had entered the city and where housing was most affordable. This neighborhood, later known as the Maxwell Street area, had previously been home to German, Bohemian, and Irish immigrants. Here, Jewish immigrants worked in the garment industry and as retailers and wholesalers in the Maxwell Street open-air market, a colorful bazaar filled with "the smell of garlic and of cheeses, the aroma of onions, apples, and oranges, and the shouts and curses of sellers and buyers."[38]

By 1910, as their economic situation improved and as African Americans began to move into the Maxwell Street neighborhood, most eastern European Jewish immigrants moved westward into Lawndale and parts of northwest Chicago. Here and elsewhere around the country, the Jews who remained behind in neighborhoods of first settlement tended to be the elderly and the poor. As immigrants climbed the socioeconomic ladder in the first decades of the twentieth century, seeking out neighborhoods with better and bigger housing, they often sought to live with their fellow Jews, creating new ethnic enclaves at the edges of America's largest cities.[39]

Figure 3.3 Cover of *Der Yiddisher Farmer; The Jewish Farmer*, April 1918, published by the Jewish Agricultural and Industrial Aid Society. For many years this monthly was "the only agricultural magazine in the world published in Yiddish." It provided advice on scientific farming and ads for services and goods.

As with the first wave of migration, however, not all post-1880 Jewish immigrants opted for urban living. In some cases, they chose to leave cities for better entrepreneurial opportunities in developing places. The Madanic family of St. Louis serves as one example of this process of secondary and tertiary migration. Hyman Madanic, together with his son Ben, came to St. Louis from Russia in 1899. From meager beginnings as sweat-shop laborers, they saved enough to open a clothing store in southern Illinois, and then a chain of stores centered around Tulsa, Oklahoma, after 1908. As of 1927, there were approximately 490 Jewish communities throughout the United States with populations between one hundred and one thousand, and another 251 communities where the Jewish population was higher than fifty but less than one hundred.[40]

In other cases, eastern European Jewish immigrants were actively encouraged to find homes and jobs beyond the East Coast. In the first decades of the twentieth century, American Jewish leaders such as Simon Wolf and Jacob Schiff worried that the continued influx of immigrants from eastern Europe would exacerbate urban overcrowding, exhaust communal resources, and provoke a backlash of antisemitic and xenophobic reactions, including legislation to restrict immigration. In response, they developed two initiatives designed to disperse eastern European Jewish immigrants across the country and to provide them with housing and work, sometimes in agriculture rather than retail.

In 1901, Jewish communal workers established the Industrial Removal Office (IRO) in New York City. Here, unemployed immigrants could apply to be sent, with financial aid, to a smaller Jewish community, where locals would help them find a job and a place to live. The IRO maintained branch committees in Jewish communities throughout the country, which kept them notified about job prospects and agreed to accept new arrivals based on monthly quotas. Between 1903 and 1917, the IRO sent over seventy-five thousand people to destinations across all forty-eight states and Canada. While some immigrants were grateful for the fresh start and the support, others despaired at the isolating conditions and lack of economic prospects they found in some rural places. One immigrant wrote to the IRO from Weatherford, Oklahoma, informing them that their substantial investment of "trouble and money" in sending him out west was "all a mistake," and that neither he nor his employer were able to make a living. The vast majority of immigrants opted to stay in New York and other major cities, which they felt offered a better quality of life.[41]

The "Galveston Plan," another initiative to send Jewish immigrants west of the Mississippi, aimed to take advantage of recent legislation establishing a port of entry at Galveston, Texas, in 1906. Jacob Schiff and other communal leaders believed that immigrants would be more likely to remain outside the East Coast if they entered the country from the Gulf of Mexico, rather than the Atlantic Ocean. Schiff hoped that this effort would allow for "a steady stream of immigrants [to] flow through New Orleans and Galveston into the territory between the Mississippi River on the east, the Pacific Ocean on the west, the Gulf on the south and the Canadian Dominion on the north."[42]

From 1907 to 1914, the so-called Galveston Plan managed to bring approximately ten thousand Jews to America, but this represented only 1 percent of the total immigration from eastern Europe during that period. Both the immigrants themselves, as well as the Russian and American governments, resisted. One immigrant who was sent to Sioux City, Iowa, through this initiative subsequently wrote to his wife in Europe, instructing her to sell their possessions and send him the money so that he could purchase a ticket for New York. As with the IRO and other efforts to settle Jews across the American continent, this project produced limited results.[43]

For decades, American Jewish communal leaders feared that the rising tide of xenophobia in American culture and politics could close the gates to immigration. In the 1920s, these fears were realized, as Congress passed legislation to severely limit immigration from southern and eastern Europe. While the quotas instituted by the National Origins Act of 1924 did not end Jewish immigration to the United States, they did mark an end to the century of migration that forever reshaped the American Jewish community. From the 1920s to the 1940s, most Jews seeking to enter the United States would have to resort to desperate, and sometimes illegal, means.

Safe Havens and Suburbs: Jewish Migrations to and within America Since 1924

Within a generation of the passage of the immigration quotas passed in the 1920s, the 1940 census revealed that, for the first time, a majority of American Jews was born in the United States. Nevertheless, despite substantial legal and logistical barriers, Jewish immigration to America continued. As historian Libby Garland has recently demonstrated, while exact numbers are impossible to pinpoint, it is likely that "tens of thousands" of Jews made their way to the United States illegally between 1921 and 1965, sometimes making use of forged documents, aliases, disguises, and other tools of deception to bypass quota limits and border agents.[44]

In 1926, Isaac Limonsky and his two sons, David and Lazer, entered the country separately with fake papers, presenting themselves as German citizens when they in fact were Lithuanian Jews. Isaac Limonsky had originally intended to emigrate to Uruguay, but a smuggler on a train to Berlin steered him toward the United States and provided him with the necessary papers. David Limonsky went first to Cuba as a legal immigrant, where he had trouble finding steady work. After returning to Europe, he met a Yiddish-speaking man named Hymie, who supplied him with an American visa and the identity of David Binder, a German citizen. Lazer Limonsky planned to sail from Berlin to Canada, where he would slip across the border into America. While at the ticket office to purchase his passage on the Cunard Line, however, he also met a smuggler who gave him German papers under the name Louis Meerowitz. Like earlier generations of Jewish immigrants, the Limonskys and their contemporaries came to America hoping to find better economic opportunities, to reunite with family members, and to evade conscription.[45]

With Hitler's rise to power in Germany in 1933, Jewish immigration took on far greater urgency amid increasing discrimination and persecution imposed on Jews under the Third Reich. Jews wishing to flee the Nazi regime for the United States faced extreme difficulties, however, both because the Germans confiscated a significant portion of their

Figure 3.4 Wilhelm, Gertrude, Victor, Henry, Rudolph, and Walter Cohen, fleeing Nazi Germany. They departed from Amsterdam, July 21, 1939, on their way to America, shortly before the outbreak of World War II.

Courtesy of Rudolph Cohen and Jewish Museum of Maryland. JMM L2003.063.5

assets as a condition for emigration, and because the State Department, reflecting strong xenophobic tendencies among both Congress and the American public, actively worked to underfill the already strict quotas. In a 1940 memo to department officials, Assistant Secretary of State Breckinridge Long recommended that consuls "put every obstacle in the way of immigrants," by means of "various administrative devices which would postpone and postpone and postpone the granting of the visas."[46]

All told, despite these hurdles, some 138,000 Jewish refugees managed to immigrate to the United States between 1933 and 1944—"certainly not all who would have wanted to come but more than any other nation admitted," as Libby Garland observes. A substantial number of them were rabbis and scholars, brought over at the invitation of organizations, universities, and Jewish institutions. The Emergency Committee in Aid of Displaced Foreign Scholars provided emigration assistance to more than three hundred leading European Jewish intellectuals who had been forced out of their positions by antisemitic legislation. Gina Castelnuovo, an Italian Jewish biologist, wrote to the Emergency Committee in April 1939, informing them that she had "lost [her] position in Italy on account of being a Jewess." Her father and other family members shared the same fate. While Niels Bohr, the Danish Nobel Prize–winning physicist, had offered Castelnuovo a temporary position in Copenhagen, the police there nevertheless informed her that she would be required to leave the country on May 25. "Now I am very troubled," she wrote, "because it is impossible to find another position in all countries of Europe," since foreigners could not secure work permits. Castelnuovo came to New York that July, where she found work in a laboratory at the Museum of Natural History.[47]

Besides the Emergency Committee, The New School for Social Research in New York City, as well as several black colleges in the South, took on refugee academics and intellectuals who taught foreign languages and the social sciences, while the Reform movement's Hebrew Union College brought Rabbi Abraham Joshua Heschel and other Jewish scholars to Cincinnati to form what became known as the "Jewish College in Exile." The list of Jewish refugees from this era who transformed American science and culture includes physicist Albert Einstein, political philosopher Hannah Arendt, psychologists Erik Erikson and Kurt Lewin, and composers Kurt Weill and Arnold Schoenberg.[48]

Most of the refugee arrivals of the 1930s were not intellectuals, however, but rather middle-class and upper-class professionals and businessmen. A group of them settled in the Washington Heights neighborhood of upper Manhattan between 1938 and 1940, where they formed a tightly knit community bound together by synagogues, clubs, periodicals, and organizations that retained both a distinctive German cultural character and a traditional Jewish flavor. Over time, German Jewish refugees established or constituted a majority of members at approximately thirty synagogues in the neighborhood, ranging from the Reform Hebrew Tabernacle to the Orthodox K'hal Adath Jeshurun. As of 1940, Washington Heights was home to eight kosher butcher shops, as well as bakeries offering German delicacies. That same year, the census reported more than twenty thousand Jews of German descent living in the neighborhood.[49]

By the end of World War II, the Nazi program of extermination reduced Europe's Jewish population from 9.5 million to 6.5 million. For most of the survivors of the Holocaust, especially those from eastern Europe, returning to their home countries was all but impossible, as in many cases their former neighborhoods were destroyed and their homes appropriated. Antisemitic hostility and violence continued in Poland and Hungary after the war. Thousands of Jewish survivors made their way to displaced persons camps, where they waited for permission to resettle. Between 1946 and 1954, 140,000 Jewish displaced persons arrived in the United States, despite continued advocacy and resistance by immigration restrictionists both inside and outside Congress. The new immigrants were aided by Jewish agencies set up to assist refugees with the resettlement process, including the American Jewish Joint Distribution Committee and the United Service for New Americans.[50]

Though most survivors desired to stay in New York and did so, they ultimately dispersed across the country in forty-six states. Echoing concerns from earlier in the century about dense concentrations of Jews in major cities inciting an upsurge in antisemitism, the United Service for New Americans and other agencies worked to settle Jews outside New York, in locations such as Columbia, South Carolina; Providence, Rhode Island; and Denver, Colorado. Once in the United States, many survivors faced a long and difficult path of adaptation, needing to cope both with the enormous trauma of their experiences in Europe and with the process of adjustment to American life. One survivor in Denver, a thirty-nine-year-old man from Poland, confided to a social worker that he was desperate to find work as means of combating his loneliness and depression. He had lost his entire family during the war and now had trouble sleeping. Another survivor confided to a social worker that "had he known what difficulties he would meet here and what adventures, he would stayed over there [in Europe]."[51]

About 1,500 survivor families got their start in America by farming, despite the fact that many of them had no prior agricultural experience. Several of them settled in Vineland, New Jersey, where they boosted a pre-existing community of Jewish farmers. Chris and Miles Lerman went to Vineland from Brooklyn, enticed by the appeal of scenic countryside living and the opportunity to rebuild a community with fellow survivors. For others, farm life served to ease their adjustment to America. As Louis Goldman, the son of survivors, recalled, "Word got around that Jews were buying farms and you could be your own boss and you didn't have to worry about the language that much." Genia Klapholz, who owned a chicken farm and organized a Jewish day school in Vineland with her husband Henry, remembered her family's stay there as their "happiest ten years in the United States."[52]

While the Klapholz family and some other Holocaust survivors sought refuge in the greener pastures of rural America, millions of Jews joined their fellow Americans in leaving cities for the suburbs after the war. Enticed by visions of single-family homes with large backyards on tree-lined streets, Jews and other Americans viewed the suburbs as the ideal place to raise families in the baby boom era. According to two-thirds of male homeowners surveyed in Levittown, New York, a desire to spend more quality time with their children motivated their family's move to the suburbs. Rabbi Albert Gordon recorded similar findings in his 1959 study, *Jews in Suburbia*, a sociological overview of American Jewish life in suburbia based largely on questionnaire responses. As one anonymous suburbanite explained to Gordon, "I moved out here for the sake of the kids. I want them to have the best that I can afford."[53]

American Jews stood at the forefront of the suburbanization phenomenon in the post–World War II decades, outpacing all other subgroups of American society in their rate of geographic mobility. During the 1950s, the number of Jewish suburbanites doubled, so that by 1960, two-thirds of America's 5.5 million Jews called suburban communities home. In this era, Jews took up residence in suburban neighborhoods at a rate four times greater than that of other Americans. Substantial Jewish communities took root in such places as Newton, Massachusetts; Skokie, Illinois; and Silver Spring, Maryland.[54]

Jewish suburbanization after World War II represented the continuation and intensification of a longer trend in American history, in which economically mobile groups migrated away from areas of first settlement to more desirable neighborhoods when such a move was financially and legally feasible. In this last respect, American Jews benefited from new developments in housing laws after the war, as in 1948 the Supreme Court struck down the restrictive covenants that had enabled residential discrimination. As white ethnics, Jews were also able to take advantage of federal housing loans and the GI Bill as they pursued homes in segregated suburban neighborhoods that were often off limits to African Americans. Real estate agents and developers, both Jewish and non-Jewish, often steered Jewish clients toward suburban neighborhoods with large Jewish populations and in close proximity to synagogues.[55]

In addition to court decisions, federal policies, and the actions of real estate agents and home buyers, the ascent of most American Jews into the middle class in this era also facilitated suburbanization. Following the Great Depression and World War II, American Jews enjoyed a period of unprecedented prosperity and continued advancement up the socioeconomic ladder. In 1900, 60 percent of the American Jewish labor force worked in blue-collar manufacturing jobs. Statistical surveys from the 1950s measuring the educational and occupational profile of postwar American Jewry, by contrast, revealed that between 75 and 96 percent of Jews earned their livelihood from non-manual labor, compared to less than 40 percent of the rest of the population. Additionally, while one in six American Jews above eighteen years old had earned a college degree as of 1953, the same held true for only one in twenty among all other Americans. The origins of American Jewish mobility preceded the war, as Jews benefited from the protections of labor unions and investments made in educating their children in the 1920s and 1930s. As sociologist Nathan Glazer remarked in assessing the socioeconomic profile of American Jewry in the 1950s, "[T]he Jewish economic advantage, already perfectly obvious in the thirties, in the form of superior education, and a higher proportion of self-employed persons, has borne fruit in the fifteen years of prosperity since 1940."[56]

As Jews rose into the ranks of the American middle class, they moved into middle-class neighborhoods. In addition to the suburbs of the Northeast and Midwest, many American Jews also migrated west and south, making their new homes in such places as Miami and Los Angeles. Many American Jews, such as Eddie Zwern, discovered these coastal paradises while serving in the army. Zwern was enchanted by California during his brief stay at Fort Ord on the Monterey Bay Peninsula. After the war, unable to afford the cross-country fare from his home in the Bronx back to the Golden State, he lied to the Army, informing them that his wife Pauline had relocated to California. Once he had earned enough for an apartment in Los Angeles, he brought his wife over, and they were soon joined by all of their siblings. Along with the Zwerns, Jews flocked to Los Angeles in the late 1940s and 1950s. From a city of 130,000 Jews before the war, Los Angeles housed three hundred thousand by 1951. By 1955, Los Angeles was home to the second largest Jewish community in America.[57]

Miami also emerged as an important Jewish center in the years after the war, as its population mushroomed from sixteen thousand to one hundred thousand within a decade. By 1960, Miami became home to the sixth largest Jewish community in the country. Scarred by rough winters in the north as well as decades of war and depression, the appeal of vacation-style living appealed to many Jews, who often came first as tourists to these cities before deciding to stay. The economies of both cities boomed in the postwar decades, providing opportunities for newcomers in retail, real estate, technology, and various industries connected to the military. A distinctively Jewish presence emerged in the Miami Beach hotel scene, with Jewish hotel owners catering to Jewish clientele with kosher kitchens and Passover holiday retreat packages.[58]

Here, along the beaches of Florida and California, as in the suburbs of northern and Midwestern cities, American Jews in the postwar period came in search of a better quality of life. Continuing a pattern set by their predecessors in earlier generations, they built new communal institutions—synagogues, schools, philanthropic organizations—designed to ease their adjustment to their new surroundings. At the same time, however, they also set a pattern that future generations of American Jews would follow. In Los Angeles and Miami, historian Deborah Dash Moore argued, Jewish culture absorbed aspects of Protestant individualism. In these coastal communities, "Jews supported Israel, joined a synagogue, or participated in Jewish politics, not due to the weight of tradition or any collective compulsion," but rather out of their own convictions and desire for self-fulfillment. In the late twentieth century, this ethos would become increasingly typical of American Jewish life across the country.[59]

In the last half of the twentieth century, America continued to provide refuge for Jews around the world, as it had done for more than three hundred years. Jews fleeing political upheaval and persecution arrived from Egypt, Cuba, and Hungary in the 1950s and 1960s. The Hart-Celler Act of 1965 eliminated the quota system of the 1920s, allowing for greater immigration from areas outside northern and western Europe. Thirty-five thousand Iranian Jews emigrated to America after the 1979 revolution, and they were joined by waves of Jewish immigration from South Africa and Israel. Significant enclaves of Syrian Jews emerged in Brooklyn, while South African Jews created new subcommunities in cities such as Houston and Los Angeles.[60]

The largest group of Jewish immigrants in this era, numbering more than four hundred thousand since the 1970s, came from the Soviet Union and its successor states. Pervasive antisemitism, a dysfunctional economy, and the conditions of life under a dictatorial regime often openly hostile toward Jews and Judaism motivated Soviet Jews to attempt to leave the country between 1967 and 1981, when the doors to emigration were closed amid a government-sponsored backlash against Zionism and Jewish culture. Tens of thousands of *refuseniks*, those Soviet Jews whose applications for exit visas were routinely denied, and who faced imprisonment and unemployment for attempting to leave, became a cause célèbre for American Jews and the international community.[61]

For Jews living in Leningrad in the 1970s, such as Marya Frumkin and Tamara Katyn, the desire to come to America echoed the longing of Jews from earlier generations, who wished to escape persecution and experience freedom. While many of them were assimilated and identified deeply with Russian culture, their passports marked them as Jewish by nationality, and they faced constant harassment and discrimination in public. Katyn "fought very hard all of the time" to maintain her position as a university professor in finance, she recalled, and she was fired once it became known that she had applied for an exit visa. Marya Frumkin described the physical and emotional agony involved in the emigration process for Jews: "You would go from line to line and they wouldn't give you the papers. And all the time you couldn't work, maybe you couldn't eat, and you never knew if they were going to let you go. I didn't believe that it was real, even after the plane was off the ground."[62]

Once in America, as with previous generations of Jewish immigrants, a majority of Soviet Jews and Jews who left after the fall of Communism chose to stay in New York, settling in neighborhoods of Brooklyn and Queens that had long been home to substantial Jewish communities, such as Brighton Beach, Boro Park, and Forest Hills. Chicago,

Boston, Los Angeles, and San Francisco also became important centers of Soviet Jewry. In adapting to American Jewish life, many immigrants embraced their Russian cultural heritage, opening and patronizing institutions for Russian music, art, gymnastics, and dance. A minority among them embraced traditional Judaism, while others associated less with religion and more with Yiddish culture as their preferred vehicle of Jewish expression. Many Jews from the former Soviet Union faced difficulties in reconciling their conception of Jewishness as an ethnic and cultural identity with the beliefs and expectations of those American Jews who defined themselves as Jewish primarily through Judaism and religious observance. Whereas American Jewish organizations often reached out to welcome them with prayer books and Jewish ritual items, many immigrants complained that what they needed most was assistance finding jobs and places to live.[63]

Nevertheless, although they often faced considerable cultural and financial challenges, many Jews from the Soviet Union rejoiced that they had arrived in a country where it was not a crime to be Jewish. "The first time I heard Yiddish spoken on the street [in Brighton Beach]," recalled one woman from Odessa, "I couldn't believe my ears. Then I saw little boys wearing yarmulkes [skullcaps worn by the religious], walking down the street unafraid, and I cried."[64] For this woman, as for generations of Jews who crossed oceans and cities in search of a better life, America has beckoned as a land of freedom and opportunity for more than 350 years.

Notes

1. Jocelyn Cohen and Daniel Soyer, "Introduction: Yiddish Social Science and Jewish Immigrant Autobiography," in *My Future Is in America: Autobiographies of Eastern European Jewish Immigrants*, eds. Jocelyn Cohen and Daniel Soyer (New York: New York University Press, 2006), 1–6; Ben Reisman, "Why I Came to America," in Cohen and Soyer, *My Future Is in America*, 35–105.

2. "Appendix: American Jewish Population Estimates, 1660—2000," in Jonathan D. Sarna, *American Judaism: A History* (New Haven: Yale University Press, 2004), 375; Ira Sheskin and Arnold Dashefsky, "Jewish Population in the United States, 2013," *American Jewish Year Book* 113 (2013), 201–77; Sergio DellaPergola, "World Jewish Population, 2013," *American Jewish Year Book* 113 (2013), 279–358. In contrast to Sheshkin and Dashefsky, whose figure of 6.5 million is used above, DellaPergola estimates the American Jewish population at about 5.4 million, below that of Israel. Both articles are worth reading for a discussion of some of the complications and controversies inherent in calculating Jewish population figures.

3. Hasia R. Diner, *The Jews of the United States, 1654 to 2000* (Berkeley: University of California Press, 2004), 3. On American Jews' experiences with antisemitism, see Leonard Dinnerstein, *Antisemitism in America* (New York: Oxford University Press, 1994). On American Jews and issues surrounding racial identity, see Eric L. Goldstein, *The Price of Whiteness: Jews, Race, and American Identity* (Princeton: Princeton University Press, 2006); and Matthew Frye Jacobson, *Whiteness of a Different Color: European Immigrants and the Alchemy of Race* (Cambridge: Harvard University Press, 1998).

4. Sarna, *American Judaism*, 36–41; Diner, *The Jews of the United States*, 53–57.

5. Jerry Z. Muller, *Capitalism and the Jews: A History* (Princeton: Princeton University Press, 2011); Rebecca Kobrin, ed., *Chosen Capital: The Jewish Encounter with American Capitalism* (New Brunswick: Rutgers University Press, 2012).

6. Eli Faber, "America's Earliest Jewish Settlers, 1654-1820," in *The Columbia History of Jews and Judaism in America*, ed. Marc Lee Raphael (New York: Columbia University Press, 2008), 21–23. On the *conversos* and the Amsterdam Jewish community, see Miriam Bodian, *Hebrews of the Portuguese Nation: Conversos and Community in Early Modern Amsterdam* (Bloomington: Indiana University Press, 1997).

7. Faber, "America's Earliest Jewish Settlers," 23–28; Diner, *The Jews of the United States*, 16–29.

8. "Abigaill Franks to Naphtali Franks, October 18, 1741," in *The Letters of Abigaill Levy Franks, 1733-1748*, ed. Edith B. Gelles (New Haven: Yale University Press, 2004), 98; Faber, "America's Earliest Jewish Settlers," 28–32; Diner, *The Jews of the United States*, 20–24, 29. Jews, Catholics, and Quakers were generally unwelcome in Massachusetts and Connecticut, colonies where a strong culture of Calvinism trumped pragmatic economic considerations.

9. "Isaac Delyon of Savannah Ships Barnard Gratz of Philadelphia Rice and Hides in Exchange for Groceries, September 24, 1760," in *The Jew in the American World: A Source Book*, ed. Jacob Rader Marcus (Detroit: Wayne State University Press, 1996), 54–55. On Jewish trading networks in the Americas, see Diner, *The Jews of the United States*, 27–28.

10. "Isaac Elizer and Samuel Moses of Newport Dispatch a Ship to Africa for a Cargo of Slaves, October 29, 1762," in *The Jew in the American World: A Source Book*, ed. Jacob Rader Marcus (Detroit: Wayne State University Press, 1996), 55–56. On Jewish participation in the slave trade, as well as Jewish attitudes toward slavery, see relevant chapters in Jonathan D. Sarna and Adam Mendelsohn, eds., *Jews and the Civil War: A Reader* (New York: New York University Press, 2010).

11. Faber, "America's Earliest Jewish Settlers," 28–29; Diner, *The Jews of the United States*, 17–20.

12. Faber, "America's Earliest Jewish Settlers," 30; Irene Neu, "The Jewish Businesswoman in America," *American Jewish Historical Quarterly* 66.1 (1976), 138–39.

13. "Barnard Gratz Writes to Brother Michael Who Was about to Come to America, November 20, 1758," in *The Jew in the American World: A Source Book*, ed. Jacob Rader Marcus (Detroit: Wayne State University Press, 1996), 53; Ira Rosenwaike, *On the Edge of Greatness: A Portrait of American Jewry in the Early National Period* (Cincinnati: American Jewish Archives, 1985), 3; Diner, *The Jews of the United States*, 27.

14. Quoted in Avraham Barkai, *Branching Out: German-Jewish Immigration to the United States, 1820-1914* (New York: Holmes and London, 1994), 5, 27.

15. Barkai, *Branching Out*, 26–29; Dianne Ashton, "Expanding Jewish Life in America, 1826-1901," in *The Columbia History of Jews and Judaism in America*, ed. Marc Lee Raphael (New York: Columbia University Press, 2008), 47; Gerald Sorin, *A Time for Building: The Third Migration, 1880-1920*, vol. 3 in *The Jewish People in America* (Baltimore: The Johns Hopkins University Press, 1992), 40–41.

16. Diner, *The Jews of the United States*, 74–75.

17. Ibid., 74.

18. Sorin, *A Time for Building*, 1–2, 7. This legislation, passed in the xenophobic era of the Red Scare and a post–World War I recession, established a quota of immigrants for any nationality at 2 percent of that group's foreign-born population as of the 1890 census. For more on the National Origins Act and its broad implications for both immigration policy and the construction of racial identity categories in America, see Mae Ngai, "The Architecture of Race in American Immigration Law: A Re-examination of the Immigration Act of 1924," *Journal of American History* 86.1 (June 1999), 67–92.

19. Eric L. Goldstein, "The Great Wave: Eastern European Jewish Immigration to the United States, 1880-1924," in *The Columbia History of Jews and Judaism in America*, ed. Marc Lee Raphael (New York: Columbia University Press, 2008), 72–73; Diner, *The Jews of the United States*, 77, 82–87.

20. Ibid., 78–81.

21. Barkai, *Branching Out*, 1–3, 17–29; Diner, *The Jews of the United States*, 82–86.

22. Menasses Hirsch letter to Babette Hirsch, March 25, 1847, American Jewish Archives, quoted in Barkai, *Branching Out*, 29–30; Jacob Rader Marcus, *Memoirs of American Jews, 1775-1865*, vol. 2 (Philadelphia: Jewish Publication Society, 1955), 48.

23. Hasia R. Diner, *A Time for Gathering: The Second Migration, 1820-1880*, vol. 2 of *The Jewish People in America* (Baltimore: The Johns Hopkins University Press, 1992), 163–65.

24. Abram Vossen Goodman, "A Jewish Peddler's Diary, 1841-1842," *American Jewish Archives Journal* 3.3 (1951): 99, accessed July 29, 2015, http://americanjewisharchives.org/publications/journal/PDF/1951_03_03_00_doc_kohn_goodman.pdf .

25. Barkai, *Branching Out*, 44–48, 81–85. On the Jewish peddler, see also Hasia R. Diner, *Roads Taken: The Great Jewish Migrations to the New World and the Peddlers Who Forged the Way* (New Haven: Yale University Press, 2015).

26. Barkai, *Branching Out*, 84–88; Diner, *The Jews of the United States*, 107–09. For a longer history of Jewish involvement in the garment trade in both the United States and Britain, see Adam D. Mendelsohn, *The Rag Race: How Jews Sewed Their Way to Success in America and the British Empire* (New York: NYU Press, 2015).

27. Lee Shai Weissbach, *Jewish Life in Small-Town America* (New Haven: Yale University Press, 2005), 51–69. For a memoir of growing up Jewish in a small Southern town, see Stella Suberman, *The Jew Store* (Chapel Hill: Algonquin Books, 1998).

28. Many local studies of American Jewish communities have been published in the last forty years. Important overviews of Jewish life in the South include Marcie Cohen Ferris and Mark I. Greenberg, eds., *Jewish Roots in Southern Soil: A New History* (Hanover: Brandeis University Press/University Press of New England, 2006); and Eli N. Evans, *The Provincials: A Personal History of Jews in the South*, rev. ed. (New York: Free Press, 1997). On Texas Jewry, see Hollace Ava Weiner and Kenneth D. Roseman, eds., *Lone Stars of David: The Jews of Texas* (Hanover: Brandeis University Press/University Press of New England, 2007). See also the resources available at the website of the Institute for Southern Jewish Life, an institution dedicated to preserving and promoting Jewish history and culture in the American South, at www.isjl.org.

29. Barkai, *Branching Out*, 58–59, 71–72; Michael A. Meyer, *Response to Modernity: A History of the Reform Movement in Judaism* (New York: Oxford University Press, 1988), 242–43, 262–63.

30. Fred Rosenbaum, *Cosmopolitans: A Social and Cultural History of the Jews of the San Francisco Bay Area* (Berkeley: University of California Press, 2009), 1–7, 25; Eveline Brooks Auerbach, "A Woman's Wagon Train Adventure," in *Jewish Voices of the California Gold Rush: A Documentary History*, ed. Ava F. Kahn (Detroit: Wayne State University Press, 2002), 111–18.

31. Barkai, *Branching Out*, 65–78, 85; Weissbach, *Jewish Life in Small-Town America*, 2–4, 13–15, 338–48. Ashton, "Expanding Jewish Life in America," 51. See Weissbach, 338–48, for demographic statistics on American Jewish communities with populations between one hundred and one thousand people between 1878 and 1950.

32. Rose Silverman, "My Future Is in America," in Cohen and Soyer, *My Future Is in America*, 189–203.

33. Diner, *The Jews of the United States*, 81, 88–93; Goldstein, "The Great Wave," 70–72.

34. Diner, *The Jews of the United States*, 94–95, 102–03, 106–11; Goldstein, "The Great Wave," 72–73. After New York City, the cities with the three largest American Jewish communities in 1927 were Chicago, Philadelphia, and Boston. For a chart of Jewish population statistics in major American cities from 1878 to 1927, see Sorin, *A Time for Building*, 137.

35. Rose Cohen, *Out of the Shadow: A Russian Jewish Girlhood on the Lower East Side* (Ithaca: Cornell University Press, 1995), 83–90.

36. Diner, *The Jews of the United States*, 105–07; Jeffrey S. Gurock, *When Harlem was Jewish, 1870-1930* (New York: Columbia University Press, 1979), 5–18. On the history of New York Jewry from colonial times to the present see Deborah Dash Moore, ed., *City of Promises: A History of the Jews of New York*, 3 vols. (New York: NYU Press, 2012).

37. William A. Braverman, "The Emergence of a Unified Community, 1880-1917," in *The Jews of Boston*, eds. Jonathan A. Sarna, Ellen Smith, and Scott-Martin Kosofsky, rev ed. (1995; New Haven: Yale University Press, 2005), 65–69. For a historical overview of Boston Jewish history, see the other essays in this volume, especially the introduction by Jonathan Sarna.

38. Irving Cutler, *The Jews of Chicago: From Shtetl to Suburb* (Urbana: University of Illinois Press, 1996), 7, 26–32, 58–66; Louis Wirth, *The Ghetto*, rev. ed. (1928; New Brunswick: Transaction Publishers, 1998), 232–33, quoted in Cutler, *The Jews of Chicago*, 66–67.

39. Cutler, *The Jews of Chicago*, 98–100; Diner, *The Jews of the United States*, 239–40.

40. Sorin, *A Time for Building*, 156; Weissbach, *Jewish Life in Small-Town America*, 28–29.

41. Diner, *The Jews of the United States*, 184–86; Sorin, *A Time for Building*, 62–65.

42. Jacob H. Schiff, "Origin of the Galveston Movement, October 25, 1906," in *The Jew in the American World: A Source Book*, ed. Jacob Rader Marcus (Detroit: Wayne State University Press, 1996), 294.

43. Sorin, *A Time for Building*, 65–66; Bernard Marinbach, *Galveston: Ellis Island of the West* (Albany: State University of New York Press, 1983), 24.

44. Edward S. Shapiro, *A Time for Healing: American Jewry since World War II*, vol. 5 in *The Jewish People in America* (Baltimore: The Johns Hopkins University Press, 1992), 125; Libby Garland, *After They Closed the Gates: Jewish Illegal Immigration to the United States, 1921-1965* (Chicago: University of Chicago Press, 2014), 1–8, 118–28.

45. Garland, *After They Closed the Gates,* 119, 126–31.

46. Garland, *After They Closed the Gates*, 184–86; Rafael Medoff, "American Jewish Responses to Nazism and the Holocaust," in *The Columbia History of Jews and Judaism in America*, ed. Marc Lee Raphael (New York: Columbia University Press, 2008), 294–98. The quote from the 1940 Breckenridge Long memo is accessible at http://www.pbs.org/wgbh/amex/holocaust/filmmore/reference/primary/barmemo.html, accessed September 10, 2015.

47. Garland, *After They Closed the Gates*, 187; Alexandra Garbarini, et al., *Jewish Responses to Persecution, Volume II: 1938-1940* (Lanham, MD: AltaMira Press, 2011), 55–56.

48. Diner, *The Jews of the United States*, 243–44; Steven M. Lowenstein, *Frankfurt on the Hudson: The German-Jewish Community of Washington Heights, 1933-1983, Its Structure and Culture* (Detroit: Wayne State University Press, 1989), 22–23. See also Gabrielle Simon Edgcomb, *From Swastika to Jim Crow: Refugee Scholars at Black Colleges* (Malabar, FL: Krieger, 1993).

49. Lowenstein, *Frankfurt on the Hudson*, 22–26, 47–51, 101–88; Diner, *The Jews of the United States*, 245.

50. Garland, *After They Closed the Gates*, 187–92; Beth B. Cohen, *Case Closed: Holocaust Survivors in Postwar America* (New Brunswick: Rutgers University Press, 2007), 8–29.

51. Cohen, *Case Closed*, 30–38, 115–21.

52. William B. Helmreich, *Against All Odds: Holocaust Survivors and the Successful Lives They Made in America* (New York: Simon and Schuster, 1992), 63–65; Oral history interview with Genia Klapholz, July 29, 1981, RG-50.462*0015, Gratz College Oral History Archive Collection, United States Holocaust Memorial Museum, accessed September 17, 2015, http://collections.ushmm.org/oh_findingaids/RG-50.462.0015_02_trs_en.pdf.

53. Steven Mintz, *Huck's Raft: A History of American Childhood* (Cambridge: Belknap Press of Harvard University Press, 2004), 277; Albert I. Gordon, *Jews in Suburbia* (1959; repr., Westport, CT: Greenwood Press, 1973), 65.

54. Diner, *The Jews of the United States*, 283–88; Riv-Ellen Prell, "Triumph, Accommodation, and Resistance: American Jewish Life from the End of World War II to the Six-Day War," in *The Columbia History of Jews and Judaism in America*, ed. Marc Lee Raphael (New York: Columbia University Press, 2008), 119–20. See also "Two Thirds of America's Jews Now Live in Suburbs, Expert Estimates," *Jewish Telegraphic Agency*, October 16, 1959, accessed January 6, 2014, http://www.jta.org/1959/10/16/archive/two-thirds-of-americas-jews-now-live-in-suburbs-expert-estimates.

55. Diner, *The Jews of the United States*, 283–85; Prell, "Triumph, Accommodation, and Resistance," 120. Non-white ethnic Americans continued to face discriminatory housing policies well after World War II. For some of the recent work on this issue, see David M.P. Freund, *Colored Property: State Policy and White Racial Politics in Suburban America* (Chicago: University of Chicago Press, 2010); and Beryl Satter, *Family Properties: How the Struggle Over Race and Real Estate Transformed Chicago and Urban America* (New York: Metropolitan, 2009).

56. Diner, *The Jews of the United States*, 285–86; Nathan Glazer, "The American Jew and the Attainment of Middle-Class Rank: Some Trends and Explanations," in *The Jews: Social Patterns of an American Group*, ed. Marshall Sklare (Glencoe, IL: The Free Press, 1957), 138–46. On the economic profile of American Jews leading up to and during the Depression, see Beth S. Wenger, *New York Jews and the Great Depression: Uncertain Promise* (New Haven, CT: Yale University Press, 1996), 10–32.

57. Deborah Dash Moore, *To the Golden Cities: Pursuing the American Jewish Dream in Miami and L.A.* (New York: Free Press, 1994), 21–24.

58. Ibid., 25–32.

59. Ibid., 263–75.

60. Diner, *The Jews of the United States*, 284, 318; Adam Chandler, "South Africa's Exodus," *Tablet*, April 5, 2012, accessed October 2, 2015, http://www.tabletmag.com/jewish-life-and-religion/96109/south-africas-exodus; Tom Teicholz, "South African Jews find a home in L.A.," *Jewish Journal* (Los Angeles), June 13, 2013, accessed October 2, 2015, http://www.jewishjournal.com/los_angeles/article/south_african_jews_find_a_home_in_l.a.

61. Annelise Orleck, *The Soviet Jewish Americans* (Westport, CT: Greenwood Press, 1999), 1–6, 49–82; Diner, *The Jews of the United States*, 342–45. See also Gal Beckerman, *When They Come for Us, We'll Be Gone: The Epic Struggle to Save Soviet Jewry* (New York: Houghton Mifflin Hardcourt, 2010).

62. Quoted in Orleck, *The Soviet Jewish Americans*, 59–61.

63. Ibid., 87–100, 132–35, 190–91.

64. Quoted in Orleck, *The Soviet Jewish Americans*, 152.

Select Bibliography

Barkai, Avraham. *Branching Out: German-Jewish Immigration to the United States, 1820-1914*. New York: Holmes and London, 1994.

Berman, Lila Corwin. *Metropolitan Jews: Politics, Race, and Religion in Postwar Detroit*. Chicago: University of Chicago Press, 2015.

Cutler, Irving. *The Jews of Chicago: From Shtetl to Suburb*. Urbana: University of Illinois Press, 1996.

Diner, Hasia R. *The Jews of the United States, 1654 to 2000*. Berkeley: University of California Press, 2004.

Ferris, Marcie Cohen, and Mark I. Greenberg, eds. *Jewish Roots in Southern Soil: A New History*. Waltham: Brandeis University Press; Hanover, University Press of New England, 2006.

Gamm, Gerald. *Urban Exodus: Why the Jews Left Boston and the Catholics Stayed.* Cambridge: Harvard University Press, 1999.

Garland, Libby. *After They Closed the Gates: Jewish Illegal Immigration to the United States, 1921-1965.* Chicago: University of Chicago Press, 2014.

Kahn, Ava Fran, ed. *Jewish Life in the American West: Perspectives on Migration, Settlement, and Community.* Los Angeles: Autry Museum of Western Heritage; Seattle: University of Washington Press, 2002.

Moore, Deborah Dash. *To the Golden Cities: Pursuing the American Jewish Dream in Miami and L.A.* New York: Free Press, 1994.

Moore, Deborah Dash, ed. *City of Promises: A History of the Jews of New York.* 3 vols. New York: New York University Press, 2012.

Raphael, Marc Lee, ed. *The Columbia History of Jews and Judaism in America.* New York: Columbia University Press, 2008.

Weissbach, Lee Shai. *Jewish Life in Small-Town America.* New Haven: Yale University Press, 2005.

CHAPTER 4

CASE STUDIES
Migration and Mobility

THE STORY of American Jewry has been one of movement—first from the Old World, then to various regions and communities across the North American continent, and then from one residential neighborhood to another. Much of this movement was occasioned by opportunity, a chance to advance occupationally or to move into better housing. From the mid-twentieth century to the present, movement from older urban neighborhoods to suburbia and from the northeast United States to the west and south has been marked.

The case studies presented here describe mobility and migration in four different locales. In Columbia, South Carolina, the storyline is one of commercial success and residential mobility. A parallel narrative on Chicago Jewry also traces the Jewish rise to civic leadership and prominence in national Jewish affairs. In Los Angeles, the Jewish story is embedded in a mosaic of ethnicities, while in New York City's Lower East Side, the mix of immigrant groups is localized in a single tenement house. Together and separately, these case studies offer models of research and collaboration that produce compelling interpretations.

Columbia Jewish Heritage Initiative

Historic Columbia

In 2008, an Institute for Museum and Library Services grant enabled Historic Columbia (South Carolina) to launch an unprecedented community engagement project. "Connecting Communities through History" invited residents of six downtown neighborhoods to co-create the histories of those places by sharing oral histories and photographs. The initiative produced new walking and driving tour brochures and wayside signage, complemented by a web-based tour. In addition to heightening community pride, the project has promoted public education and local heritage tourism.[1]

In 2011, Historic Columbia added to the initiative with a thematic tour that focused on the histories of African Americans in South Carolina's capital city. As Historic Columbia's website puts it, "Since its creation in 1786, Columbia has featured a large African American population whose labor, skills, and vision have been integral in the city's physical, spiritual, and social evolution. During the course of four centuries the city's black community transformed itself from that of a predominately enslaved population to a society whose members overcame the restrictions of Jim Crow and charted the course of the Civil Rights era."[2]

The new tour programs drew the interest of Columbia's Jewish community, which has a long history in that city. Jewish merchants and storekeepers were in residence from Columbia's founding in 1786 and the number of Jewish residents, though modest (about 2,750 in 2001), is at an all-time peak. In April 2014, Jewish community leaders approached Historic Columbia about expanding its "existing community-based initiative to include a thematic exploration of local Jewish history." Working cooperatively, Historic Columbia, the Columbia Jewish Federation, and the Jewish Community Center invited discussion and comment from state and local organizations interested in Jewish religious, educational, and cultural activities. These focus groups identified a number of issues, among them the need to document the impact of Jews on the city's history and a lack of community cohesion comparable to that of other local ethnic groups.[3]

To launch the Columbia Jewish Heritage Initiative, which is designed to collect stories, images, and documents and to make them accessible in a variety of print and web-based platforms, Historic Columbia has organized a coalition of interested organizations. In addition to the Columbia Jewish Federation and the Jewish Community Center, partners include the Richland Library, the Jewish Historical Society of South Carolina, and the College of Charleston, which houses the Jewish Heritage Collection in its library. Early on, the project received a critical infusion of public financial support from the Central Carolina Community Foundation, followed by grants from the City of Columbia and the South Carolina Humanities Council. The initiative is also strongly supported through private contributions.

Rather than reinvent the wheel, Historic Columbia's project has gathered information and expertise from across the state: the Jewish Historical Society and the College of Charleston have worked together in partnership for many years to gather documents, photos, and oral histories. In this new initiative, therefore, Historic Columbia volunteers are being trained to conduct oral histories, while the Jewish Historical Society and the College of Charleston manage the transcription of the interviews, copies of which will be deposited in both Charleston and Columbia.[4]

Since historic sites and neighborhoods are the building blocks of Historic Columbia's efforts to highlight the city's history, early attention is being given to the stories of downtown Jewish residents who have moved out into other urban and suburban neighborhoods. As in other locales, ethnic succession in particular neighborhoods creates a thick layering of experiences and memories. Ultimately, Historic Columbia aims to weave stories of Jewish life in Columbia into its inclusive interpretive program to create a multiethnic narrative. But for the moment, according to executive director Robin Waites, the task is to tease out and understand the Jewish storyline in greater specificity and detail before trying to braid it into the community-wide narrative.[5]

In the interim, Historic Columbia has begun to leverage its alliances with other organizations to jump-start public programming related to Jewish Columbia. Each year, the Jewish Historical Society of South Carolina convenes two statewide meetings, one in Charleston, its headquarters, and one in another South Carolina city. In November 2015, the Jewish Historical Society partnered with Historic Columbia and the rest of the Columbia Jewish Heritage Initiative coalition to hold its fall meeting in Columbia and the nearby town of Orangeburg. The conference program included sessions on Columbia's Jewish merchants and industrialists, dedication of historical markers, and walking tours of the Orangeburg Jewish cemetery and of Columbia's commercial district. The walking tour in Columbia is an opportunity for Historic Columbia to pilot a Jewish walking tour that debuts in May 2016. Meanwhile, Historic Columbia continues to seek out community-based events and programs, such as the fall and spring Jewish Food Festivals coordinated by two of the local synagogues, and to use them as opportunities for gathering new stories, photos, and documents.[6]

Aside from its burgeoning community engagement programs, Historic Columbia has a lot on its plate. Historic Columbia manages six sites in the city, five of which are historic houses (including the Woodrow Wilson Family Home: A Museum of Reconstruction). Not a single staff member of the organization is Jewish or has a background in Jewish history or culture. Yet by counseling with Jewish residents and with Jewish community leaders and by collaborating with strategic partners who bring expertise to the project, Historic Columbia has already been successful in casting an inclusive net, bringing new voices into its public interpretive program and broadening its base of support. The Columbia Jewish Heritage Initiative is a model of what can be accomplished in breaking new ground in regional Jewish history by deploying an engaged, strategic collaborative process.

Shalom Chicago

Chicago History Museum

When the Chicago History Museum was awarded a 2016 National Medal of Honor by the Institute of Museum and Library Services (IMLS), the IMLS cited the Museum's "collaborative efforts with various neighborhoods and community groups . . . in catalyzing new opportunities for local involvement." One of the projects referenced by the IMLS was *Shalom Chicago*, a 2012-2013 project that offered visitors "an intimate insight to some very personal histories of the Chicago Jewish community." Olivia Mahoney, the curator and project leader for *Shalom Chicago*, described her work as continuing "the Museum's efforts to reach out to different communities in Chicago and tell a broader and more inclusive history of the city."[7]

Since *Shalom Chicago* was the museum's first effort to tell the story of Chicago Jews, Mahoney began her work by creating a network of local Jewish organizations and individuals to serve as advisors, in-house reviewers, and links to local Jewish communities. She

Figure 4.1 Visitors in the Chicago History Museum's exhibition, *Shalom Chicago*, looking at objects related to street markets in the Maxwell Street neighborhood.
Courtesy of the Chicago History Museum.

followed this up with trips to visit exhibitions at Jewish museums in New York, Philadelphia, and Baltimore in order to clarify interpretive themes and to better understand the strengths and weaknesses of different interpretive approaches. Her search for resources, information, and loans was facilitated by several of the Chicago History Museum's Jewish board members and by a collaboration with the Spertus Institute for Jewish Learning and Leadership, which loaned materials for the exhibition, provided staff expertise, and co-sponsored public programs.[8]

The exhibition set out three primary themes for its narrative: to tell "how immigrant Jews and their descendants adapted to American society while retaining a distinct religious and cultural identity," to show "how Chicago Jews contributed to the city's growth and development," and to relate how "Chicago Jews helped define what it means to be Jewish in America."[9] The exhibition narrative unfolded chronologically, with major sections on successive waves of Jewish immigrants from German-speaking central Europe, Yiddish speakers from eastern Europe, refugees from Nazi Germany, and Jews from the Soviet Union.

To make the story immediate and personal, the exhibition employed first-person narratives and quotes. In each major section of the exhibition, key narrators were profiled; some of the profiles were followed by an audio program in which the "narrators" speak in first-person voice about a significant aspect of their lives. In the opening section of the exhibition, for example, Abraham Kohn (1819–1871), a Bavarian Jew and clothier, tells how he established Chicago's first Jewish congregation in 1847, and Fannie (Guggenheimer) Alschuler (1846–1909), originally from Baden, describes her early life in Chicago around 1871. Other key figures included businessman and philanthropist Henry Greenebaum (1833–1914), who came from Germany in 1848; Russian metalsmith Falick Novick (1878–1958), who arrived in Chicago in 1907; labor activist Bessie Abramowitz (1889–1970), a Russian-born garment worker who helped lead a major 1910 strike; Ukrainian artist Todros Geller (1889–1949), who settled in the city in 1918; and Bernard Kronthal and Trude Heimann, who fled Nazi Germany in the 1930s with help from distant family members.[10]

The heart of the exhibition is the section devoted to Jewish life during the heyday of the eastern European immigration. From around ten thousand Jews in 1870, Chicago Jewry grew to three hundred thousand in 1930. The growth was fueled mostly by immigrants from Russia, Ukraine, Poland, Lithuania, Hungary, and Romania who were pushed by antisemitic laws and sporadic violence and pulled by America's economic opportunity. *Shalom Chicago* devotes much of its three thousand square feet of space to painting a rounded portrait of this diverse wave of immigrants as they settled into the city, found work and started families, organized congregations and communal institutions, and expressed themselves in art and culture.

Some parts of the Chicago story are well-known. Jewish business successes and occupational mobility followed a national pattern. Many new immigrants began as peddlers and moved on to retail, especially in clothing and mail order. The towering figure is Julius Rosenwald, the son of a Springfield, Illinois, merchant, who grew Sears Roebuck into the world's largest retailer from 1895 into the 1920s, but there are other success stories that run in parallel, including the Chicago Mail Order Company and Spiegel, May, Stern & Company, both of which enjoyed long success in mail order sales of consumer goods. Aside from working in the garment industry, Jews "made boots and shoes, manufactured furniture, packed meat, brewed beer, and ran major department stores."[11] Names like Hart, Schaffner & Marx (clothing manufacture), headquartered in Chicago, remain prominent even today.

The exhibition deploys three hundred objects, images, and texts to offer a rounded picture of the community. The three major movements in American Judaism are represented by Chicago rabbis who achieved national prominence: Emil G. Hirsch (1851–1923), a proponent of radical reform, helped organize the 1893 World Parliament of Religions and taught philosophy and rabbinic literature at the University of Chicago; Solomon Goldman (1893–1953), a leading Conservative rabbi, co-authored the pageant, *The Romance of a People*, at the 1933 Chicago World's Fair and served as president of the Zionist Organization of America in 1938–1940; and Orthodox Rabbi Saul Silber (1881–1946), who founded and led Hebrew Theological College, a bastion of modern Orthodoxy. All three were themselves immigrants—Hirsch from Luxembourg, Goldman from Russia, and Silber from Lithuania.

For several generations, Jewish Chicago was concentrated in a few urban neighborhoods, which were dotted with synagogues and other communal organizations. One that played a critical role was the Chicago Hebrew Institute (CHI), which was founded in 1903. Originally a small settlement house, it became a community center offering educational, cultural, and social activities. Unusually, CHI was founded and governed by the people it served; its goal was to help immigrant Jews to "become part of American Society while retaining their religious and cultural identity." As the Jewish community began to spread out to the suburbs, the CHI followed, first to North Lawndale, where it was re-named the Jewish People's Institute, and then as part of the Jewish Community Centers in both the suburbs and the city.

Another notable organization, the Anti-Defamation League, has its roots in Chicago. It was founded in 1913 by Chicago lawyer Sigmund Livingston in response to the lynching of Leo Frank (see chapter 10). Its aim is "to stop the defamation of the Jewish people and to secure justice and fair treatment to all." Livingston campaigned against antisemitism in movies, books, and newspapers, in Jewish quotas at colleges and universities, in restrictive covenants, and in campaigns sponsored by the Ku Klux Klan and Henry Ford. Today, the Anti-Defamation League is one of America's leading civil rights and human relations agencies.[12]

Shalom Chicago carries the story of Chicago Jews into the present. The later sections of the exhibition track Jewish residential mobility from the neighborhoods of first- and second-generation settlement on the south and west sides out into the suburbs and throughout the metro area. The exhibition concludes with a look at present-day Chicago and a chorus of contemporary voices. Objects, text, and audio stations were complemented with hands-on interactives and a range of educational and public programs. The exhibition was also augmented by a book-length publication that came about unexpectedly: two visitors to the exhibition were so impressed that they offered to sponsor a catalog, also titled *Shalom Chicago*, which was published just before the exhibition closed, giving the project an extended life.

The *Shalom Chicago* project proved to be a popular and critical success. Adding to its series of programs on religious, cultural, and ethnic communities, the Chicago History Museum has come to exemplify inclusiveness and community engagement.

97 Orchard Street

Lower East Side Tenement Museum

In 1988, Ruth Abram and Anita Jacobson were looking for a vacant storefront on the Lower East Side, searching for a place in which to interpret New York City's immigrant history. By accident, they stumbled on 97 Orchard Street, a five-story tenement building erected in 1863. They discovered that the building's owner had sealed its upper floors in 1935, rather than bringing the apartments up to code, in effect creating a time capsule of immigrant life. Subsequent research showed that roughly seven thousand immigrants and their families had called 97 Orchard home between 1863 and 1935, including many Jewish newcomers from central and eastern Europe.[13]

Today, the Lower East Side Tenement Museum has restored seven apartments at 97 Orchard to represent a variety of immigrant families. These period reconstructions of tenants' apartments range from the German Jewish Gumpertz family c. 1874 to the Italian Catholic Baldizzi family in the 1930s. In 2012, the Tenement Museum opened a new Shop Life program in the basement, featuring Bavarian immigrant John Scheider's saloon and barroom (1864–1880s) and incorporating stories of some of the many other businesses that occupied the basement space. As this book goes to press, the Tenement Museum is preparing to open three additional apartments at a second tenement (103 Orchard Street), which will represent more-recent immigrant families: "the Epsteins, Jewish survivors of the Holocaust who came to 103 Orchard in the 1950s, the Saezes, Puerto Rican migrants who moved in during the 1960s, and the Wongs, who immigrated from Hong Kong in the 1960s."[14]

Guided tours, led by museum educators, are the Tenement Museum's core program, in both the residential units and the basement commercial space. The educators introduce the site-specific stories, circulate primary sources, and provide essential context. They also answer visitor questions and facilitate conversations among their visitors. The educators help visitors to place themselves in the specific circumstances confronting each tenant family at a particular moment in time and to evoke larger historical and contemporary questions. The ninety-minute Shop Life tour, for example, "focuses on immigrant entrepreneurship, community, and notions of success." The tours animate the families and "show them directly reacting to conflict and articulating multiple perspectives." In short, the period reconstructions "immerse visitors in the past, inspire their curiosity and become the stage upon which they can imagine history."[15]

A striking feature of the Tenement Museum's interpretive program is the museum's readiness to revisit and revise key elements based on new scholarship and visitor responses. One instance relates to the apartment occupied by Abraham and Fannie Rogarshevsky and their six children in the 1910s. The Rogarshevsky home was originally set in 1918, just after Abraham's death. The apartment was "dressed" in traditional Jewish mourning, with cloths covering the mirrors, a table laid out with food for the mourners, and other elements of lived religion. However, the setting and situation failed to arouse strong responses among visitors, unlike the Levine family apartment set in the 1890s, which provoked a good deal of curiosity and comment. To rectify the situation, in 2010 the Museum re-cast the space to reflect family preparations for the Sabbath eve (Friday evening) meal. The refurnished space helped educators and visitors to explore the tension between traditional Sabbath observance and the pressures of earning a living by working on Saturday and thereby desecrating the Sabbath. The new focus situated the Rogarshevsky family in the process of adapting to harsh realities; it also addressed working conditions in the modern factories that were replacing sweatshops, notably the 1911 fire in the Triangle Shirtwaist Factory that took the lives of 146 workers.[16]

The Tenement Museum's interpretive practice is notable for its intensive use of current scholarship in a variety of disciplines. In addition to social and cultural historians, the museum engages preservationists and architectural historians, anthropologists, material culture and oral history specialists, and interpretive consultants. Detailed studies of building materials and furnishings are complemented by research in public records, family memorabilia, and oral histories. By using experts in different ethnic histories, the museum is able to draw on cross-cultural insights and to sharpen contrasts as well as commonalities in shaping the dramatic situations that focus the public tour program. Unlike many consultancies, the museum encourages its scholars to actively apply their insights to the settings, visitors, and educators. This deep engagement precludes a watering down of history, producing "a distillation of material and a concentrated look at particular moments."[17]

The museum's interpretive program provides a rich, multicultural perspective on New York's long and celebrated immigrant history. By carrying the story into more recent decades at 103 Orchard Street, the museum underscores the continuity of immigration into the contemporary moment, making immigration an immediate and concrete issue rather than a distanced or abstract matter. Also, by documenting the presence of Germans, Italians, and other groups, it revises visitor preconceptions that the Lower East Side was an exclusively Jewish phenomenon, making for a more nuanced understanding of the Lower East Side, even among the museum's Jewish visitors. As one observer puts it, "drawing visitors into a critical examination of immigrant history—one that recognizes commonality and conflict alike, . . . encourages them to reflect on the immigrant present through the immigrant past."[18]

The Tenement Museum holds great promise as a model for other museums and historic sites interpreting Jewish life in America, not to speak of many other ethnic and cultural groups. The museum's interpretations of Jewish life in one key locale emphasizes the diversity of Jewish immigrants and their interactions with other immigrant peoples, points that are salient in many communities. In addition, the museum's process of research and program development is replicable by many other history organizations, large and small alike. Its methods of guiding and facilitating and its emphasis on setting up historically authentic situations and inviting visitors to engage the issues and the tensions of lived experience are also exemplary and can be applied to a variety of contexts, from the evolution of religious life to war-time decision-making.[19]

Jews in the Los Angeles Mosaic

Autry Museum of the American West

When Prussian immigrant Harris Newmark arrived in Los Angeles in 1854, he felt he "had landed on another planet." Seven years later, Los Angeles still failed to impress. Newcomer Eugene Meyer, a native of Strasbourg, came to work in a general store owned by Solomon Lazard, but he was "so disappointed that he wanted to leave within forty-eight hours." Still, Newmark, Meyers, Lazard, and other pioneering Jewish settlers stuck it out. The sleepy southern California town offered unusual opportunities for earning a living and also for empowering Jewish residents as leaders in the growth and transformation of the community.[20]

Los Angeles offers one telling instance of Jewish settlement in cities, towns, and villages across the United States in the decades before the Civil War. A century earlier, the tiny minority of Jews living in the American colonies were concentrated in a few commercial centers along the Atlantic coast. By 1860, though still a small minority of the American population, Jews resided in hundreds of communities, large and small. Moreover, Jewish immigrants—mainly from German-speaking lands in Europe—were part of a mass migration from central and western Europe that was inflecting both local communities and the nation. In Los Angeles, for example, foreign-born residents constituted only about 2 percent of the population in 1844; by 1870, 28 percent of LA residents were foreign-born.[21]

LA Jews in 1870 represented a variety of Jewish ethnicities. The Lazards came from France, the Newmarks were Prussian-born, and Eugene Meyer was from Alsace. They were soon joined by immigrant Jews with roots in German states such as Bavaria and Polen, many of the latter of Polish descent. As early as the 1870s, a few Jews trickled in from eastern Europe, then, after 1900, came an influx of Sephardic Jews from Rhodes. In the 1930s, Jewish refugees from Nazism arrived in Los Angeles, followed after World War II by Holocaust survivors, then Jews from Iran, the Former Soviet Union, and Israel. If Los Angeles in the twenty-first century had become a mosaic of ethnicities, its Jewish residents were themselves a microcosm of American diversity.[22]

In fact, by the early twenty-first century, Los Angeles had a Jewish population larger than Jerusalem. Surprisingly, it was only in 2013 that a major exhibition on LA Jewish history was organized, by the Autry Museum of the American West. As part of its mission to be inclusive of the many peoples of the West, in 2002 the Autry opened an exhibition on "Jewish Life in the American West," which dealt with aspects of Jewish life from the 1830s to 1920 and was accompanied by a catalog edited by Ava Kahn, PhD. The exhibition proved to be very popular, but many visitors wondered why Los Angeles was represented by only a few objects and some brief references to Hollywood. Even before the exhibition closed, the Autry decided to mount a second show, focused on LA Jewry.[23]

As recently as 2003, there was little scholarly writing on the history of LA Jews, and most of the primary resources for researching that history were in private hands. To fill this gap in American Jewish history, David Myers, a professor of Jewish history at the University of California, Los Angeles (UCLA), started a project to collect resources to document the history of LA Jewry. Meanwhile, Stephen Aron, another UCLA history professor, was leading the Autry's Institute for the Study of the American West. Myers and Aron taught a seminar on LA Jewish history in 2005. The Autry recruited Karen S. Wilson, who had recently completed an MA on Jews in Los Angeles and was a student in the UCLA seminar, as the project curator. One of the key goals of the project was to re-examine LA Jewish history in its own terms rather than as a replication of Jewish life in New York City, the dominant paradigm in American Jewish historiography.[24]

To discover what made LA Jews unique and how they thought of themselves, the project drew on a variety of local resources. The Skirball Cultural Center had collected some LA material and the Jewish Historical Society of Southern California had established an archive of historical materials. The University of Southern California had created a multimedia installation on LA Jews, and the Jewish Federation of Greater Los Angeles had mounted an exhibition to celebrate its centennial. The Autry project team drew on these resources and also organized an extensive network of families and community organizations to identify additional resources and information. The project established two advisory bodies, one of academic scholars and a second of community historians; the former reviewed draft exhibition text, while the latter were especially productive in reviewing the story boards and suggesting resources for the exhibition. In the end, the

Figure 4.2 Visitors to *Jews in the LA Mosaic* exhibition engaging with one of the interactive maps.

Photograph by Bonnie Perkinson. Courtesy of Autry Museum of the American West. Autry 126.

exhibition occupied five thousand square feet with 150 objects, eighty photographs, five videos, two audio excerpts, and listening stations featuring fifty songs.[25]

Both the exhibition and the accompanying book of essays focus "on two historical interactions—the impact of the Jewish community on the evolution of Los Angeles and the way the city, with its multiethnic population, has changed and molded its Jewish residents, in the process creating a Jewish persona distinct in attitude and lifestyle from its East Coast and Midwestern cousins," according to Tom Tugend in the *Jewish Journal*.[26] Although the evolution of neighborhood life was not among its key themes, the exhibition gave substantial attention to life in the Boyle Heights area and to later migrations into West Los Angeles and beyond to the suburbs. In fact, geographic mobility within the metro area occupied a space at the heart of the exhibition.

The exhibition featured a digital map showing areas of Jewish residence in LA County from the 1850s to 2012. A series of maps plot the locations of Jewish communal organizations, showing an outward spread from the center of Los Angeles over the generations. And right in the middle of the exhibition, the project team designed a "Public Square"— echoing the Los Angeles Plaza, near which early Jewish settlers had resided. The Public Square featured a large three-dimensional map of LA County, dotted with pegs in the major neighborhoods of today. Using strands of yarn they could attach to the pegs, visitors were invited to trace the movements of their own families over multiple generations. The result was a tapestry of threads representing LA residential mobility. A second map asked visitors to hang acrylic tiles on hooks where they lived, creating clusters of tiles by area of residence. In addition to giving visitors space into which they could put themselves into the story, the two interactives provided information to both the project team and to subsequent visitors. The activities also helped to demonstrate that LA Jewish life had transcended Boyle Heights, the classic center of immigrant Jewish life from the 1910s into the 1940s.[27]

Neighborhood life in Boyle Heights was re-interpreted. The epicenter of Jewish life for two generations, Boyle Heights was itself "hopelessly heterogeneous," being home to many ethnic communities. One of the key offshoots of the Autry exhibition is an online project "Mapping Jewish LA" sponsored by UCLA and curated by Dr. Wilson. The website "links the history of Jewish neighborhoods and communities throughout Los Angeles with historical maps, cultural artifacts and archival materials." The history of Jewish geographic mobility is graphically represented in a series of maps that mirror the digital maps created for the exhibition, giving the Autry project an extended afterlife.[28]

The intention of the project team, says Karen Wilson, the project curator, was to make "the focus more outward, rather than the inward focus of most exhibitions about Jews. We were not trying to display only artifacts and stories that would resonate with Jews, but, rather, offer artifacts and stories that would resonant with anyone living in Los Angeles, foregrounding the experiences of Jewish Angelenos." The Autry project is noteworthy, too, for its extensive partnerships and collaborations with historical organizations and museums, community organizations, academic institutions, and area residents. The project also benefitted from professional expertise, notably the participation of scholars from UCLA. The model of intensive community engagement and strategic partnerships can be applied to a variety of projects ranging from walking tours to websites.

Notes

1. Robin Waites, telephone interview with the author, November 4, 2015. Historic Columbia website "Connecting Communities through History," http://www.historiccolumbia.org/education/community-engagement/connecting-communities-through-history; and "Neighborhood Tours," accessed March 2, 2016, http://www.historiccolumbia.org/take-a-tour/neighborhood-tours.

2. Historic Columbia website, "African American Historic Sites Tour," accessed March 2, 2016, http://www.historiccolumbia.org/take-a-tour/neighborhood-tours.

3. *Encyclopedia of Southern Jewish Communities* website, "Columbia, South Carolina," accessed March 2, 2016, http://www.isjl.org/south-carolina-columbia-encyclopedia.html; and Historic Columbia website, "Columbia Jewish Heritage Initiative," accessed March 2, 2016, http://www.historiccolumbia.org/CJHI.

4. College of Charleston website, "Jewish Heritage Collection," accessed March 2, 2016, http://jhc.cofc.edu/.

5. Robin Waites, telephone interview with the author, November 4, 2015.

6. Jewish Historical Society of South Carolina website, "Journal [Fall 2015]," accessed March 2, 2016, http://jhssc.org/wp-content/uploads/2015/09/Fall_2015a.pdf; and Robin Waites, telephone interview with the author, November 4, 2015.

7. Institute of Museum and Library Services Citation, April 1, 2016. Chicago History Museum press release, "Shalom Chicago: New Exhibit at Chicago History Museum," November

10, 2012, accessed April 19, 2016, http://chicagomuseumblog.com/2012/11/10/shalom-chicago-new-exhibit-at-chicago-history-museum/; and Kerry Reid, "'Shalom Chicago': History Museum's new exhibition tells story of Chicago Jewish Community," *Chicago Tribune*, October 17, 2012, accessed April 19, 2016, http://articles.chicagotribune.com/2012-10-17/entertainment/ct-ent-1018-museum-shalom-20121017_1_chicago-history-museum-first-jewish-congregation-olivia-mahoney.

8. Olivia Mahoney, telephone interview with the author, April 15, 2016.

9. Chicago History Museum, *Shalom Chicago* exhibition script (Introduction).

10. Ibid.

11. Chicago History Museum, *Shalom Chicago* exhibition script.

12. Anti-Defamation League website, "About the ADL," accessed April 20, 2016, http://www.adl.org/about-adl/.

13. Tenement Museum, "Our Story," accessed February 3, 2016, https://www.tenement.org/about.html. See also, Sharon Seitz, ed. *A Tenement Story: The History of 97 Orchard Street and the Lower East Side Tenement Museum* (Lower East Side Tenement Museum: New York, 2004); and Andrew Dolkart, *Biography of a Tenement House in New York City: An Architectural History* (Sante Fe, NM: The Center for American Places, 2006).

14. Russell A. Kazal, "Migration History in Five Stories (and a Basement): The Lower East Side Tenement Museum," *Journal of American Ethnic History* 34, no. 4 (Summer 2015): 77–78, 87.

15. Kazal, "Migration History," 78; Annie Polland, "Ivory Towers and Tenements: American Jewish History, Scholars, and the Pubic," *American Jewish History* 98, no. 2 (April 2014): 41–43.

16. Polland, "Ivory Towers and Tenements," 42–44. See also Annie Polland, "Working for the Sabbath: Sabbath in the Jewish Immigrant Neighborhoods of New York," *Labor: Studies in Working-Class History of the Americas* 6, no. 1 (Spring 2009): 33–56.

17. Polland, "Ivory Towers and Tenements," 42, 44–45, 49.

18. Kazal, "Migration History," 86–89.

19. Hasia R. Diner, Jeffrey Shandler, and Beth S. Wenger, eds., *Remembering the Lower East Side: American Jewish Reflections* (Bloomington: University of Indiana Press, 2000); Frederick M. Binder and Donald M. Reimers, *All the Nations under Heaven: An Ethnic and Racial History of New York City* (New York: Columbia University Press, 1995); and Annie Polland and Daniel Soyer, *Emerging Metropolis: New York Jews in the Age of Immigration, 1840-1920* (New York: New York University Press, 2012).

20. Karen S. Wilson, "Becoming Angelenos," in Karen S. Wilson, ed., *Jews in the Los Angeles Mosaic* (Autry National Center of the American West in association with University of California Press: Los Angeles, 2013), 13–14.

21. Karen S. Wilson, "Becoming Angelenos," 11, 15.

22. Karen S. Wilson, telephone interview with the author, August 11, 2015.

23. Stacy Lieberman, telephone interview with the author, May 22, 2015. Karen S. Wilson, telephone interview with the author, August 11, 2015.

24. Karen S. Wilson, telephone interview with the author, August 11, 2015. Robin Keats and Meg Sullivan, "Jews in the other promised land: a story that UCLA helped the Autry to tell," *UCLA Today* May 13, 2013, accessed February 23, 2016, http://newsroom.ucla.edu/stories/artifacts-tell-story-of-jews-in-246044. See also, Karen S. Wilson, "Introduction," in Karen S. Wilson, ed., *Jews in the Los Angeles Mosaic*, 3–8.

25. Karen S. Wilson, interview. Tom Tugend, "How the Jews changed L.A.," *Jewish Journal*, May 1, 2013, accessed February 23, 2016, http://www.jewishjournal.com/cover_story/article/how_the_jews_changed_los_angeles.

26. Tugend, "How the Jews changed L.A."

27. Wilson, interview.

28. "Mapping Jewish LA," accessed February 23, 2016, http://www.mappingjewishla.org/.

CHAPTER 5

FAMILY AND FESTIVALS

Jewish Domestic Life

O N JUNE 27, 1787, Dr. Benjamin Rush (1746–1813), a noted physician, civic leader, educator, and humanitarian (as well as a signer of the Declaration of Independence) was invited to attend a Jewish wedding. The marriage of Rachel Phillips and Michael Levy followed Jewish tradition. The service began with prayers, followed by the signing of a marriage contract (*ketuba*), in which the bridegroom committed to support his bride. Bride and groom were then escorted to the *chuppah*, or wedding canopy "composed of red and white silk . . . supported by four young men (by means of four poles), who put on white gloves for the purpose."

> As soon as this canopy was fixed, the bride, accompanied with her mother, sister, and a long train of female relations, came downstairs. She was led by her two bridesmaids under the canopy. Two young men led the bridegroom after her and placed him, not by her side, but directly opposite to her. The priest now began again to chaunt [*sic*] an Hebrew prayer, in which he was followed by part of the company. After this he gave to the groom and bride a glass full of wine, from which they each sipped about a teaspoonful. Another prayer followed this act, after which he took a ring and directed the groom to place it upon the finger of his bride.

The wedding ceremony concluded with the groom shattering the wine glass, symbolizing, as Dr. Rush was told, "the brittleness and uncertainty of human life and the certainty of death, and thereby to temper and moderate their present joys."[1]

Although invited by the bride's father, Jonas Phillips, to dine with the other guests, Dr. Rush left after taking some wine and a piece of wedding cake. Before his departure, however, Mrs. Phillips "put a large piece of cake into [his] pocket!" Reflecting on the wedding, Dr. Rush wrote, "During the whole of this new and curious scene my mind was not idle. I was carried back to the ancient world and was led to contemplate the Passovers, the sacrifices, the jubilees, and other ceremonies of the Jewish Church."[2]

Some of the more nuanced meanings of the ceremony escaped even Dr. Rush's interested eye. The *chuppah*, for example, exemplifies "the home that the Jewish husband and wife intend to build lovingly together in the future," characterized by a commitment to leading a Jewish life. The canopy with its open sides also recalls the desert tent of Abraham and Sarah, symbolizing the Jewish tradition of hospitality and, therefore, service to society. This amalgam of commitment to family and tradition, domestic life and communal obligation, makes the Jewish home a valuable lens through which to view important aspects of American Jewish history.[3]

Ideals, Myths, and Realities

Marriage (of one kind or another) is a fundamental institution in all known cultures. A wedding ceremony typically kicks off a new cycle of domestic life, one in which the new family unit is charged with a few fundamental responsibilities. In Jewish tradition, extending back into biblical times, these responsibilities include companionship and intimacy ("A man . . . shall cling to his wife, so that they become one flesh." Gen. 2:24), procreation and the raising of children ("Be fertile and increase." Gen. 1:28), transmission of cultural heritage ("Teach [the laws and commandments] to your children." Deut. 11:19), and the task of earning a living ("By the sweat of your brow shall you get bread to eat." Gen. 3:19). To these ideals—and they are ideals, not descriptions of reality— Jewish tradition added two other requirements: the family was to be patriarchal with the husband dominant ("Your urge shall be for your husband, and he shall rule over you." Gen. 2:16) and the family was to be pious and pure ("You shall be to Me a kingdom of priests and a holy nation." Ex. 19:6). Rabbinic Judaism, which guided traditional Jewish life over two thousand years from late antiquity into the present, elaborated on these fundamentals in Jewish law and custom, producing "a powerful myth about the strength and stability of the Jewish family through the ages."[4]

The disruptions of modernity, including demographic shifts, migration, industrialization, and secularization, greatly affected the structure, size, character, economy, customs, and commitments of Jewish families in Europe, even in the less-developed countries of eastern Europe. And as change increasingly took hold, nostalgia for an idealized "traditional" family grew apace. By the second half of the nineteenth century, observers were lamenting the passing of the patriarchal, pious, three-generation household embedded in a dense matrix of extended kin. This model of Old World Jewish family life did not, however, necessarily reflect the realities of traditional Jewish life. By the mid-eighteenth century, most residential family units in east central Europe were nuclear families. They might live in multifamily dwellings—and often did so—but their households were discrete. Average family size was 4.4 people, living typically in two or three rooms. Households remained the primary economic unit, though kin networks were often critical to success in commerce and trade. Conversely, business relationships often led to marriage. Kin networks were also important for assisting sick, young, or aging family members,

הַגָּדָה שֶׁל פֶּסַח.

יְמֵי חַיֶּיךָ, הָעוֹלָם הַזֶּה. כֹּל יְמֵי חַיֶּיךָ, לְהָבִיא
לִימוֹת הַמָּשִׁיחַ:

בָּרוּךְ הַמָּקוֹם בָּרוּךְ הוּא. בָּרוּךְ שֶׁנָּתַן תּוֹרָה

denotes this time only; but ALL the days of thy life, denotes even at the time of the Messiah.

Blessed be the Omnipresent; blessed is he, blessed is he who hath given the law to his people Israel, blessed be he: the

Figure 5.1 The costs of acculturation. The Wicked Child is depicted in American dress and smoking at the traditional Passover seder. From *Services for the First Two Nights of Passover* published by J. H. Kantorowitz, New York, 1887.

since care was typically given within the household. Marriage within the Jewish community was the norm, and many Jewish marriages were arranged rather than the products of romantic love and individual choice.[5]

In America during the colonial and early national periods, marrying another Jew was a more challenging proposition due to the imbalance of men and women. Intermarriage was a common occurrence and many of those marriages were non-conversionary. Many in-group marriages were still arranged, typically with the consent of the betrothed. But even within arranged marriages there was strong affection, both for spouses and for children. The household was generally composed of parents and children, sometimes with the addition of an aging parent or other dependent relative and sometimes with boarders, apprentices, servants, and slaves. The household remained the locus of economic activity, with women and children actively working. Kin networks were relied on in business relationships and sometimes as a source of marriageable mates. Like other early American families, Jewish families still experienced high rates of infant mortality, early death, and serial marriage—certainly as compared to our contemporary families. However, given the small number of Jews and sparse primary sources, we still have much to learn about the character of Jewish family life in early America.[6]

We also have a lot to learn about Jewish family structure and function in nineteenth-century Europe and America. Jews in western and central Europe—the primary sources of Jewish emigration to America between 1820 and 1880—lived in small domestic units, mostly in households composed of nuclear families (parents and children), with limited obligations to extended kin. In Alsace, for example, only 10 percent of Jewish households comprised extended families (though about 30 percent of Jewish families had close kin living nearby). Households might also include one or more boarders, kin, employees, or servants. Many women worked to help support their families in addition to managing their households; children, too, worked in the family economy. "Young Jewish people spent relatively little time in school," writes Hasia Diner. "Sons commonly worked with parents in preparation for adulthood." These trends carried over into nineteenth-century America.[7]

Immigrant women participated actively in family businesses. Josephine Goldmark recalled that it was "the custom among middle-class Jews [in the nineteenth century] . . . of taking part in their husbands' businesses." Women regularly worked in family stores. Widows, out of necessity, carried on family businesses on their own, and sometimes women created their own businesses. Once they were married, women typically ceased to work for wages outside the home, but contributed to the family income by taking in boarders and lodgers or by part-time work outside the home. In 1879, "the Lissner family, German immigrants to Oakland, could not exist on Louis's meager earnings from pawnbroking, so Matilda raised chickens and peddled eggs in the neighborhood." Only in a few very successful families were wives able to lead a more leisured life, devoted to managing their households and removed from involvement in the family business.[8]

The Modern Family Emerges

The overwhelming majority of contemporary American Jews descend from the mass immigration from eastern Europe, 1880 to 1924. More than for any other group of

European immigrants, this was a migration of families: the Jews who came here, mostly came to stay. Between 1908 and 1924, one-third of all immigrants returned to their home countries, compared to 5–15 percent of Jewish immigrants. The need to support families weighed heavily on Jewish newcomers. As Samuel Joseph observed in 1914, "Jewish immigrants are burdened with a far greater number of dependents than any other immigrant people." To stay afloat, Jewish immigrants took in boarders and sent their children out to work. Despite myriad anecdotes of Jewish parents sacrificing for their children's education and the well-documented occupational and economic mobility of the second generation, Jewish children in New York City accounted for a higher proportion of family income than in other immigrant groups.[9]

Myth and memory characterize these immigrants as uniformly pious, stringently observant of the Sabbath and festivals, *kashrut* (dietary rules), and family purity. In fact, however, the newcomers were not the most learned or pious, and many had already begun to move away from traditional Jewish culture and observance. While some were driven from their homes by violence and many came to escape oppressive restrictions and

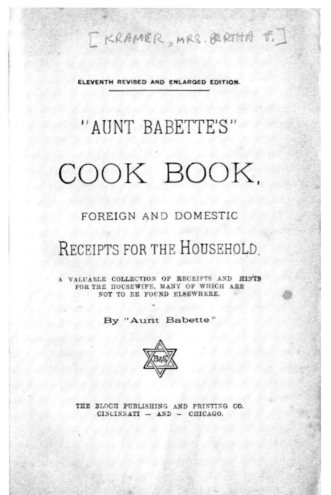

Figure 5.2 Cover of the second American Jewish cookbook. *Aunt Babette's Cook Book,* The Bloch Publishing and Printing Company, Cincinnati, Ohio, 1889. Though featuring a Jewish Star of David on its cover, the author, Bertha E. Kramer, included recipes for Oysters Baked on Shell and Royal Ham Sandwiches among other non-kosher dishes.

Courtesy of the Jewish Museum of Maryland.

antisemitism, most came to America for its freedom and economic opportunity. Like previous generations of Jewish immigrants, these newcomers struggled to acculturate and accommodate to the norms and values of American society.[10]

Contemporary observers, contemplating the newcomers, saw a spectrum of homes and families. In 1902, Esther Jane Ruskay extolled the Jewish home's "beautiful ceremonies, healthful restraints, and simple pleasures," thanks to which the American Jew lived a "temperate, well-ordered life, with none of the evils and none of the fears of this modern age to puzzle or threaten him." Charity workers saw a quite different reality: "The tenement is killing the Jewish home, of which we have all been proud." Desertion, in particular, cast "discredit on our people's reputation for domestic virtues," and illegitimacy threatened Jewish women's reputations.[11] Meanwhile, some families experienced a wrenching reversal of roles, as acculturated children guided their "green" parents in the strange new ways of American life.[12]

These dislocations and disruptions were real, of course. About 10 percent of the Jewish women receiving community relief in New York, for example, had been abandoned by their spouses, and 20 percent of the Jewish children sheltered by municipal institutions were from deserted families. During the era of mass migration, Jewish orphanages sprang up to shelter children who had been abandoned or lost a parent or whose families could no longer afford to support them. Yet we need to avoid exaggerating the more dramatic dysfunctions of family life during the era of mass migration. Instead, we will want to look at the extra-familial factors that helped to stabilize Jewish family life during the first and second generations of eastern European immigration. For one thing, the process of chain migration—following kin, friends, and neighbors to the same destination—helped to ensure that newcomers had connections with earlier arrivals who could help them in adjusting to their new homes. *Landsmanshaftn*, fellowships of newcomers from the same locale or region, sustained that support, offering a range of assistance from camaraderie to burial insurance. Free loan societies extended credit, while retailers sold on credit to peddlers, and wholesalers and manufacturers did the same for retailers, creating an informal system of financing. The ethnic enclave itself, with its multifamily housing, its shops, stores, and eateries, its markets, and its Yiddish vernacular, provided a sense of familiarity and security. And kinfolk were often close by, a source of comfort and common aspirations. "The extended Jewish family played a critical role as an economic unit or network," writes Gerald Sorin. "Relatives deployed their collective resources, borrowed from one another, hired, trained, sustained, and encouraged one another."[13]

Anxieties about the Jewish family, however, transcended those about its integrity and material conditions of life. What Jenna Joselit terms "cultural thresholds of alarm" were crossed in the lapsing of traditional Jewish observance. The Jewish home in the interwar years had moved from being a "domestic Temple" to "little more than a hotel," complained one observer. The Jewish home had become "a place to eat, a place to sleep, and a place from which to flee the moment one has made use of its hotel functions." Traditional Jewish rituals such as Sabbath observance and the maintenance of *kashrut* were languishing: a 1931 survey showed that 60 percent did not light Sabbath candles and 80 percent did not keep kosher. Our Jewish families, Rabbi Leon Lang argued in 1939, are "families of Jews but not Jewish homes."[14]

Concerns like these were exacerbated by Jewish mobility. As early as 1920, American-born children outnumbered their immigrant parents. And, with impressive speed, the second generation began to make their way outward and upward. The ethnic enclaves, present everywhere that Jews concentrated in significant numbers—from East Baltimore to Boyle Heights in Los Angeles—were typically working- and lower-middle class neighborhoods. As soon as family incomes grew, Jews began moving away from these fabled neighborhoods to areas of better housing. Acculturation and mobility proceeded apace. As one observer noted, "Today in America, Jewry, like a chameleon, has taken on the color of its new surroundings. Its soul remains divided between the memory of its Eastern heritage—of traditions nursed through centuries of ghetto life—and the interests of the community, which has received it. Its thought has been cast increasingly in the American vernacular."[15]

"It's the second-generation Jews with all the outward characteristics minus beard and mustache, playing baseball, great fight fans, commercial travelers, clean-shirted, white collared, derby-hatted, crease-trousered. The women are stylish and stout, social workers, actresses, stump-speakers, jazz dancers with none of the color and virtues of the erstwhile bearded bewigged parents," wrote one observer. And the changes transcended outward appearance. Gender roles and aspirations were changing in the interwar years. "In the Old World," writes Henry Feingold, "the sexes remained largely separate for work and

Figure 5.3 The Rosenberg-Blackman family gathered for Sabbath in Portland, Oregon, c. 1922.
Courtesy of the Oregon Jewish Museum and Holocaust Education Center. OJM 04266.

play. . . . In the America of the twenties, Jewish men and women were finally coming to live in the same world." The result was an increase in wage earning among women, a decline in arranged marriages, and a rapid adoption of birth control. Changes in gender roles and aspirations affected the Jewish family, as the traditional emphasis on modesty began to erode. This put new strains on the institution traditionally tasked with transmitting religious observance. Moreover, the second generation was in transition at a time of rapid social change in America itself. Feingold has offered a striking image of that transition: "The Jews of the twenties were changing their cultural garments while riding on an escalator."[16]

By the start of World War II, the density and vitality of first-generation enclaves was in decline, while new areas were being populated by middle-class Jewish families living in nuclear households and practicing birth control. The early decline in family size, coupled with occupational mobility and growing abundance (despite the rigors of the Great Depression), set the stage for American Jewry's domestic moment in the postwar years.

Mid-Century and Beyond

"By 1940 American Jews had adopted the model of the middle-class American family more successfully than any other immigrant group," write Geldman and Geffen. "Fictional Jewish families as portrayed by Jewish authors in the 1940s are unmistakably middle-class American families who also happen to be Jewish." Even in the depths of the Depression, Jewish occupational mobility—fueled by careers in independent business and the professions—lay a foundation for postwar prosperity. Social mobility was accompanied by residential mobility. The pressures of depression and war had forced many families to double-up. After years of housing starvation, the postwar building boom led to an unprecedented growth of the suburbs.[17]

Jews were among the most eager to transplant themselves from the city to the suburbs. By 1960, a majority of American Jews lived in suburbia. This mass residential movement transformed Jewish family life. In the old first- and second-generation neighborhoods, grandchildren often lived in proximity to their grandparents. Geographic dispersion reduced regular contact, distancing many suburban families from tradition. "A Sunday visit to *bubbie* [grandmother] and *zaidie* [grandfather] in the city might take in shopping at the Jewish bakery, bookstore, or kosher butcher. [But] such casual activities were the most intensive Jewish cultural encounters some third- and fourth-generation children would experience." The thick ethnic culture of earlier generations was becoming attenuated. And the thinning of social interaction in the suburbs meant a greater reliance on formal activities such as synagogue attendance or youth group meetings. For newly suburbanized Jews, the family became dependent on the "Jewish skills and knowledge of community professionals. . . . Even such classic family rites as lighting Hanukkah candles or participating in a Passover *seder* no longer took place at home, but in the synagogue, under the direction of a rabbi or teacher."[18]

"The number of Jews who kept kosher, observed the Sabbath, and had a serious interest in Jewish ideas and books, declined during the building boom," writes Edward

Shapiro. "For most suburban Jews, the major role of Judaism was now the celebration of life-cycle events." The rituals that were most frequently observed were oriented toward children—ritual circumcision, bar and bat mitzvah ceremonies, and a few festivals. The focus on children was part and parcel of a family life that had become increasingly child-centered, in part because the number of children in families that were not Orthodox remained small. Low levels of fertility in Jewish families (due to birth control and late marriages) were offset only by the high rate of Jewish nuptiality: a 1982 study reported that as many as 98 percent of Jewish men at age forty-five had been married.[19]

Concern for the needs of children is a long-established tradition in Jewish family history. But in the postwar decades, suburban Jewish families were unusually attentive to their offspring. In fact, many second- and third-generation Jewish parents acknowledged that the move to the suburbs was "for the sake of the children." With greater economic means, Jewish parents tended to indulge their children with "the best of everything"—and this included, observes Marshall Sklare, "clothing, medical attention, entertainment, vacations, schools, and myriad other items." Parental interest in gratifying their children extended also to home rituals. Those rituals that involved children and were fun experiences tended to endure or even intensify. In suburbia, for example, the festival of *Sukkot* (Tabernacles), which involves the construction of a temporary structure, the *sukkah*, became more popular. Building a *sukkah* was the perfect suburban project, a family-centered, do-it-yourself activity.[20]

Affluence also altered the role of Jewish men and women. By the 1950s, many Jewish women in suburbia were full-time homemakers and mothers. Fathers, preoccupied with earning a living, relinquished their traditional role as the principal transmitters of Jewish heritage and culture. "The Jewish woman has acquired her new position of leadership by default," writes Albert I. Gordon. "So completely engrossed in business affairs . . . [the husband] generally gives little attention to spiritual and cultural matters that involve his home and family." Values as well as affluence accounted for this most domestic of times: the postwar cult of domesticity "defined women's highest calling as mother and wife," argues Edward Shapiro.[21]

In mid-century, Jewish institutions had developed fixed assumptions about the Jewish family. It was composed of two parents and their children, labor and responsibilities were strictly divided by gender, and children were the focus of family life and activities. Yet by 1990, the most common household in the Jewish community was composed of one adult Jew living alone. The next most common was a household of two adult Jews. Only 14 percent of Jewish households comprised two Jewish adults living with one or more children under age eighteen. And contemporary American Jews were living in a variety of family constellations: "as singles of all ages; empty nest couples whose children have left home and will not again return; senior adults living alone or in communities and facilities, widowed or married; dual-career spouses; single parents, whether by death of one's spouse, loss or divorce; and non-traditional couples, gay men and lesbian women." The "typical household" is more than likely to be atypical in one way or another.[22]

Throughout American history, Jews have lived in a variety of household types. But the contemporary Jewish family lives in an unusually varied and complex range of circumstances. Why is this so? One reason is a decline in the numbers of married Jews. In 1970, nearly 80 percent of all adult Jews were married; a generation later (1990), that proportion had dropped to two-thirds. Age at first marriage had increased. In 1970, 17 percent of Jewish men were single at ages twenty-five to thirty-four; by 1990, this number had increased to 50 percent. Women followed a similar pattern. Jewish women tend to be highly educated and many are pursuing careers. Feminism, too, has changed many women's attitudes toward themselves, giving many the confidence to determine their own paths. "Over the past thirty years," write Geldman and Geffen, "being single in America has developed into a lifestyle." Complementing the trend toward postponement of marriage, divorce rates, single motherhood, and cohabitation without marriage have increased. Today, a third of all Jewish children "live in homes touched by divorce: about 10 percent of Jewish children live in single parent homes and 20 percent live in households in which at least one spouse has been divorced," according to Sylvia Fishman.[23]

But the most egregious change in Jewish family life has come about through intermarriage. Into the 1960s, rates of intermarriage remained relatively low. But since the 1960s, rates of intermarriage outside the Orthodox community have increased dramatically. Today, out-marriage may account for as many as half of all non-Orthodox marriages. Clearly Jews are now widely "regarded as acceptable partners for non-Jews and the opposition from the non-Jewish family has declined markedly," write Geldman and Geffen. Since many of these out-marriages are non-conversionary, there is now a high incidence of intermarried and multicultural families among American Jews. This, of course, has had an unintended consequence of some note: some tens of millions of non-Jewish Americans now have a Jewish relative by marriage and/or by descent.[24]

"A low birth rate, high intermarriage, and the diverse forms of family life present new and different challenges to the American Jewish family," argue Geldman and Geffen. In response, the American Jewish community has developed a range of initiatives designed to support and strengthen the family, most especially in its role as the transmitter of Jewish heritage. Voluntary communities or communities of choice, such as the *havurot* (fellowships), are used by some as a substitute for the traditional family network. Family education programs and professional training for family educators aimed at engaging Jewish families in cultural, religious, and communal activity have proliferated. Programs have been developed to bring Jewish young adults to Israel (free of charge) and to connect them to their roots, while the March of the Living and other programs related to the Holocaust are designed to instill a sense of shared destiny. A plethora of Jewish start-ups, pop-ups, innovative projects, and philanthropic initiatives have emerged in recent decades in a diffuse effort to promote Jewish renewal.[25]

The contemporary Orthodox community continues to grow through a high birthrate and large families, as well as through the adherence of converts and non-Orthodox Jews. As of this writing, it appears that American Jewish families—and the American Jewish community at large—falls into three broad categories: traditionally observant (Orthodox) Jews, liberal Jews (Conservative, Reform, and Reconstructionist), and secular Jews who identify themselves in relation to Jewish culture. Today, American Jewish families, with all their diversity, more strongly resemble those of non-Jewish neighbors than the

Jewish family of a hundred or even fifty years earlier. The trends and transitions discussed here make it hard to predict what the family will look like in the next generation or two, but the resilience of Jews and of their cultural traditions make it likely that the Jewish family in its myriad forms will endure and perhaps even flourish.

Domestic Traditions: Family Purity

Traditional Jewish marriage, such as that with which this essay opens, actually begins with the act of *kiddushin* (sanctification). At a point prior to the wedding ceremony, the man gives to his chosen bride a ring or money in the presence of witnesses, making her forbidden to all other men. In this interim stage, she is now *mikuddeshet* (sanctified to her husband-to-be). The root word *kadosh* (holy) informs the marital relationship, the Jewish home, and the Jewish people: "You shall be . . . a holy nation." Since God abides in the entire universe, holiness is not confined to the synagogue (or Temple), but must permeate the home as well.

One of the essentials of the traditional Jewish home is "family purity." "Blood is holy. It symbolically carries the soul of animate creatures. That is why it is spilled out for sacrifices, and why meat, in order to be kosher, is salted so that all the blood is removed," writes Rabbi Alan Suskin. Menstruation, therefore, in which there is an emission of blood, makes the menstruant (temporarily) ritually impure. She must, therefore, refrain from sexual relations during her period, following which, she is required to immerse herself in a ritual bath (*mikveh*). "At the mikveh the woman prepares herself by bathing, brushing her teeth, cleaning under her nails, removing all jewelry, and so forth, to make sure that her body is perfectly clean before entering the waters. She then goes into the water and immerses, and recites a prescribed blessing. The procedure is similar for a woman who has given birth. . . . Like all human behaviors, one's sexual life can be lived in a holy way. Jewish law provides instruction regarding how one can bring *kedushah* (holiness) into relationships."[26]

Immersion in the mikveh was not limited to women. Men, too, immersed themselves in the mikveh on various occasions. Bridegrooms entered the mikveh on their wedding day, men immersed themselves before the annual Day of Atonement (Yom Kippur), and in some Hasidic communities it was customary for men to attend the mikveh weekly on the eve of the Sabbath. All of these practices were customary. It is mandatory, however, for converts to Judaism to enter the mikveh as an integral part of the conversion process.[27]

Domestic Traditions: The Kosher Home

The Jewish home is marked in a number of ways. From the outside, the chief symbol of a Jewish home is a small container called a *mezuzah* (literally, doorpost). This is affixed at the front door of a Jewish home (and on other interior doorways as well). The mezuzah contains a small piece of parchment on which has been inscribed, in Hebrew, the verse from Deuteronomy 6:9: "inscribe them on the doorposts of your house and on your gates." There are many views as to the significance of the mezuzah, but two views are especially prevalent today: the mezuzah protects us, not against external harm but against sinning, and it reminds us every time we enter and leave that worldly affairs are not so important as the awareness of God and our responsibility to lead a responsible life.[28]

Within the house, a key marker of Jewish identity is the kosher kitchen. For more than two thousand years, Jews have been linked by religious observances that include *kashrut*, a code of eating prescribed in the Bible. Separation of "meat" and "dairy" in kosher cooking has produced an elaborate system of distinctive foodways and culinary practice designed in part to mark off Jews from others and in part to promote intentional eating. The laws and customs of kashrut have evolved over time, and in America abundance has made observance of kashrut ever-more refined and detailed: Orthodox visitors to the Shapiro House at Strawbery Banke in Portsmouth, New Hampshire, for example, are shocked to discover that a century ago Jews washed both meat and dairy dishes using the same basin (quite unlike today's state-of-the-art two-sink, two-dishwasher kosher kitchens). Custom and culinary practice have also been influenced by the cuisines and food cultures of Jews' neighbors, as Jews adapted local foodstuffs to traditional precepts. Just recently, the Conservative movement announced that rice and beans may be cooked and eaten during Passover—a practice that had long been honored among Sephardic and Mizrachi (Middle Eastern) Jews.[29]

What Jews eat, when, and with whom they eat it help to define them as a community. Food is a means to observe and to celebrate; foodways embody Jewish values and symbols. These, however, have been greatly modified in America, first by the fact of food abundance that has distinguished America from most other countries, and then by regional and ethnic cuisines, which have produced some remarkable regional variants like matzah ball gumbo. The growth of the food industry has revolutionized the pantries of American Jews, while expanding the availability of kosher foods. And in recent decades a succession of national reform campaigns for better nutrition, food safety, environmental protection, and social justice have also influenced Jewish eating. Kashrut has, in turn, had a profound effect on American foodways, leading one writer to describe America as a "kosher nation."[30]

Domestic Traditions: Sabbath and Festivals

In keeping with its role as a miniature Temple, the Jewish home is the venue for celebrating important festivals in the weekly and annual festival cycle. The most important of these festivals is *Shabbat*, the Jewish Sabbath. It was said by the great Yiddish writer Ahad Ha'am that "More than the Jewish people have kept the Sabbath, the Sabbath has kept the Jewish people." Shabbat is a weekly day of rest for man and beast. Shabbat celebrates the creation of the world (when God rested on the seventh day) and commemorates the Exodus from Egypt, an event that freed the Jewish people from slavery. Like all Jewish festivals, the Sabbath begins at sundown the evening before: the Sabbath eve meal, therefore, falls on Friday evening. The traditional Sabbath rituals include songs welcoming the Sabbath Queen, the lighting of Sabbath candles (with blessing), recitation of the *kiddush* (the blessing over wine), ritual washing of hands (also with a blessing), and a blessing

Figure 5.4 Sam, Jen, and Richard Polt welcome the Sabbath in Needham, Massachusetts, 2008. Note the Sabbath candles, the kiddush cup, and the cover for the braided Sabbath challah.

Courtesy of the Jewish Museum of Maryland and Audrey Polt. JMM CP 14.2010.031.

over the traditional braided bread (*challah*). As the most important festival in the Jewish calendar, the Sabbath is typically celebrated with a special meal, followed by singing and recitation of grace. The Sabbath candlesticks, the kiddush cup, and an elegant challah cover are among the most visible and most frequently used ritual objects found in Jewish homes. The Sabbath day ends after sundown, when three stars can be observed.[31]

Other Jewish festivals are celebrated at home as well. The most notable is probably the biblical pilgrimage festival of *Pesach* (Passover). The Passover *seder* (literally, order) features a dramatic ritual meal that is based on a traditional liturgy embodied in the *haggadah* or narrative. Passover is the most generally observed of Jewish festivals in the annual calendar and the Jewish festival most familiar to non-Jewish Americans (since the Last Supper was a Passover seder). The Pesach liturgy retells the story of the Exodus from Egypt and incorporates discussion and study. The symbols of the festival—among them, *matzah* (unleavened bread), *maror* (bitter herbs), and *pesach* (paschal lamb)—are called out for special attention; candle-lighting, kiddush, ritual washing of hands, recitation of blessings, and grace are counterpointed by a lavish meal. For centuries, the Passover seder has been an occasion for gathering of family and friends, for storytelling and reminiscence, and for discussion of social and political issues of the day. Since World War II, a host of new haggadahs have been produced to meet various interests—women's haggadahs and haggadahs of social justice, personal narratives, and handmade haggadahs. And as significant events occur, mention of them has entered the Passover liturgy: the Holocaust, the murder of European Jewry by the Nazi regime, for example, is now universally commemorated during the seder.[32]

Other festivals also have their domestic expressions, typically a special festival cuisine. The biblical pilgrimage festival of *Shavuot* (Pentecost), which is celebrated seven weeks after Passover, commemorates the giving of the Ten Commandments to the Israelites at Mount Sinai and also the beginning of the early harvest in the land of Israel. It is customary to eat dairy food on Shavuot to recall the journey from Egypt, characterized in Exodus 3:8–17 as a journey "from the misery of Egypt to a land flowing with milk and honey." The Hanukkah festival, known as the Feast of Lights, recalls an incident in the restored Temple (165 BCE) when a single cruse of oil burned for eight days. Foods, such as potato pancakes (latkes), that are fried in oil are traditional Hanukkah fare. The carnival-like festival of Purim celebrates the saving of Persian Jewry described in the Book of Esther. It is customary for families to exchange gifts of goodies, including the traditional tri-cornered *hamantashen* pastry named for Haman, the leading adversary of the Jews. Many other Jewish festivals involve domestic rituals and special prayers. But what is really important to note is that home celebrations of many Jewish festivals have been influenced and shaped by the conditions of American liberty, abundance, and diversity. In fact, Jewish domestic rituals and celebrations now include national holidays, most notably Thanksgiving.[33]

Domestic Traditions: Life Cycle Rituals

The most familiar Jewish life cycle events are typically celebrated in synagogue rather than in the home. Weddings, of course, and bar and bat mitzvah ceremonies are usually held in synagogue. But equally important life cycle events are traditionally marked within the Jewish home, among them the birth of a son and the death of a family member.

On the eighth day after the birth of a son, Jewish families perform the ancient ceremony of *brit milah* (ritual circumcision), a ritual that welcomes the newborn into the covenant (*brit*) and community of Israel (that is, the Jewish people). The ceremony centers on the circumcision and naming of the newborn child. The site of the circumcision ceremony is not mandated by law, but many such ceremonies are conducted in a home setting. A professional *mohel* (ritual circumciser) usually conducts the ceremony and performs the removal of the foreskin. During the ceremony, the baby is given his Hebrew name (in eastern European tradition, the name of a deceased relative whom the parents wish to honor) and usually is "redeemed" from service in the temple by his father; this ancient custom involves payment to a synagogue in return for which the newborn is excused from preparing for the rabbinate. A key part of the event is a festive meal, often accompanied by traditional dishes such as bagels and spreads. The naming of a newborn daughter, in contrast, is traditionally done in the synagogue, though these ceremonies, too, are now taking place in the home.[34]

Food is also an integral element of the Jewish mourning ritual known as *shiva* (literally, seven). When a Jew loses a close relative—father, mother, son, daughter, brother, sister, or spouse—he or she is traditionally required to sit shiva (a week) at home, where the mourner is visited and comforted. "Every law and every custom of Jewish mourning and comforting has, at its core, the overwhelming motivation to surround those who are dying and those who will grieve with a supportive community. While some may argue that facing death and coping with grief heighten one's feeling of aloneness, the Jewish approach places loss and grief in the communal context of family and friends." Weekday prayer services are held in the house of mourning, either in the house of the deceased or where the deceased's family is sitting shiva. It is customary to recite psalms of consolation and for the mourners to recite the kaddish, a prayer of sanctification. It is considered an act of loving-kindness to attend services and to console the bereaved family. It is also a communal responsibility to provide food with which to feed the family in mourning and its guests. Those in mourning rise from sitting shiva for Sabbath and festivals and at the end of the shiva week.[35]

The Jewish wedding, with which we began this chapter, also has a dimension of domestic ritual. During the wedding ceremony proper, it is customary to recite the *sheva berakhot* (seven blessings). "While today most newly married couples are eager to sneak away for honeymoon time alone . . . Jewish tradition held that the bride and groom needed time with the community to help start their marriage out on the right foot. For the seven days following the wedding, the bride and groom were treated like a queen and king, and were invited to dine at the home of a different friend or relative on each night. These festive meals were called 'sheva berakhot.' Following dinner, the seven blessings would be recited again. . . . During generations when marriages were arranged and couples may have met just before marriage the sheva berakhot meals served as a way for the couple to get to know each other, while being supported by the community."[36]

The re-casting of traditional rituals and the creation of new rituals is an ongoing process among American Jews. As one writer puts it, "Jewish rituals have emerged and evolved as a means to connect with history, with community or with notions of the Divine. For this reason, new rituals are a barometer of both the vibrancy of Jewish life and the particular dynamics of the community at the time in which they emerge. As Judaism continues to reshape itself to the contours of contemporary life, ritual has become one of the most compelling facets of modern Jewish expression."[37]

Notes

1. "A Philadelphia Wedding, 1787: Letter of Benjamin Rush to His Wife," *Publications of the American Jewish Historical Society* 42, no. 2 (December 1952): 189–92.

2. Ibid.

3. Meir Soloveichik, "'The First Truly American Jew': Jonas Phillips and the Promise of the New Republic," in *By Dawn's Early Light: Jewish Contributions to American Culture from the Nation's Founding to the Civil War* (Princeton: Princeton University Library, 2016), 28.

4. See, for example, "Husband and Wife" and "Parent and Child" in *Encyclopaedia Judaica*, 2nd ed. (Farmington Hills, MI: Thomson Gale, 2007); Paula Hyman, "The Modern Jewish Family: Image and Reality; in David Kraemer, ed., *The Jewish Family: Metaphor and Memory* (New York: Oxford University Press, 1989), 179.

5. Gershon David Hundert, "Jewish Children and Childhood in Early Modern East Central Europe," in Kraemer, ed., *The Jewish Family*, 81–94.

6. Paula Hyman, "Introduction" and "Afterword" in Steven M. Cohen and Paula E. Hyman, eds., *The Jewish Family: Myths and Reality* (New York: Holmes and Meier, 1986), 3–13, 230–35.

7. Paula Hyman, "The Modern Jewish Family," 179–80; Hasia R. Diner, *A Time for Gathering: The Second Migration, 1820-1880* (Baltimore: Johns Hopkins University Press, 1992), 20, 81–84.

8. Hyman, "The Modern Jewish Family," 184–85; Diner, *A Time for Gathering*, 81–84; Francine Klagsbrun, "Changing Roles of Jewish Women," in Norman Linzer, et al., eds., *Crisis and Continuity: The Jewish Family in the 21st Century* (Hoboken, NJ: Ktav Publishing House, 1995), 53–55. Susan A. Glenn, *Daughters of the Shtetl: Life and Labor in the Immigrant Generation* (Ithaca: Cornell University Press, 1990), 8–89.

9. Annie Polland and Daniel Soyer, *Emerging Metropolis: New York Jews in the Age of Immigration, 1840-1920* (New York: New York University Press, 2012), 112, 122.

10. Arden J. Geldman and Rela Mintz Geffen, "Family, American Jewish," in *Encyclopaedia Judaica*, 2nd ed. (Farmington Hills, MI: Thomson Gale, 2007), 695–96.

11. Jenna Weissman Joselit, "Modern Jewish Family in the United States," in *JWA Encyclopedia*, accessed March 11, 2016, http://jwa.org/encyclopedia.

12. Geldman and Geffen, "Family," *Encyclopaedia Judaica*, 6: 696.

13. Polland and Soyer, *Emerging Metropolis*, 103–23; Gerald Sorin, *A Time for Building: The Third Migration, 1880-1920* (Baltimore: Johns Hopkins University Press, 1992), 82–83, 92–93, 157; Reena Sigmund Friedman, *These Are Our Children: Jewish Orphanages in the United States, 1880-1921* (Hanover, NH: University Press of New England, 1995).

14. Joselit, "Modern Jewish Family," in *JWA Encyclopedia*; Henry L. Feingold, *A Time for Searching: Entering the Mainstream, 1920-1945* (Baltimore: Johns Hopkins University Press, 1992), 35–61.

15. Geldman and Geffen, "Family," in *Encyclopaedia Judaica*, 2nd ed., 6: 697; Joselit, "Modern Jewish Family," in *JWA Encyclopedia*. See also Jenna Weissman Joselit, *The Wonders of America: Reinventing Jewish Culture, 1880-1950* (New York: Hill and Wang, 1994); and Sarah L. Braunstein and Jenna Weissman Joselit, eds., *Getting Comfortable in New York: The American Jewish Home, 1880-1950* (New York: The Jewish Museum, 1990).

16. Henry Feingold, *A Time for Searching*, 36–42, 47–48. For some of the anxieties that accompanied acculturation and adaptation, see Riv-Ellen Prell, *Fighting to Become Americans: Jews, Gender, and the Anxiety of Assimilation* (Boston: Beacon, 1999).

17. Geldman and Geffen, "Family," in *Encyclopaedia Judaica*, 2nd ed., 6: 699; Edward S. Shapiro, *A Time for Healing: American Jewry since World War II* (Baltimore: Johns Hopkins University Press, 1992), 155–57.

18. Geldman and Geffen, "Family," in *Encyclopaedia Judaica*, 2nd ed., 6: 700–01; Edward S. Shapiro, *A Time for Healing*, 143–49, 167.

19. Edward Shapiro, *A Time for Healing*, 149–50; Jay Y. Brodbar-Nemzer, "The Contemporary American Jewish Family," in Darwin L. Thomas, ed., *The Religion and Family Connection: Social Science Perspectives* (Provo, UT: Brigham Young University, 1988), 66–87.

20. Geldman and Geffen, "Family," in *Encyclopaedia Judaica* 6: 701.

21. Francine Klagsbrun, "Roles of Jewish Women," in Linzer, et al., eds., *Crisis and Continuity*, 55–56; Albert I. Gordon, *Jews in Suburbia* (Boston: Beacon Press, 1959), 59–60; Edward Shapiro, *A Time for Healing*, 143.

22. Geldman and Geffen, "Family," in *Encyclopaedia Judaica* 6: 702.

23. Ibid.; Klagsbrun, "Changing Roles," 57.

24. Geldman and Geffen, "Family," in *Encyclopaedia Judaica* 6: 703–04; Jennifer A. Thompson, *Jewish on Their Own Terms: How Intermarried Couples Are Changing American Judaism* (Rutgers, NJ: Rutgers University Press, 2014).

25. Geldman and Geffen, "Family," in *Encyclopaedia Judaica* 6: 703–04.

26. My Jewish Learning website, Rabbi Alana Suskin, "Menstruation and 'Family Purity,'" accessed March 16, 2016, https://www.jewishvirtuallibrary.org/jsource/Judaism/niddah.html.

27. Mikvah.org website, Rivkah Slonim, "Understanding Mikvah," accessed March 16, 2016, http://www.mikvah.org/article/understanding_mikvah_and_the_laws_of_family_purity_.

28. Richard Siegel, et al., eds., *The Jewish Catalog: A Do-It Yourself Kit*, 1st ed. (Philadelphia: The Jewish Publication Society, 1973), 12–13.

29. David Kraemer, *Jewish Eating and Identity through the Ages* (New York: Routledge, 2007); Avi Y. Decter and Juliana Ochs Dweck, eds. *Chosen Food: Cuisine, Culture, and American Jewish Identity* (Baltimore: Jewish Museum of Maryland, 2011); Maddie Beihl, Telephone interview with the author, January 30, 2016; Marcie Cohen Ferris, *Matzoh Ball Gumbo: Culinary Tales of the Jewish South* (Chapel Hill: University of North Carolina Press, 2005).

30. Decter and Dweck, *Chosen Food*, 1–3. Sue Fishkoff, *Kosher Nation* (New York: Schocken Books, 2010).

31. Abraham Joshua Heschel, *The Sabbath: Its Meaning for Modern Man* (New York: Farrar, Straus and Young, 1961); Susan Nashman Fraiman, "Sabbath," in *Encyclopaedia Judaica*, 2nd ed., 17: 616–22; Reform Judaism.org website, "Shabbat," accessed March 16, 2016, http://www.reformjudaism.org/jewish-holidays/shabbat.

32. Philip Goodman, *The Passover Anthology* (Philadelphia: Jewish Publication Society, 1961).

33. Michael Strassfeld, *The Jewish Holidays: A Guide and Commentary* (New York: Harper & Row, 1985); Arthur Waskow, *Seasons of Our Joy: A Handbook of Jewish Festivals* (New York: Bantam Books, 1982); Marlena Spieler, *Jewish Festival Food: Eating for Special Occasions* (London: Lorenz Books, 2015); Dianne Ashton, *Hanukkah in America: A History* (New York: New York University Press, 2013); Beth S. Wenger, "Rites of Citizenship: Jewish Celebrations of the Nation," in Marc Lee Raphael, ed., *The Columbia History of Jews and Judaism in America* (New York: Columbia University Press, 2008), 366–84.

34. Juliana Ochs Dweck, "'Who Can Cater a Bris in Queens?' Circumcision Meals in Contemporary America," in Decter and Dweck, eds., *Chosen Food*, 54–65.

35. My Jewish Learning website, Ron Wolfson, "How To Make a Shiva Call," accessed March 17, 2016, http://www.myjewishlearning.com/article/how-to-make-a-shiva-call/. See also Jack Riemer, ed., *Wrestling with the Angel: Jewish Insights on Death and Mourning* (New York: Schocken Books, 1995).

36. My Jewish Learning website, Gabrielle Kaplan-Mayer, "The Sheva Berakhot," accessed March 17, 2016, http://www.myjewishlearning.com/article/the-sheva-berakhot/.

37. Steinhardt Foundation website, Eli Valley, "New Jewish Ritual," accessed March 17, 2016, http://www.steinhardtfoundation.org/wp-install/wp-ontent/uploads/2013/10/winter_2010.pdf. See also Vanessa L. Ochs, *Inventing Jewish Ritual* (Philadelphia: Jewish Publication Society, 2007); Rela M. Geffen, ed., *Celebration & Renewal: Rites of Passage in Judaism* (Philadelphia, Jewish Publication Society, 1993).

Select Bibliography

Cohen, Steven M., and Paula E. Hyman, eds. *The Jewish Family: Myths and Reality*. New York: Holmes and Meier, 1986.

Decter, Avi Y., and Juliana Ochs Dweck, eds. *Chosen Food: Cuisine, Culture, and American Jewish Identity*. Baltimore: Jewish Museum of Maryland, 2011.

Diner, Hasia R. *Her Works Praise Her: A History of Jewish Women in America from Colonial Times to the Present*. New York: Basic Books, 2002.

Diner, Hasia R. *A Hungering for America: Italian, Irish, and Jewish Foodways in the Age of Migration*. Cambridge, MA: Harvard University Press, 2001.

Donim, Hayim Halevy. *To Be A Jew: A Guide to Jewish Observance in Contemporary Life*. New York: Basic Books, 1972.

Friedman, Reena Sigmund. *These Are Our Children: Jewish Orphanages in the United States, 1880-1925*. Hanover, NH: University of New England Press, 1994.

Geffen, Rela M., ed. *Celebration and Renewal: Rites of Passage in Judaism*. Philadelphia: Jewish Publication Society, 1993.

Geldman Arden J., and Rela Mintz Geffen, "Family, American Jewish," in *Encyclopaedia Judaica*, 2nd ed. Farmington Hills, MI: Thomson Gale, 2007.

Glenn, Susan A. *Daughters of the Shtetl: Life and Labor in the Immigrant Generation*. Ithaca: Cornell University Press, 1990.

Goldman, Karla. *Beyond the Synagogue Gallery: Finding a Place for Women in American Judaism*. Cambridge: Harvard University Press, 2000.

Joselit, Jenna Weissman. *The Wonders of America: Reinventing Jewish Culture, 1880-1950*. New York: Hill and Wang, 1994.

Joselit, Jenna Weissman. "Modern Jewish Family in the United States," *JWA Encyclopedia* [http:// jwa.org/encyclopedia].

Klapper, Melissa R. *Jewish Girls Coming of Age in America, 1860-1920*. New York: New York University Press, 2005.

Kraemer, David C. *Jewish Eating and Identity through the Ages*. New York: Routledge, 2007.

Kraemer, David C., ed. *The Jewish Family: Metaphor and Memory*. New York: Oxford University Press, 1989.

Linzer, Norman, et al., eds. *Crisis and Continuity: The Jewish Family in the 21st Century*. Hoboken, NJ: Ktav Publishing House, 1995.

Nadell, Pamela S., and Jonathan D. Sarna, eds. *Women and American Judaism: Historical Perspectives*. Hanover, NH: University Press of New England, 2001.

Nadell, Pamela S. *Women Who Would Be Rabbis: A History of Women's Ordination, 1889-1985*. Boston: Beacon Press, 1998.

Ochs, Vanessa L. *Inventing Jewish Ritual*. Philadelphia: Jewish Publication Society, 2007.

Prell, Riv-Ellen, ed. *Women Remaking American Judaism*. Detroit: Wayne State University Press, 2007.

Spieler, Marlena. *Jewish Festival Food: Eating for Special Occasions*. London: Lorenz Books, 2015.

Strassfeld, Michael. *The Jewish Holidays: A Guide and Commentary*. New York: Harper & Row, 1985.

CHAPTER 6

CASE STUDIES
Domestic Life

JEWISH DOMESTIC life cuts across most of the other themes discussed in this book. Tenement homes, usually located in New York City and most often on the Lower East Side, during the peak years of Jewish immigration (1880–1924) are stock items in American movies. The Jewish mother and the Jewish kitchen—inextricably linked in American popular culture—are standard features of Jewish shtick. So are the frequently caricatured excesses of traditional Jewish weddings. Kosher foodways remain a standard feature of Jewish life, at least in the minds of many non-Jews. And a growing number of Americans have attended bar and bat mitzvah services and have at least a passing familiarity with a Sabbath service.

We are still waiting for American history organizations to tackle the Jewish mother or the Jewish feminist movement, but in the meantime a number of institutions have organized interpretive programs on aspects of Jewish domestic life and culture. This selection of case studies highlights, in turn, the home life of an early merchant family in Norfolk, Virginia; the 1920s home of eastern European Jewish immigrants in Portsmouth, New Hampshire; Jewish families settling in the Upper Midwest; the Jewish contribution to American cookery; and a Frank Lloyd Wright home built for Stanley and Mildred Rosenbaum in Florence, Alabama.

Moses Myers House

Chrysler Museum of Art

In 1787, Moses Myers (1752–1835), a Jewish merchant, married and moved to Norfolk, Virginia. Five years later, he bought a large lot and built a two-story brick townhouse with a pedimented gable and a portico around the front door. Here, Myers and four later generations of his family made their home, adding wings and reconfiguring the interior to suit their evolving needs. Today, the Moses Myers House is an historic house museum owned by the City of Norfolk and managed by the Chrysler Museum of Art.[1]

The Myers House is notable on a number of counts. Myers was Norfolk's first resident Jew and was prominent in the town's commercial and civic affairs. He served on the Common Council, was a major in the local militia, was appointed superintendent of the Norfolk branch of the Bank of Richmond, and was a founder of the Norfolk Chamber of Commerce. The family's household affairs and business life are unusually well-documented in an extensive archive, which today is part of the Chrysler's library and which provides an exceptional resource for architectural restoration and interpretation of the site. The Myers House—furnished to c. 1820—features a wealth of furniture, art, and decorative items, about 70 percent of which are original to the site and the Myers family. The house itself is an urban dwelling, quite different from the plantation homes open to visitors in the area; its 1796 octagonal-ended dining wing is attributed to architect Benjamin Latrobe.[2]

Visitors to the Myers House can experience the home in two distinct ways. Unobtrusive, free-standing pedestals offer interpretation to those who choose to guide themselves. Most visitors, however, choose to tour with a trained guide, who tailors a narrative to meet visitors' particular interests. The house features notable architectural details, important works of art (including companion portraits of Moses and Eliza Myers by Gilbert Stuart), and a variety of period furniture, glass, silver, and ceramics. One upstairs room interprets the life and accomplishments of Barton Myers (1853–1927), Moses Myers' great-grandson, a civic and business leader in Norfolk. A second room is devoted to the life of Moses Myers.

The Moses Myers room interprets him as a typical merchant and entrepreneur whose business ventures spanned the Atlantic world. Moses Myers was born in New York City. His father, Haym Myers, a native of Amsterdam, came to the colonies in the 1740s as a *shochet* (ritual slaughterer) and established himself as a merchant. His mother, Rachel Louzada, was a descendent of a family that had lived in New York since 1689. After military service in the American Revolution, Moses Myers entered a commercial partnership with Samuel Myers (no relation), the son of noted colonial silversmith Myer Myers. They established offices in Amsterdam and St. Eustatius, an island in the Caribbean Netherlands. The Myers's firm failed in 1784, but a partial repayment of debt enabled Moses to move to Norfolk and begin rebuilding his business. Myers "opened a small store selling naval supplies, corn, animal hides, tobacco, and lumber. From this humble beginning, Myers's business thrived, growing into a major import-export operation as Norfolk emerged as a significant port in the early republic era. According to historian Malcolm Stern, Myers 'had dealings in practically every seaport on both sides of the North Atlantic.'" In the 1810s, Myers's business was hurt by the British blockade during the War of 1812, and in 1819 was bankrupted by the collapse of the First National Bank. He was appointed collector of the port of Norfolk by President John Quincy Adams in 1827.[3]

Moses Myers's commercial and civic activities exemplify those of the prominent Jewish merchants of his time. Especially notable are the overlap of mercantile and family networks. Moses Myers brought his son John into his firm as a partner in 1809; after the War of 1812, John established a branch of Moses Myers & Sons in Baltimore. Two other Myers sons, Sam and Myer, also played roles in the family business—and both married daughters of Joseph Marx of Richmond, a friend and business associate of Moses Myers.[4]

Myers and his family were clearly identified as Jews, but their level of Jewish observance is not known. In the early nineteenth century, there were only a handful of Jewish families resident in Norfolk. The only documented communal institution was a Jewish cemetery established in 1819. Worship services may have been held in private homes and a chance discovery of Torah Scrolls in 1840 is suggestive of communal worship, but there is no evidence of a formal congregation during Moses Myers' lifetime.[5]

Whether the Myers family observed the rules of *kashrut* is questionable. Norfolk did not have a resident *schochet* (kosher slaughterer) at the time, and evidence from the Myers Family Papers indicate that the family consumed *treyfe* (forbidden, non-kosher) foods such as ham and turtle, though the meat may have been intended to feed their slaves and servants. A letter from John Myers to his brother Samuel, dated March 1, 1810, exhorts Samuel to eat "raw oysters and eggs." No Jewish ritual objects associated with the Myers family have been identified, and none are on display in the Myers House. The Myers family's concern for marrying Jewishly is in tension with their seeming disregard of traditional religious observance. Both aspects of their identities as American Jews are characteristic of the period: as Jonathan Sarna notes, traditional religious practice spanned a broad spectrum of observance. The Moses Myers House offers an exceptional view of the early American Jewish mercantile elite, thoroughly grounded in a trove of family documents.[6]

The Shapiro House

Strawbery Banke Museum

In 1898, Schepsel Milhandler, a recent immigrant from Ukraine, arrived in Portsmouth, New Hampshire. Milhandler promptly changed his name to Samuel Shapiro and went to work to bring over other members of his family, starting with his eldest brother, Simon. In a typical instance of chain migration, the Shapiros were able to pay the way for seventeen relatives to travel from Ukraine to Portsmouth. One of the newcomers was Samuel's younger brother, Abraham (Avrum) Shapiro, who married another new immigrant, his brother's sister-in-law, Sarah (Sheva) Tapper. Abraham and Sarah purchased a home in the Puddle Dock neighborhood, an old part of town largely populated with immigrants, including about 150 Jews and their families.[7]

A Jewish presence in Portsmouth. New Hampshire, was noted as early as 1780, when Abraham and Rachel Isaac were mentioned in Charles Warren Brewster's *Rambles About Portsmouth* (1869). By the late 1880s, a community was beginning to form: there were sixteen Jewish families living in Portsmouth and men gathered for worship in private homes. In 1905, a congregation was formally organized, which rented a room for meetings and religious services and hired a religious leader who also functioned as the local *schochet* (kosher butcher) and *mohel* (ritual circumciser). The new congregation purchased land for a cemetery (previously they buried their dead in a nearby community) and in 1911/1912, the congregation purchased a Methodist church for use as a synagogue. By 1919, Puddle Dock featured two kosher butcher shops, a Jewish bakery, and three Jewish-owned grocery stores, in addition to Temple Israel.[8]

Puddle Dock remained a crowded, low-income neighborhood. In 1958, a non-profit preservation organization, Strawbery Banke Museum, was incorporated to utilize federal funds for historic preservation instead of razing buildings for urban renewal. In the 1960s, more than forty "deteriorated" structures were saved, specifically those houses built before 1820. By the 1980s, Strawbery Banke had become a major museum, with education as well as preservation at the core of its mission. Today, Strawbery Banke "is unique among outdoor history museums in presenting an authentic neighborhood, with most of the [forty-two] historic buildings on their original foundations." It is also unique among such museums in showcasing the everyday life of a Jewish family.[9]

How did this come about? In the 1990s, State Senator Elaine Krasker, a member of the Shapiro family, was serving on the board of Strawbery Banke. The board chair suggested to her that one of Strawbery Banke's houses should be restored as the home of Jewish immigrants. Ms. Krasker initiated a family fundraising effort, and the house Strawbery Banke chose for restoration had been the home of Abraham and Sarah Shapiro from 1909 to 1928. An intensive oral history project collected thirty interviews from older members of the community; a grant from the National Endowment for the Humanities helped Strawbery Banke to develop a comprehensive interpretive program focused on the Shapiro family's domestic life. The Shapiro House is now the most-visited of the more than forty historic structures owned and managed by the Strawbery Banke Museum.[10]

The Shapiro House has been restored to 1919, when Abraham, Sarah, and their nine-year-old daughter Mollie were in residence, together with one or two boarders. Visitors enter through the back door, passing through a small backyard with a garden and coming directly into the kitchen. Here they encounter a costumed interpreter playing the role of Sarah (Sheva) Shapiro, busily cooking traditional eastern European dishes. In a heavy Yiddish accent, Mrs. Shapiro welcomes visitors, displays the dishes she is preparing on her coal-burning stove, and talks about maintaining a kosher lifestyle. Visitors are drawn in by the down-home odors and many relate to the traditional European foods: visitors of Italian descent see the mandlebrot as biscotti, while those with Polish ancestors know kreplach as pierogi.[11]

A highlight of the visit is the small bathroom just off the kitchen. Installed in 1911/1912, it was the first indoor bathroom in the Puddle Dock neighborhood and retains a fascination for contemporary visitors. Guests proceed into the dining room—with a table set for the Sabbath eve dinner, replete with Sabbath candles, kiddush cup, and challah—and an audio program that re-creates a conversation among the Shapiro family about preparations for the Sabbath. The front parlor features an eight-minute looping video that provides background on the extended Shapiro family and their lives in Puddle Dock.[12]

Figure 6.1 Visitors to the Shapiro House kitchen are greeted by Sarah (Sheva) Shapiro, portrayed by Barbara Ann Paster, who is making latkes and applesauce.

Photographed by Ralph Morang, 2008. Courtesy of Strawbery Banke Museum. SBanke 5652.

Upstairs on the second floor, guests can view the two bedrooms occupied by Mollie and her parents. Mollie's nightdress is draped on her bed along with Abraham's *tallit* and *t'filin* (prayer shawl and phylacteries). Interpretive panels explain the complex relationships of the twenty-seven Shapiro family members who lived in the neighborhood and the lives of the boarders who resided in the third-floor garret and who shared the Shapiros' dining room and bathroom. Here, in a dress-up space, children can try on boys' and girls' clothing from 1919. An exhibition on the archaeology of the site features evidence of toys and childlife. Before they leave the Shapiro House, guests are encouraged to visit the nearby Temple Israel, the center of Jewish communal life, in which members of the Shapiro family played leadership roles.[13]

The Shapiro House is a featured stop on Strawbery Banke's thematic immigration tour, and many elements reflect the transition from immigrant to American ways. As Sarah remarks to her guests, "My daughter Mollie learned about bananas at school." Shapiro House guests learn about chain migration, the role of extended family, and the maintenance of Old World traditions and Jewish rituals even as they are immersed in the daily life of a working family. By all accounts, the Shapiro House works effectively for a wide range of visitors. To Strawbery Banke's credit, the museum is now launching a review of its interpretive program, including that at the Shapiro House, to begin preparing for a new generation of public programs.[14]

Unpacking on the Prairie

Minnesota Historical Society, State Historical Society of Iowa, and Iowa Jewish Historical Society

In late 1953, Minneapolis resident Edith Linhoff Edelman was honored by the Junior Chamber of Commerce for her seasonal decorations. Unlike the other honorees, Ms. Edelman was chosen for her display of Hanukkah symbols. As she recalled, "[We] made a huge blue and white 'Dreidle' or spinning top. We decorated our windows with colorful transparent paper and they looked like stained-glass windows depicting the story of Chanukah."[15]

The Jewish festival of Hanukkah commemorates the 165 BCE victory of Judah Maccabee and his family over Syrian-Greek forces that had occupied the land of Israel and desecrated the Jerusalem Temple. For centuries, Jews commemorated the restoration of the Temple by lighting oil lamps or candles for eight nights, by eating traditional foods, and by giving children Hanukkah *gelt* (coins). However, Hanukkah was always treated as a minor festival, unmentioned in the Hebrew Bible, except in the United States, where as Elizabeth Pleck puts it, "Hanukkah candles burn considerably brighter . . . than among Jews living in other parts of the world."[16] As Dianne Ashton argues, Hanukkah was continually revised in response to communal concerns and social conditions. During the nineteenth century, as domestic celebrations of Christmas grew ever more elaborate, child-centered families of American Jews countered by making Hanukkah the Jewish alternative to Christmas. By the 1950s, when the Edelman family was honored, window displays expressed Jewish confidence in their acceptance as citizens and manifested Jewish claims to a place in the public square.[17]

A photograph of Ms. Edelman receiving her prize from the Junior Chamber of Commerce was featured in an exhibition organized and traveled by the Minnesota Historical Society, 1998–2002, titled *Unpacking on the Prairie: Jewish Women in the Upper Midwest*. The traveling show was based on a major exhibition and book developed by the Minnesota Historical Society in collaboration with the Jewish Historical Society of the Upper Midwest.[18] In its traveling version, the exhibition comprised thirteen two-sided panels with graphic rails and vitrines, two media carts, and an object cart with hands-on artifacts and a puzzle. The exhibition traveled to half a dozen sites in Minnesota, as well as venues in Michigan, South Dakota, North Dakota, Iowa, Alberta, and Washington, DC. Its primary theme was "the process of transporting, transmitting and transforming Jewish religion and culture" in the Upper Midwest, and one of its primary sections focused on "Women's efforts in maintaining and transforming domestic religious culture . . . and their roles as keepers of family memories."[19]

When *Unpacking on the Prairie* reached Des Moines in 1998, the State Historical Society of Iowa and the Iowa Jewish Historical Society presented two complementary exhibitions. The first was a traveling installation titled "Passages" by San Francisco–based artist Beth Grossman that explored the historical memory of immigration. The second was an original exhibition on "The Iowa Story," curated by David Gradwohl, a professor emeritus of anthropology at Iowa State University.

The Iowa exhibition gave prominent attention to Jewish foodways, home rituals, and traditions of *tzedakah* (philanthropy) in a section titled "Making a Jewish Home." Sabbath and festival meals were represented in photographs, table settings, children's books for the Jewish holidays, utensils, and ritual objects; among the highlights were a milk can for collecting kosher milk for Passover, used by Sarah Leah Lipoladsky Rosenberg from the 1920s to the 1940s, and a *hachmesser* or chopping knife with handle, used by Anna Hanin of Sioux City to prepare gefilte fish.[20] Iconic objects such as these, complemented by family photos and settings, and interpreted with text in question-and-answer format, clearly describe a distinctive religious culture transported and adapted to New World circumstances.

In a perceptive review that appeared in the *Des Moines Register*, art critic Lenore Metrick wrote that the exhibition embodied the Jewish tradition of discourse and commentary. She quotes Virginia Woolf, "Let us never cease from thinking—what is this 'civilization' in which we find ourselves? What are these ceremonies and why should we take part in them?" Metrick writes, "[These] questions from 1938 seem at the heart of the current exhibit," and goes on to say, "From the outset, the exhibit attempts to provoke the viewer to wonder, 'Who am I?' in relation to the lives portrayed here."[21] These are meaningful concerns, and they underline the value of collaborations between secular and Jewish historical organizations as well as the value of joining art and history in an integrated program.

American Foodways: The Jewish Contribution

University of Michigan Library

"Kitchen Judaism" has sometimes been given a pejorative connotation, but foodways represent where Jews are from, declare to whom or what they belong, and reveal the beliefs they hold close. Whether coming from Brazil to New York in the seventeenth century or from Israel to Los Angeles in this century, Jews have improvised with tradition to create new culinary repertoires. They have created cuisines both nostalgic and innovative, honoring old country foods while adapting new tastes and ingredients. Meanwhile, traditional Jewish foods (or approximations of them) have been widely adopted by Americans of varied backgrounds, reflecting an ongoing cultural exchange.[22]

In fall 2013, the University of Michigan Library hosted *American Foodways: The Jewish Contribution*, a major exhibition co-curated by Janice Bluestein Longone and Avery Robinson. The exhibition featured material from the Special Collections Library's Janice Bluestein Longone Culinary Archive, which comprises more than twenty-five thousand items and is one of the nation's largest collections of culinary Americana. The Library Lobby displayed Jewish charity cookbooks from all fifty states and Washington, DC, while the Hatcher Special Collections Library showcased a variety of related material, including cookbooks, advertisements, recipes, reports, and ephemera. Items were selected to represent a range of different tropes and experiences from Jewish culinary practice in America, such as markets, dining out, and food festivals, starting with Asser Levy, one of the first licensed butchers in early New Amsterdam, to a 2013 Yiddish Food Festival in Arkansas.[23]

The *American Foodways* project includes a number of culinary rarities. Among them is an original copy of the earliest American Jewish cookbook—the 1871 *Jewish Cookery Book, or Principles of Economy Adapted for Jewish Housekeepers* by a Philadelphia Jewish woman, Esther Levy, about whom little is known. Other highlights include *The Market Assistant* (1867) by Thomas F. DeVoe, which details all the meats, fish, wild game, and produce available in the early public markets of New York, Philadelphia, and Boston, as well as menus from famous delicatessens such as the 2nd Avenue Deli (New York), Rascal House (Miami), and Zingerman's (Ann Arbor).[24]

Even before Jewish authors and organizations were publishing cookbooks, a number of American cookbooks were incorporating Jewish recipes. *The Virginia Housewife or Methodical Cook* by Mary Randolph (1824), considered the first regional American cookbook, noted the merits of kosher meat: "Few persons are aware of the injury they sustain by eating the flesh of diseased animals. None but the Jewish butchers, who are paid exclusively for it, attend to this important circumstance." An 1845 edition of *Modern Cookery in All Its Branches* includes a recipe for "compote of oranges—a Hebrew dish," while *Mrs. Hale's New Cook Book* (1857) offers recipes for a "stewed fish, Hebrew fashion" and fried salmon, also in the "Hebrew fashion." Sarah Tyson Rorer (1849–1937), the founder of modern dietetics, founder-principal of the Philadelphia Cooking School, and the domestic editor of the *Ladies Home Journal*, included a full section of Jewish recipes in her 731-page tome, *Mrs. Rorer's New Cook Book: A Manual of Housekeeping*, published in 1902.

The core of the exhibition was composed of charity cookbooks, the cookbooks produced by various organizations to raise money for philanthropic purposes. Frequently, these publications describe the work of the sponsoring organization and the importance of philanthropic giving. Ads offer a glimpse of Jewish commercial life as well. The earliest of these Jewish charity cookbooks, as distinct from commercial cookbooks, was published in 1888—*The Fair Cookbook* from "the ladies" of Congregation Emanu-El in Denver. Charity cookbooks "were a critical means for women to collaborate, raise money, and record their cultural and familial food histories."[25] These home-grown cookbooks were made for real people by real people, and the recipes tend to have been thoroughly vetted by dozens of families, sometimes over several generations. These cookbooks tell us a lot about what particular communities were eating, to what degree they reflect traditional Jewish practice, and how it was adapted and mingled with other culinary traditions. As one observer notes, "The changing demographics and concerns of American Jewry become obvious in these personal epicurean diaries."[26]

Jewish charity cookbooks also reflect traditional values of philanthropy and communal obligation. They document the advent or expansion of synagogues, Jewish community centers, and other community organizations. And they exemplify the diversity of Jewish culinary practice over space and time. In them, we can discover successive waves of Jewish immigration, each with its distinctive culinary favorites. One recent example benefits the Resettlement Service of Southfield, Michigan, which assists immigrants from the Former Soviet Union: its title is *With a Russian Flavor*. Other cookbooks bring in regional variations. From Honolulu comes the *When You Live in Hawaii You Get Very Creative During Passover Cookbook*; from Asheville, North Carolina, comes *Lox and Grits:*

THE
WHEN YOU LIVE IN
HAWAII
YOU GET VERY CREATIVE DURING
PASSOVER COOKBOOK
Congregation Sof Ma'arav

Figure 6.2 Cover of a cookbook published by Congregation Sof Ma'arav in Honolulu, Hawaii, 1989. Note the combination of chopsticks with traditional chicken soup and matzah balls.

Courtesy of the Jewish Museum of Maryland. JMM CP 77.2011.1.

Jewish Kitchens in Appalachia; and from Tulsa, Oklahoma, we get *Home on the Range: A Roundup of Recipes and Jewish Traditions from Oklahoma Kitchens.*[27] Jews living in different regions have produced some remarkable variants—matzah ball gumbo in the south, potato latkes with maple syrup in New England, and salmon gefilte fish in the northwest, to name just a few.[28]

The negotiation of Jewish women with American food is reflected in ads, recipes, and other publications from processed food makers. Crisco, for example, was introduced to the marketplace by Proctor & Gamble in 1912. Yiddish and English magazine ads declared that "the Hebrew race . . . had been waiting for four thousand years" for this vegetarian shortening. Heinz Baked Beans proudly displayed its *hechsher* (seal of rabbinic approval) from the Union of Orthodox Jewish Congregations in America. And for years, Maxwell House Coffee published *haggadot* for use at the annual Passover seder. Needless to say, Jewish food manufacturers such as Manischewitz and Horowitz Margareten competed in the market for Passover and kosher foods.[29]

The *American Foodways* project not only drew visitors from across the United States but also prompted an intensive collecting effort: souvenirs and ephemera associated with Jewish food festivals and other contemporary foodways were gathered in, greatly expanding the Longone Archives' collections. The two hundred items in the *American Foodways* exhibition offered viewers of many backgrounds an American narrative grounded in the universal need for food and the nearly universal interest in foodways. The project also succeeded in conveying a key interpretive theme: "what we eat and how we eat it are central to identity, marking points of distinction, assimilation, and cultural transfer."[30]

The Rosenbaum House

Frank Lloyd Wright Rosenbaum House Foundation
and the City of Florence

On August 23, 1940, Mildred and Stanley Rosenbaum moved into their new home in Florence, Alabama, a house designed by noted architect Frank Lloyd Wright. Stanley Rosenbaum grew up in Florence, where his father, Louis, owned a small chain of movie theaters. Stanley Rosenbaum attended Harvard and the University of Denver. At the time of his marriage, Stanley worked in the family's movie theater business. When he retired from that business in 1960, he joined the faculty of Florence State University (now the University of North Alabama), where he taught for many years. His wife, Mildred (Mimi) Bookholtz, was a New York City native who had studied music and art at Hunter College and Columbia Teachers College. She had also worked as a model, appearing in several national magazines.[31]

When the young couple decided to settle in Florence, Louis Rosenbaum gave them $7,500 and a piece of land as a wedding present. The Rosenbaums sought advice from a friend, Aaron Green, then an architecture student at Cooper Union, who recommended Wright for the commission. In 1936/1937, Wright had designed a home for Katherine and Herbert Jacobs near Madison, Wisconsin. This was Wright's first "Usonian" house, a modest structure designed to introduce a new, modern standard in American homebuilding.[32]

Wright was an advocate of "organic architecture" that blended into its landscape and created a harmonious interior. To relate the house to its natural surround, Wright did away with a front porch, downspouts, and prominent chimneys. "The materials of the Usonian house were to be nature's own: wood, stone, or baked clay in the form of bricks, and glass curtain walls, clerestories, and casement windows sheltered under overhanging soffits." The design of the Rosenbaum House also featured an advanced heating system that piped hot water under concrete slab floors and a carport, a Wright invention. The structure was designed to grow with its resident family.[33]

The Rosenbaums contracted Wright in April 1939. Construction started in January 1940, but completion was delayed due to inexperienced labor, scarce materials, and bad weather. Budgeted to cost $7,500, the house cost was around $14,000. It was also troubled by problems—the roof leaked and the chimneys were defective. Still, the Rosenbaums contracted Wright a second time in 1946 to design an addition that would accommodate their growing family. When the addition was finished in 1948, it had a larger kitchen, a dormitory for the couple's boys, a guest bedroom, and a second carport. The Rosenbaum House was the first Usonian home to be expanded, and it remains the only Wright structure in Alabama.[34]

Choosing a contemporary architect and novel design were consonant with the Rosenbaums' cosmopolitan attitudes. The Rosenbaums were civic-minded and progressive, in keeping with family tradition. Louis Rosenbaum served as president of the local synagogue seven times between 1924 and 1953, and in 1937 his generosity saved the Florence United Methodist Church from losing its building through foreclosure. Louis and Stanley donated $40,000 to help fund the city's first public library. Father and son were founders of a local chapter of the Alabama Council on Human Relations, which advocated for racial equality. When the local black library fell into disrepair, Stanley moved to integrate the main library; he also persuaded the Ford Motor Company, which had opened a factory in nearby Sheffield, to integrate its cafeteria. The Ku Klux Klan burned a cross in the Rosenbaums' yard.[35]

Mildred and Stanley Rosenbaum continued to live in their home, raising four sons, one of whom, Jonathan Rosenbaum, became a noted film critic. Stanley died in 1983. After his death, Mildred devoted herself to weaving and to preserving the Rosenbaum House, pioneering strategies for the protection of historic residential properties. In 1991, she was the first recipient of the Wright Spirit Award from the Frank Lloyd Wright Building Conservancy. Mildred stayed on in the house until 1999, when she negotiated a sale to the city of Florence that provided for its complete restoration and preservation. The original Wright furniture was included in the sale, and the contents of the house were documented and removed during the restoration. The city spent $600,000 to restore the house, opening it as a public museum.[36] Today, the Rosenbaum House continues to interpret the architectural ideas of Frank Lloyd Wright and the history of the Rosenbaum family. This landmark structure is not only one of the finest examples of Wright's groundbreaking architecture, but also a remarkably preserved Jewish home.

Notes

1. Chrysler Museum website, "The Moses Myers House," accessed February 26, 2016, http://www.chrysler.org/about-the-museum/historic-houses/the-moses-myers-house/; Crawford Alexander Mann III, telephone interview with the author, February 25, 2016.

2. Chrysler Museum website, "The Myers Family," accessed February 26, 2016, http://www .chrysler.org/about-the-museum/historic-houses/the-moses-myers-house/the-myers-family/; Crawford Alexander Mann III, telephone interview with the author, February 25, 2016.

3. Chrysler Museum website, "The Myers Family," accessed February 26, 2016, http://www .chrysler.org/about-the-museum/historic-houses/the-moses-myers-house/the-myers-family/; Encyclopedia of Southern Jewish Communities website, "Norfolk, Virginia," accessed February 28, 2016, http://www.isjl.org/virginia-norfolk-encyclopedia.html; Malcolm H. Stern, "Moses Myers and the Early Jewish Community of Norfolk," Journal of the Southern Jewish Historical Society 1, no. 1 (November 1959): 5–13.

4. Chrysler Museum website, "The Myers Family," accessed February 26, 2016, http://www .chrysler.org/about-the-museum/historic-houses/the-moses-myers-house/the-myers-family/;

Encyclopedia of Southern Jewish Communities website, "Richmond, Virginia," accessed February 28, 2016, http://www.isjl.org/virginia-richmond-encyclopedia.html.

5. Chrysler Museum website, "The Myers Family," accessed February 26, 2016, http://www.chrysler.org/about-the-museum/historic-houses/the-moses-myers-house/the-myers-family/; Crawford Alexander Mann III, telephone interview with the author, February 25, 2016; *Encyclopedia of Southern Jewish Communities* website, "Richmond, Virginia," accessed February 28, 2016, http://www.isjl.org/virginia-richmond-encyclopedia.html; *Encyclopedia of Southern Jewish Communities* website, "Norfolk, Virginia," accessed February 28, 2016, http://www.isjl.org/virginia-norfolk-encyclopedia.html; Stern, "Moses Myers," 8–9.

6. Chrysler Museum website, "The Myers Family," accessed February 26, 2016, http://www.chrysler.org/about-the-museum/historic-houses/the-moses-myers-house/the-myers-family/; Crawford Alexander Mann III, telephone interview with the author, February 25, 2016; *Encyclopedia of Southern Jewish Communities* website, "Richmond, Virginia," accessed February 28, 2016, http://www.isjl.org/virginia-richmond-encyclopedia.html; *Encyclopedia of Southern Jewish Communities* website, "Norfolk, Virginia," accessed February 28, 2016, http://www.isjl.org/virginia-norfolk-encyclopedia.html; Jonathan Sarna, *American Judaism* (New Haven: Yale University Press, 2004), 22–27, 45–47; Myers Family Papers, transcription of letter, John Myers to Samuel Myers, March 1, 1810, and Myers Household Account Ledger, October 1, 1824.

7. Elaine Krasker, telephone interview with the author, January 29, 2016; Strawbery Banke Website, "Shapiro House," accessed January 27, 2016, http://www.strawberybanke.org/index.php?option=com_content&view=article&id=115&Itemid=168.

8. Temple Israel Website, "History," accessed January 28, 2016, http://www.templeisraelnh.org/welcome/about-us/history/.

9. Strawbery Banke Website, "Timeline," accessed January 27, 2016, http://www.seacoastnh.com/timeline/strawberybanke.html; "Home," accessed May 8, 2015, http://www.strawberybanke.org/; Elizabeth Farish, telephone interview with the author, August 11, 2015.

10. Elaine Kasker, telephone interview with the author, January 29, 2016; Maddie Beihl, telephone interview with the author, January 30, 2016.

11. Rabbi David Senter and Elissa Kaplan Senter, telephone interview with the author, January 28, 2016; Maddie Beihl, discussion with the author, January 30, 2016; Joan Nathan, "Rosh Hashana, Circa 1919," *New York Times*, September 16, 2009, accessed January 28, 2016, http://www.nytimes.com/2009/09/16/dining/16rosh.html?pagewanted=all&_r=1.

12. Beihl, telephone interview with the author, January 30, 2016.

13. Senter, interview with the author, January 28, 2016; Beihl, interview with the author, January 30, 2016.

14. Ibid.

15. "Unpacking on the Prairie," brochure, 1998, Minnesota Historical Society.

16. Elizabeth H. Pleck, "Hanukkah in America: A History by Dianne Ashton" (book review), *American Jewish History* 98, no. 4 (October 2014): 351.

17. Dianne Ashton, *Hanukkah in America: A History* (New York: New York University Press, 2013), 1–14 and *passim*.

18. Linda Mack Schloff, *"And Prairie Dogs Weren't Kosher": Jewish Women in the Upper Midwest* (St. Paul, MN: Minnesota Historical Society, 1996).

19. "Traveling Exhibition," flier, Minnesota Historical Society, n.d [c. 1998].

20. "Unpacking on the Prairie: The Iowa Story," exhibition checklist compiled by David Gradwohl, April 3, 1998.

21. Lenore Metrick, "Unpacking on the Prairie," *Des Moines Register*, May 17, 1990.

22. See, for example, Joan Nathan, *Jewish Cooking in America* (New York: Knopf, 1994); Hasia Diner, *Hungering for America: Italian, Irish, and Jewish Foodways in the Age of Migration* (Cambridge, MA: Harvard University Press, 2003); and Sue Fishkoff, *Kosher Nation: Why More and More of America's Food Ansers to a Higher Authority* (New York: Schocken, 2010). Avery Robinson, telephone interview with the author, March 2, 2016.

23. University of Michigan Library website, "American Foodways: The Jewish Contribution," accessed March 8, 2016, http://www.lib.umich.edu/online-exhibits/exhibits/show/jewishfoodways.

24. Sharon Pomerantz, "The Joy of Jewish Cookbooks," *The Forward* website, December 9, 2013, accessed March 7, 2016, http://forward.com/culture/188402/the-joy-of-jewish-cookbooks/#ixzz429kmUOPp.

25. Steve Friess, "Not a Chef, Not a Restaurateur, but an Expert on Jewish Culinary Literature," *Tablet* website, August 21, 2013, accessed March 9, 2016, http://www.tabletmag.com/jewish-life-and-religion/141323/longone-culinary-expert.

26. Ahava Ehrenpreiss, "Recipes for Jewish American Life," December 25, 2013, accessed March 9, 2016, *Washtenaw Jewish News* website; Mary Bilyeu, "American Foodways Exhibit at Hatcher Library," September 2013, accessed March 9, 2016, http://washtenawjewishnews.com/PDFs/WJN-Sept13-web.pdf.

27. University of Michigan Library website, "American Foodways: The Jewish Contribution," http://www.lib.umich.edu/online-exhibits/exhibits/show/jewishfoodways/item/4637?exhibit=117&page=874.

28. Sharon Pomerantz, "The Joy of Jewish Cookbooks"; Avi Decter and Juliana Ochs Dweck, "Introduction," in Avi Y. Decter and Juliana Ochs Dweck, eds. *Chosen Food: Cuisine, Culture and American Jewish Identity* (Baltimore: Jewish Museum of Maryland, 2011), 1–3.

29. Hasia R. Diner, "'Our Parents Were Hungry and We Are Sated': The Immigrant World of American Jewish Food," in Avi Y. Decter and Juliana Ochs Dweck, eds., *Chosen Food*, 14.

30. Decter and Ochs, "Introduction," in *Chosen Food*, 1.

31. Frank Lloyd Wright Rosenbaum House website, "Learn about the Rosenbaum Family," accessed April 18, 2016, http://wrightinalabama.com/?p=415. See also, Barbara Kimberlin Broach, *Frank Lloyd Wright's Rosenbaum House: The Birth and Rebirth of an American Treasure* (San Francisco: Pomegranate, 2006).

32. Rosenbaum House website, "Learn about the Rosenbaum Family."

33. Usonia 1 Jacobs House website, "Historical Background," accessed April 19, 2016, http://www.usonia1.com/01_hist.html; Encyclopedia of Alabama website, "Rosenbaum House Museum," accessed April 18, 2016, http://www.encyclopediaofalabama.org/article/h-2397.

34. Encyclopedia of Alabama website, "Rosenbaum House Museum," accessed April 18, 2016, http://www.encyclopediaofalabama.org/article/h-2397.

35. Institute for Southern Jewish Life website, *Encyclopedia of Southern Jewish Communities*, "Florence/Sheffield, Alabama," accessed April 19, 2016, ISJL - Alabama Florence Encyclopedia - Institute of Southern Jewish life.

36. Wikipedia website, "Jonathan Rosenbaum," accessed April 17, 2016, https://en.wikipedia.org/wiki/Jonathan_Rosenbaum; *Times Daily* website, "Mildred Rosenbaum," accessed April 18, 2016, http://www.timesdaily.com/archives/article_7b346425-44bc-52fb-9365-2ddb48c64c63.html.

CHAPTER 7

DIVERSITY AND RESPONSIBILITY

Creating Jewish Community

IN 1843, a group of young men established a new fraternal and service organization in New York. B'nai B'rith was a departure from previous Jewish organizations, which were based on religion: members were required only to affirm their allegiance to Judaism or to the Jewish people. As Stephen Whitfield notes, "This definition of a Jew was not ecclesiastical, not ancestral, not legal. It was subjective—if you call yourself a Jew, you're a Jew."[1] The new organization reflects the special opportunities and challenges of affirming Jewish identity and community in an open society. Jews had traditionally accepted that the realization of Jewish identity took place within the religious community. But in America, being Jewish became a choice, indeed a choice in which identity could be severed from worship and belief, expressed instead as "peoplehood."

Meanwhile, traditional religious communities, too, were transformed in America: unlike Europe, throughout the colonial and early national period, local congregations were dominated by lay leaders rather than by ordained rabbis, forging their own paths to Jewish observance and worship. The arrival of trained clergy eventually produced a diversified structure unknown in Europe. Jewish communal and philanthropic organizations also evolved within new templates, producing an array of local and national institutions that sought to renew Jewish life, to serve Jews in need, and to define Jewish community in America.

Jewish communal organizations were responding to what Hasia Diner describes as "an unself-conscious recognition of need: need for economic security, need for support in time of crisis, need for friendship, and need for community. American Jews engaged in these activities because they wanted to and because they had to."[2] Over the century of migration from 1820 to 1920, America's Jewish population grew, developed, and broadened, and the American Jewish community evolved into a geographically pervasive, religiously diverse, and socially complex entity.[3] Evidence of the struggle to forge a Jewish identity and to build community is found in communities large and small throughout North America—in synagogues, cemeteries, hospitals, and schools; in Jewish community centers and social service agencies, schools, and summer camps; in informal fellowships and fraternal orders; in virtual communities and townscapes. This chapter describes the context in which some of the many notable expressions of Jewish community appeared and tells the story of how they evolved over more than three centuries of Jewish life.

Early Communal Institutions

The first effort to establish a Jewish community in North America began in New Netherland (later New York) with the arrival of twenty-three Dutch Jews fleeing from Recife, Brazil, following its capture by the Portuguese. In Recife, Jews had made up nearly half the colonial population and supported two synagogues. But the governor of New Netherland, Peter Stuyvesant, objected to their taking up residence since they were not adherents of the Dutch Reformed Church. After lengthy debate, the Dutch East India Company ruled that the Jews were allowed to "live and remain there, provided the poor among them shall not become a burden to the company or the community, but be supported by their own nation."[4] Despite restrictions, conversions, and returns to the Netherlands, the small community persisted. By 1655, this nascent community had already acquired a *Sefer Torah* (scroll containing the first five books of the Hebrew Bible) and had gathered for private worship. That year, the Jews requested permission to "purchase a burial ground." And in 1664, when the English captured New Netherland and re-named it New York, Jews along with other Dutch residents, were granted "liberty of conscience in divine worship and church discipline."[5]

By the 1690s, New York Jews had leased a house for religious worship, and by the 1700s this was known as the "Jew synagogue." The house next door was rented to "the Jew Rabby [teacher]." Wealthy Jewish merchants bought a plot of land in 1728 large enough to accommodate a *mikveh* [ritual bath] and constructed the first purpose-built synagogue in North America (1730). A year later, the congregation erected a two-story structure to serve as a school and administrative offices, and in 1758 the congregation bought a third building to house its *shamash* [caretaker].[6]

The pattern of community development pioneered in New York persisted through the colonial period and well into the nineteenth century. Typically the first communal institution with an enduring physical presence was the Jewish burial ground, since death could strike at any time and Jewish tradition required interment within a day or two of death. Gathering for worship, in contrast, could be done informally in any venue, often a private home or a rented building. In Leavenworth, Kansas, for example, the Mount Zion Cemetery Association was founded in 1857 (just three years after Kansas was organized as a Territory), while Congregation B'nai Jeshurun, the first synagogue in Kansas, was not organized until two years later. The same pattern is seen in Las Vegas, New Mexico, and other emergent Jewish communities. Purpose-built synagogue structures (some with attached ritual baths) could wait, though they, like cemeteries, continue to mark Jewish communal presence across the continent.[7]

In 1775, there were five established congregations, each with its own synagogue: New York; Newport, Rhode Island; Philadelphia; Savannah, Georgia; and Charleston, South Carolina. As Hasia Diner has shown, in each the process followed a sequence: "initial settlement, consecration of a cemetery, formation of a congregation, and the building of a synagogue. In each Jews both accepted their status within a larger society and sought to expand the rights they enjoyed. They forged bonds with each other and tried to establish a comfortable relationship with the Christian majority."[8] To lead a full Jewish life meant that Jews who chose to identify with a community generally chose to live near or among other Jews as constituents of a synagogue-community.

By the time of the Civil War, Jewish communities—fueled by immigration from central Europe and explosive growth in America's western territories—had been established in cities and towns, not only along the eastern seaboard, but also in the Midwest, the South, and the far West. A key feature of these new congregations was the leadership of lay people. The absence of an organized clergy to rule on religious matters had led to an atmosphere of religious diversity (or laxity). The first ordained rabbis arrived in America only in the 1840s—and what they discovered on their arrival was discouraging. As Rabbi Abraham Rice (1800–1862), who arrived in America in 1840 and was the first ordained rabbi to serve an American congregation, observed: "I dwell in complete isolation without a teacher or a companion in this land whose atmosphere is not conducive to wisdom . . . the character of religious life in this land is on the lowest level; most of the people are eating non-Kosher food, are violating the Shabbos [Sabbath] in public . . . and there are thousands who have been assimilated among the non-Jewish population, and have married non-Jewish women. Under these circumstances, my mind is perplexed and I wonder whether a Jew may live in a land such as this."[9]

Renewal and Reform

Even before Rabbi Rice arrived in America—followed by a growing number of other trained rabbis—efforts were being made to renew traditional Judaism. As early as the 1820s, a younger generation of Jews in New York and Charleston, the two largest Jewish communities, took steps to address what they saw as "apathy and neglect" toward Judaism. In New York, younger members of Congregation Shearith Israel broke away to establish an independent society "to promote the study of our Holy Law and . . . to extend a knowledge of its divine precepts, ceremonies, and worship among brethren generally, and the enquiring youth in particular." The dissidents justified their secession on the grounds that each individual should worship "according to the dictate of his conscience" and because their original congregation had worshipped using the Sephardi rites, rather than the Ashkenazi tradition of the majority of congregants. In Charleston, the dissidents called for a return to pristine Judaism, shorn of rabbinic embellishments, and a much-shortened prayer service conducted largely in English.[10]

Figure 7.1 The 1794 synagogue building of Congregation Beth Elohim in Charleston, South Carolina, c. 1812, drawn by John Rubens Smith. The building's exterior resembled a church in Georgian style, suggesting an effort to blend in.

Courtesy of the Prints and Photographs Division, Library of Congress (John Rubens Smith Collection).

While the New Yorkers proposed to revitalize Judaism within the framework of Jewish law, suggests Jonathan Sarna, the Charleston reformers believed that Judaism itself needed to be reformed. "Both secessions," writes Sarna, "challenged the authority of the synagogue community, insisting that America recognize their right to withdraw and worship as they saw fit." Unlike Europe, where there was typically one synagogue in each community, by the Civil War every major Jewish community in America had at least two synagogues. No one synagogue represented the community as a whole. Instead, synagogues reflected the free choice and diversity of America, and this shifted the balance between congregation and adherents: synagogues became "much more concerned to attract members than to discipline them."[11] By the mid-nineteenth century, American congregations represented a spectrum of policy and practice, ranging from traditional Orthodoxy to radical Reform.[12]

Striving for Unity

Despite the diversity of Jewish religious culture, constant efforts to reform or renew Judaism, and the geographic dispersion of American Jews, several efforts were mounted in the nineteenth century to unify American Jewry. A key leader in aiming for unity at mid-century was Isaac Leeser (1806–1868), the *hazzan* [prayer leader] of Congregation Mikveh Israel in Philadelphia. Largely self-educated, Leeser published books and articles, as well as a widely disseminated monthly newspaper, *The Occident and American Jewish Advocate*, which reported on Jewish communal affairs in cities and towns across the country. He also completed the first Jewish translation of the Hebrew Bible into English (1853), which became the standard text for nineteenth-century American Jewry.[13]

A keen and well-informed observer, Leeser was a staunch advocate for Jewish tradition. But he was also committed to "Jewish regeneration" and advocated adaptation to American conditions, including delivery of synagogue sermons in English (1830). Among his many efforts to promote traditional observance and a unified American Jewry, Leeser tried to launch both a Jewish publication society and a Jewish seminary (Maimonides College) for the training of an American rabbinate, but both initiatives failed.[14]

In 1855, Leeser and Isaac Mayer Wise (1815–1900), leading light of the Reform movement, convened a "national conference" of clergy and lay representatives to discuss a common liturgy, Jewish education, and some kind of overarching ecclesiastic assembly. But both Orthodox and radical Reform leaders boycotted the conference. American Jews fell into two camps, Orthodox and Reform. A few years later, however, a number of congregations organized a Board of Delegates to "keep a watchful eye on all occurrences at home and abroad." But the board represented fewer than one-fifth of American synagogues and, according to Dr. Sarna, "made no pretense at promoting religious unity."[15]

Yet a third effort to promote Jewish unity was launched in 1873—by lay leaders rather than by clergy. The Union of American Hebrew Congregations, based in Cincinnati, embraced a full spectrum of congregations aiming to preserve Jewish identity and to train English-speaking rabbis and teachers. To these ends, the Union established Hebrew Union College in 1875, the first successful Jewish seminary in America. Both the Union of American Hebrew Congregations and Hebrew Union College seemed to presage the triumph of modern Reform Judaism in America, but as immigrants arrived in growing numbers from eastern Europe, Orthodox congregations continued to grow. A decisive break came in 1883, signaled by controversy over the notorious "treyfa banquet," in which non-kosher food was served to a gathering of Jewish leaders, many of whom observed kashrut (traditional dietary restrictions).[16]

As the nineteenth century drew to a close, Jewish leaders seeking a middle ground began to organize what came to be called Conservative Judaism. By 1920, three separate and distinct movements had emerged—Reform to the left, Orthodoxy to the right, and Conservative Judaism in the center. Traditionalists and reformers alike had launched American Jewry on the path toward a quasi-denominational model unknown in Europe and one that has continued into the present.[17]

Communal Welfare

Despite ideological differences, European traditions of mutual responsibility, philanthropy, and assistance to those in need persisted among American Jews. Initially, synagogues provided relief for the needy, but as waves of new immigrants arrived in the nineteenth and early twentieth centuries, congregational support no longer sufficed.

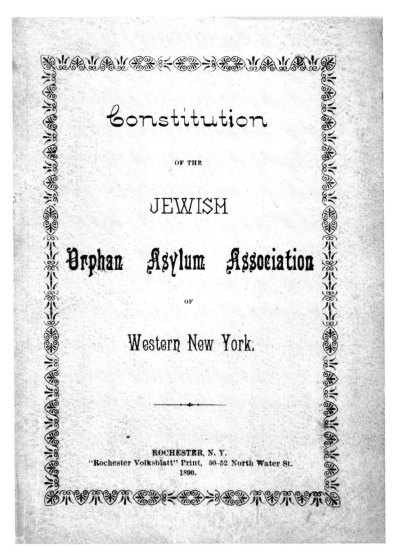

Figure 7.2 *Constitution of the Jewish Orphan Asylum Association of Western New York*, printed by Rochester Volksblatt in Rochester, New York, 1890. For several generations, orphanages were key institutions of social welfare in Jewish communal life.

Courtesy of the Library of the Jewish Theological Seminary (Abraham and Deborah Karp Collection). JTS B(NS)A123, JTS catalog number 46.

Instead, "participation in philanthropic projects and membership in organizations devoted to the relief of distress involved almost all Jews," writes Hasia Diner. "While male and female societies functioned separately, and in some cities, different ethnic groups formed their own charities and operated apart from their brethren, philanthropy served, by and large, as a communal umbrella."[18]

Early in the nineteenth century, Jews had begun to organize benevolent societies to serve local needs. Many of these originated as burial societies, subscribing to the traditional view that burial of the dead was an act of benevolence, and a communal and not just a private matter. Some of these societies added other acts of loving-kindness to their mission, including visitations to the sick and infirm, relief for the poor, and assistance to widows and orphans. The societies also used dues to provide interest-free loans. The Chevras Bikur Cholim Uk'vuras Meisim (Society for Visiting the Sick and

Burying the Dead), for example, was founded in 1848 in Fort Wayne, Indiana; another, founded in 1867 in Helena, Montana, "devoted thousands of dollars in relieving the distressed and afflicted." In addition to their communal obligations, Jewish benevolent organizations also took on social functions. The Hebrew Benevolent Society in Santa Cruz, California (founded in 1875), which included most Jewish men in town, also brought together their families: "business was transacted, then the meeting adjourned, [followed by] a hop, playing on the piano, a dinner, toasts, speeches, compliments, and good night to all."[19]

Jewish women organized themselves in female benevolent associations. In fact, the Female Hebrew Benevolent Society, founded in 1819 in Philadelphia, was the first non-synagogue Jewish charity in America.[20] Like their male counterparts, they participated in preparations for burial—washing and dressing the body. Also like the men's societies, women's organizations tended to the sick and needy. In New Haven, Connecticut, Ahavas Achos (Love of Sisters) sat with the dying and provided relief for female poverty and distress. "And, as with the male societies," writes Diner, "women at their meetings also enjoyed themselves and sponsored picnics, 'dime parties,' and theatricals for pleasure and to fill up the association's treasury."[21] Both men's and women's benevolent societies, then, fused sociability and ritual.[22]

"Immigrant Jews needed each other in a foreign land," writes Howard Rock, "and common ties of ethnicity, language, and culture remained strong."[23] But new kinds of institutions were needed to satisfy the desire for bonding. One of the earliest of these efforts to create community was the B'nai B'rith (1843), the fraternal and benevolent organization started by German immigrant Jews in New York concerned with "the deplorable condition of Jews." Members sought to support the sick, poor, and needy, and to help immigrants integrate into American society. Their first concrete action was to provide insurance to members that would help pay for their funeral expenses and offer a modest stipend to members' bereaved families.

Within a few years, the organization embraced "the elevation of the masses in a moral and intellectual direction," developing discussion groups, cultural programs, and, in New York, Covenant Hall (1851), the first Jewish community center, and the Maimonides Library Association (1852).[24] Mid-century also saw the establishment of Jewish literary societies, which discussed cultural matters, sponsored lectures on a variety of topics, and encouraged fraternal feeling. As Jews grew in number and moved into new locales, B'nai B'rith lodges and young men's literary societies proliferated across the country, constituting what one observer has termed "secular synagogues."[25]

In time, many of the charitable organizations created by Jews began to be modeled on Protestant American institutions. In traditional Jewish practice, the principles of *tzedakah* (literally "justice") obligated the giver and were predicated on close ties between donor and recipient. In contrast, over the course of the nineteenth century, Christian and nonsectarian charities worked to rationalize philanthropy: charity was deemed a privilege and not a right, with the organizations determining who among the needy were deserving of support. By 1900, Jewish organizations, too, began to emphasize the idea of "the deserving poor" as well as the values of thrift and sobriety.[26]

Also, Jews, like other Americans, began to promote the movement toward unified community-wide charity, to avoid competition for funds and to eliminate redundant services. In many cities, including Kansas City, Portland, Denver, Indianapolis, St. Louis, Omaha, and Atlanta, established German Jewish communities founded settlement houses, immigrant aid organizations, orphanages, and other organizations to assist the large numbers of eastern European newcomers who were flooding their communities. However, at the first opportunity, the newcomers began to establish their own community institutions. In Cleveland, for instance, the Germans organized the Russian Refugee Society and the Hebrew Temporary Home, but in 1897 the new arrivals established their own Hebrew Shelter Home. By 1903, leaders of both the "Germans" and the "Russians" came together to organize a federation of Jewish agencies to conduct a combined annual fundraising campaign.[27]

By the beginning of the First World War, most of the largest Jewish communities had begun to organize federations of charitable and communal organizations, which have been prominent features in dozens of Jewish communities for the past century.[28] Today, Jewish federations can be found in more than 150 communities, from Portland, Oregon, to Palm Beach, Florida.

Communities Informal and Intentional

Ethnic Neighborhoods

As the nineteenth century came to a close, religious and welfare organizations dotted the Jewish landscape in communities throughout the continent. But there were also an array of other expressions of community, each of which helped to mark its locale as a Jewish place. The most important of these was the Jewish neighborhood. Because Jewish life traditionally involved gathering for prayer, study, and mutual assistance and because the feeling of community was intensified by the proximity of relatives, friends, fellow congregants, and countrymen, Jews tended—like other immigrant groups—to concentrate in particular neighborhoods within their place of residence.

The great paradigm for these ethnic neighborhoods was New York's Lower East Side, which in its heyday (the 1910s and 1920s) was the epicenter of immigrant Jewish life in New York and also its most densely populated neighborhood. Its streetscape lined with stores, pushcarts, and markets selling "Jewish foods," its kosher restaurants, its multitude of store-front synagogues and Jewish organizations, its bustle of Yiddish-speaking people, and its worklife (dominated by the clothing industry) gave the Lower East Side a palpable sense of cohesion and community.[29] These urban neighborhoods of first-generation settlement proliferated in the Northeast and the Midwest in the first decades of the twentieth century, especially in large cities like Chicago, Boston, Detroit, Newark, Pittsburgh, and Cincinnati. As Gerald Sorin notes, "The larger the city immigrant Jews settled in, the more likely their community would resemble the Lower East Side of New York: Yiddish-speaking Jews living in large concentrations and working among people very much like themselves." But Sorin adds, "Immigrants in the smaller cities and towns of the interior, on the other hand, were far less dependent on the garment industry and the ethnic economy, generally, and more likely to be self-employed.

They were also more dependent on the English language and more likely to have cultural interchange with Gentiles."[30]

Even before the height of mass migration from eastern Europe, there were distinctly Jewish neighborhoods. In the colonial and early national periods, Jews clustered around their synagogue; at the height of Jewish migration from central Europe (1840–1870), German-speaking Jews also tended to reside in areas of first-generation settlement. But generalizations need to be made with qualifications. In Baltimore, for example, it was long assumed that Jews in the 1840s were concentrated within a few blocks of the Lloyd Street Synagogue in East Baltimore, the first purpose-built synagogue in Maryland. However, research by Eric Goldstein has shown that the Lloyd Street location was chosen because it was roughly equidistant from several distinct clusters of Jewish settlement and therefore equally convenient—or inconvenient—for its scattered congregants. The real burgeoning of East Baltimore as a quintessential Jewish neighborhood did not happen until the early twentieth century.[31]

Still, in the century from 1840 to 1940, one can identify densely Jewish areas in cities and towns across the country. Strawbery Banke, a neighborhood in Portsmouth, New Hampshire, famous today for its innovative museum complex, was known locally as a Jewish neighborhood in the first decades of the twentieth century. So was Boyle Heights in Los Angeles between the world wars, likewise the West Colfax section in Denver, Decatur Street in Atlanta, and the Marion Street Corridor in Columbia, South Carolina. In time, as Jews acculturated and adapted, they moved from areas of first settlement to better housing in more desirable neighborhoods. The path of Jewish mobility can often be traced in surviving synagogue buildings, many re-purposed as churches, as congregations followed their members to new neighborhoods.[32]

Landsmanshaftn

Another expression of community that is especially characteristic of the eastern European immigrants who arrived from 1880 to 1924 are the *landsmanshaftn* [hometown societies] that were organized by groups of newcomers from the same town or region in Europe. In smaller communities, most Jews participated in the same community organizations, regardless of their place of origin. But in larger towns and cities, associations could differentiate by ethnicity and region. Among the earliest of these landsmanshaftn, was the Netherlander Israelitisch Sick Fund Society (1859), followed by hundreds of other associations that helped to sustain "the scent of the same earth," as one immigrant put it. The societies assisted their members by providing insurance, medical attention, death benefits, loans, and a network that helped to fuel social mobility. As Daniel Soyer argues, organizations like Anshei Viskover (Men of Viskov) or the Satanover Benevolent Society reflect nostalgia for the old life, but also vehicles for adapting to the new.[33]

Agricultural Colonies

Landsmanshaftn and other community organizations were essentially grassroots projects. But there was another category of intentional communities that is worthy of special attention. The mass migration of Jews from eastern Europe reached epic proportions starting in the 1880s. Some well-placed German Jewish leaders, observing the dense concentrations of relatively poor newcomers, were concerned about their prospects in overcrowded urban enclaves; they were also troubled by the shadow the eastern European immigrants cast on their now-established predecessors. Accordingly, some Jewish leaders organized efforts to disperse the newcomers. One project, the "Galveston Plan," encouraged immigrant Jews to disembark at the Galveston, Texas, port of entry and to settle in more westerly communities such as Fort Worth, Oklahoma City, Omaha, and Minneapolis. A second initiative, the Industrial Removal Office (1901), assisted individuals and families to re-locate from cities like New York, Philadelphia, and Boston to communities where work opportunities might be better. By 1917, more than 75,000 people had been re-settled by the Industrial Removal Office in nearly 1,700 locales across the United States, though many such re-locations failed to provide the promised opportunities.[34]

A third dispersal initiative, settlement of immigrant Jews in agricultural colonies, involved far fewer people, but has left an indelible mark on Jewish memory and on the historical landscape. Various organizations, notably the Baron de Hirsch Fund, sponsored agricultural settlements from Woodbine, New Jersey, to Oregon. The settlers were motivated and energetic, but their colonies were typically sited in inhospitable locations. The agricultural colony on Sicily Island near Bayou Louis in Louisiana, for example, was wiped out by floods; the settlers at Cotopaxi in Colorado, discovered that only one hundred of their 1,780 acres were fit for cultivation; and the colony of Painted Woods, located near Bismarck, South Dakota, was doomed by drought and prairie fires. As a result, most of these intentional communities were short-lived, though romance and nostalgia have preserved their stories.[35]

Seeking a National Voice

In the first decades of the twentieth century, at the height of Jewish immigration to America, the scale, diversity, and dispersion of Jews led to new initiatives in search of a national Jewish voice. One set of interrelated efforts focused on the renewal of Jewish life and culture in America, including the Jewish Publication Society, Gratz College, the Jewish Chautauqua Society, and the American Jewish Historical Society (1892), the first ethnic history organization in the United States.[36] A second approach was represented by the National Council of Jewish Women (1893) and national fraternal organizations such as B'nai B'rith, B'rith Sholom, and Brith Abraham. Each of the three emergent religious movements—Orthodox, Reform, and Conservative—had established a seminary by 1900, but their differences precluded any unified voice in national affairs.

Well-established German Jewish leaders, seeking to aid fellow Jews in Europe through diplomacy and resistance to immigration restriction, organized the American Jewish Committee in 1906. The American Jewish Committee, however, was dominated by a small elite, unrepresentative of the mass of new Jewish immigrants. The Federation of American Zionists—which morphed into the Zionist Organization of America—was

Figure 7.3 The Hebrew Immigrant Aid Society (HIAS) was founded in New York in 1881 to assist Jewish refugees from Russia. HIAS provided new immigrants with shelter, meals, housing, translators, jobs, and transportation. *The Jewish Immigrant* cover (January 1909) shows Lady Liberty opening the "gates of righteousness" to the newcomer.

Courtesy of the Hebraic Section, Library of Congress.

organized in 1897; however, both the Federation of American Zionists and later the Zionist Organization of America were hampered by constant discord among its various factions, suffering steep rises and falls in membership and influence. In 1918, the American Jewish Congress was organized by eastern European Jewish leaders as a more democratic alternative to the American Jewish Committee; it sought to address the rights of Jewish minorities in post–World War I Europe. At the local level, the federation movement brought together various local organizations, but the federations did not begin to develop a coordinated national voice until the National Council of Jewish Federations and Welfare Funds was established in 1931.[37]

Coordinating the diversity of American Jewish voices was challenging even in moments of crisis. When the First World War devastated Jewish communities in Europe, several distinct groupings sprang into action to provide relief to their immiserated brethren. In October 1914, Orthodox Jews organized the Central Committee for the Relief of Jews Suffering Through the War. This was followed within days by a meeting of forty organizations convened by the American Jewish Committee, which established the American Jewish Relief Committee. But months later, labor groups organized the People's Relief Committee, leaving three major organizations working to assist European Jewry.[38]

Despite overlap and redundancy, even the proliferation of national Jewish organizations enriched the communal culture of local Jewish communities. Most of the national organizations were either federations of pre-existing local community groups, or had spawned local chapters, or both, complementing the array of strictly local expressions of community. The result was a dense web of fraternal, Zionist, defense, and philanthropic organizations in dozens of communities across the continent.

Between the Wars

The First World War had slowed immigration from war-torn Europe; in 1921 and 1924, despite fierce lobbying by Jewish groups, Congress passed legislation that reduced the migration of "undesirable" eastern and southern Europeans—including Jews—to the merest trickle compared with the pre-1914 floods. At the heart of the new legislation were nativist attitudes and growing fears that White Anglo-Saxon Protestant America would be undermined by the influx of unassimilated immigrants who could not be truly Americanized. Antisemitic impulses also underlay a rash of efforts to establish Jewish quotas at leading colleges and universities, social exclusion, and discrimination in employment (especially in large corporations) and housing.[39]

Despite overt and covert expressions of antisemitism, during the 1920s Jews continued to acculturate and to make headlong progress toward the middle class. Jewish newcomers continued to manifest an entrepreneurial spirit in niche, marginal, and new lines of business. Their children continued to be disproportionately represented in colleges, universities, and professional schools. And as they prospered, many Jews moved out of older immigrant neighborhoods into areas of second- and third-generation settlement.[40]

Evidence of growing prosperity can be seen not only in the building of new synagogues in the more desirable neighborhoods where Jews began to settle but also in the establishment of Jewish country clubs. The earliest of these were organized before World War I as a way to counter exclusion from mainstream clubs. By 1924, there were sixty-nine Jewish country clubs (of which some, founded by German Jews, excluded Russians!). The 1920s also saw the burgeoning of Jewish resort areas, notably Atlantic City and the Catskills. The latter, popularly known as "the borscht belt," developed a distinctive style and culture, one that had profound influence not only on Jews, but on Americans in general.[41]

In 1923, a newly minted Reform rabbi, Benjamin Frankel, established the first Hillel Foundation at the University of Illinois, Urbana-Champaign. Hillel was a response both to social exclusion and to a religious vacuum. As Howard Sachar puts it, Hillel "was a mixture of social activities interspersed with Sabbath and holiday services, courses in Hebrew and the Bible, and personal counseling." Within a couple of years, Hillel became a program of B'nai B'rith, and foundations were started at Wisconsin, Ohio State, and Michigan. Over time, Hillel chapters proliferated, often providing service to both their campuses and to local Jewish communities, especially in smaller towns dominated by a college or university. Today, Hillel chapters can be found on 550 campuses across the United States.[42]

The *embourgoisement* of American Jewry, so evident in the 1920s, came to an abrupt halt with the advent of the Great Depression. Instead, this "moratorium on upward mobility" threw thousands into poverty, homelessness, and despair, straining the resources of Jewish communal agencies. In 1931, a nationwide study of thirty Jewish welfare agencies showed a 42 percent increase in relief recipients in the first nine months of the year. A report by the New York Federation of Jewish Charities contended that "the normal absorption of Jews within the American economic structure is now practically impossible." The pressure for relief accelerated the trend of forming community-wide Jewish federations for combined planning and fundraising: in 1936 there were 145 Jewish federations—forty-eight of which had been established after 1931.[43]

On the Suburban Frontier

The Second World War and the destruction of European Jewry in the Holocaust left American Jewry as the preeminent Jewish community in the world (40 percent of all Jews). The war also marked a watershed—the steep decline of antisemitism in America. By 1940, a majority of American Jews were native-born, and by mid-century American Jewry had become a phenomenon—a population without a substantial working class. In 1948 to 1953, fourteen federations found that 75 to 98 percent of their local communities were engaged in white-collar work. Overall, Jews were the most highly educated population in America, leaders in intellectual life, the arts, academia, and business. They were also the most philanthropic: although only 3 percent of the population, the United Jewish Appeal became the most successful of all postwar philanthropies.[44]

Postwar Jews were on the move geographically as well as socioeconomically, from city centers to suburbia, from small towns to larger communities, and from one region to another. In the late 1940s, two-thirds of all American Jews lived in New England and the Mid-Atlantic; by 1990, only half of all Jews lived in the Northeast. The fastest-growing Jewish communities were in the Sun Belt. Edward S. Shapiro documents the flow of Jews westward and southward by citing the dates each community established its own federation: St. Petersburg in 1950; Orange County, California, in 1964; Mobile in 1966; and Las Vegas in 1973. By 1990, more Jews lived in Phoenix than Pittsburgh.[45]

In suburbia, Jews continued to cluster together, but the thick culture of the older immigrant enclaves appeared to thin out. "American Jews seem to have opted for a Judaism of affiliation without ritual observance of synagogue attendance," observes one historian. "Worship in non-Orthodox congregations increasingly became a spectator rather than a participant activity." Still, a majority of suburban Jews affiliated with a congregation, drawn into membership for the education of their children and their programs of social, cultural, and even athletic activities. From the 1950s through the 1970s (and beyond), the nexus of suburban Judaism was the synagogue center, with catering halls, game rooms, and gymnasiums housed in elaborate, pretentious buildings. Rabbi Arthur Hertzberg called these synagogues "temples of Jewish togetherness."[46]

Meanwhile, Jewish philanthropy continued to gain symbolic stature: half of all suburban Jews contributed to their federation campaigns or to the United Jewish Appeal (in

Figure 7.4 An intentional community and immersive experience in Jewish living, many postwar summer camps promoted Jewish literacy and practice. Here, campers gather for Friday evening services at Camp Ramah in Wisconsin in the 1950s.

Courtesy of Camp Ramah in Wisconsin.

support of Jews in Israel and other countries abroad). Status began to flow from synagogues into Jewish federations (the principal arm of Jewish fundraising); "I am because I give" became a key marker of Jewish identity. In some suburban communities, the culture of affiliation was epitomized by the Jewish Community Center, which expanded to become community campuses that embraced the Jewish Community Center, the headquarters of the local federation, the offices of social service agencies, day schools, housing for seniors, and occasionally even a cultural center.[47]

Identification through affiliation seemed inadequate to many communal leaders. Instead, they invested in two complementary forms of immersive Jewish experience—the Jewish day school and the Jewish summer camp. Day schools can trace their history back to the nineteenth century, but the proliferation of day schools is mostly a postwar phenomenon. Both community-wide and denominational day schools grew rapidly in number, especially in recent decades. Today, Jewish day schools number in the hundreds nationwide.[48]

The other distinctive form of immersive living that began to burgeon in the 1950s and 1960s was the Jewish summer camp. Day camps and their equivalents go back to the beginning of the twentieth century, as do some early efforts to provide working women recreational time in country settings. During the interwar years, summer camps were established that catered exclusively to Jewish campers, ranging from Maine to the Ozarks. But mostly these efforts did not have a distinctively Jewish purpose. In the postwar period, however, overnight camps were established to provide "a worthy use of summer." Some were denominational, such as Camp Ramah (with eight camps sited from New England to California) sponsored by the Conservative Movement, or the sixteen camps (from Wisconsin to Mississippi) sponsored by the Reform Movement. Others were sponsored by Zionist groups, such as the Habonim [Labor Zionist] camps (seven camps ranging from Maryland to Vancouver), while others, such as Capital Camps, were sponsored by local groups. In these new seasonal communities, campers studied Hebrew and Jewish culture, engaged in regular worship services, and joined in activities designed to promote *ruach* (Jewish spirit). Today, synagogue centers, Jewish Community Centers, day schools, and Jewish summer camps continue to mark the American landscape from coast to coast.[49]

Crises and Responses

The social and cultural upheavals of the 1960s and 1970s resonated within the Jewish community. The blandness—some would say sterility—of much congregational life, the thinning of Jewish culture, and a largely passive population were concerns even in the 1950s. But in the wake of counter-cultural activism, these concerns became causes. At the same time, American Jews confronted some of the trade-offs of assimilation—among them a growing number of Jews who identified as secular or cultural Jews and a rising rate of intermarriage that threatened the viability of Jews and Judaism in America. By 2000, the rate of intermarriage had risen to more than 30 percent of all non-Orthodox marriages. Anxieties led first to efforts to prevent intermarriage, then to measures to bring these new multicultural families into Jewish congregations and communities.[50]

Another wave of change that swept Jewish life from the 1960s on was Jewish feminism. Women had long been mainstays of synagogues and of Jewish organizational life, but now their leadership and initiatives became more explicit and more focused. In 1973, a National Jewish Women's Conference was convened in New York; that same year, Rachel Adler published an essay titled "The Jew Who Wasn't There." Women's groups sprang up, independently and then within congregations and other Jewish organizations, ranging from consciousness-raising to study and advocacy. The Jewish Feminist Organization was established in 1974 as a national umbrella; it and numerous local groups pressed for change in synagogue and community. Within a relatively short time, the liberal movements of Judaism began to count women as part of the traditional *minyan* [quorum of ten adults] required for prayer, calling women to the Torah, and ordaining women as rabbis and cantors. New rituals were adopted, such as a special Passover seder for women, while old rituals were revived and adapted. The result, says Hasia Diner, "showed how women's activism and their explorations of Judaism inspired a new zest for Jewish themes," opening new space for women in American Judaism.[51]

At the same time, young Jews seeking meaning and spirituality began to form *havurot* [fellowships] for worship and study. These small, intimate, egalitarian gatherings were a marked contrast and challenge to "establishment" Judaism. As Howard Sachar writes,

"[T]hese circles were affiliated with synagogues; others developed on their own. In whichever form, all functioned democratically, without 'official' rabbinical supervision. Indeed, some became almost defiantly antiestablishmentarian in their approach to Jewish worship and social commitment. By the late 1980s, *havurah* chapters were to be found in every major Jewish community in the land. They represented yet another American version of grass-roots democracy."[52]

Amid the ferment of late-twentieth-century Jewish life, a whole panoply of new Jewish institutions emerged. One type—the Holocaust center—came out of a growing consciousness of the Shoah (Holocaust). In addition to the United States Holocaust Memorial Museum in Washington, District of Columbia (1993), major Holocaust museums were opened in Los Angeles (1993) and New York (1997). By 2015, there were more than 150 Holocaust museums and education centers in communities across the nation. Jewish museums also burgeoned: in 1977, when the Council of American Jewish Museums was organized, there were only seven professionally staffed institutions, but by 2015, it had grown to more than seventy museums, galleries, and historic sites. At the same time, local Jewish history organizations multiplied, creating archives, preserving sites, and developing expansive programs of education and engagement. (See chapter 14.)

Interest in Jews and Judaism flowered on American campuses as well as in the community. As late as the 1950s, Jewish studies as an academic discipline was confined to the three major rabbinical seminaries, Dropsie College, Brandeis University, and a handful of other colleges and universities. By 1966, there were more than sixty full-time positions in Jewish studies in American universities, with enrollments of more than ten thousand students. The Association for Jewish studies was founded in 1969 and by 1990 had more than one thousand members. That year, there were six hundred positions in Jewish Studies. The new programs appealed both to Jews and Gentiles, the latter in particular in colleges outside the Northeast. "The growth of Jewish studies signified the academy's recognition that American Jews had become part of the American mainstream, that Judaism was as legitimate a faith as Christianity, and that Jewish culture could be studied for its own sake, not merely as a prelude to Christianity," writes Edward Shapiro. Today, campus-based Jewish studies programs engage dozens of local communities through lectures, symposia, and other public activities, including many towns with only small numbers of Jewish residents.[53]

Advances in Jewish studies, however, did little to stem rising rates of intermarriage, so Jewish leaders turned to new kinds of immersive, experiential programs to engage and inspire young Jews. The March of the Living was established in 1988 to bring high school students from around the world to Auschwitz and Birkenau, where they spend a week, climaxing in a march from the concentration camp to the killing center, followed in many cases by a week in Israel to commemorate Yom Ha-Zikaron (Remembrance Day). A complementary program—Birthright Israel—is aimed at Jewish young adults aged eighteen to twenty-six and offers a free ten-day trip to Israel. Its purpose, as stated by the sponsoring organization, is "to generate a profound transformation in contemporary Jewish culture and a connection between Israelis and their peers in the Diaspora." To date, more than a quarter million American Jews have participated in this novel form of temporary Jewish community.[54]

Jewish Community Today

In October 2013, the Pew Research Center issued a 200-page report titled "Portrait of Jewish Americans." Although the report confirmed that "American Jews overwhelmingly say they are proud to be Jewish and have a strong sense of belonging to the Jewish people," the report also noted that the nature of Jewish identity is changing, with many Jews—especially young adults—identifying as Jewish on the "basis of ancestry, ethnicity or culture," rather than religion. As might be expected of any study of a population so scattered and so diverse, the Pew report became the subject of intense debate within the Jewish community. Some challenged its methodology (including its population estimates), others its findings. But at least two propositions appear to be uncontested—the diversity of Jewish identity (and hence, of community) and the continuing transformation of community from one generation to another.[55]

Efforts to steer the ongoing transformation of community are in full flower. The Orthodox community, which has been growing in numbers and influence (despite the sectarian stance of the ultra-Orthodox) has expanded its efforts to educate and renew commitment to traditional Judaism. The liberal movements in Judaism, meanwhile, have focused energies on in-reach and welcome to the intermarried, the lesbian, gay, bisexual, queer, and transgender community, and other underserved Jewish populations. Major Jewish philanthropies have joined wholeheartedly in these efforts: it is hard to think of a major Jewish foundation that is not actively supporting some form of innovative program of Jewish renewal, especially those targeted at the next generation of American Jews. The results of these manifold efforts to re-engage Jews in Jewish conversations, as a surrogate for Jewish community, are not clear, but the variety of initiatives suggest that diversity will continue to increase within a stable population.[56]

What is clear, however, is that American Jews, and particularly the younger generation, have embraced the digital universe and online modalities to engage, mobilize, advocate, converse, study, and convene. A wide range of online communities have been formed to promote everything from systematic study of traditional Jewish texts to meetings of "Mash-Up Americans." Meanwhile, the Internet has enabled individuals and small groups of Jews to create a host of informal pop-up communities that range from one-time gatherings to regular events. In coming years, as American Jews expand their virtual, ephemeral, and informal associations, the forms and meanings of Jewish community will continue to multiply and evolve.[57]

Notes

1. Stephen J. Whitfield. "Between Memory and Messianism: A Brief History of American Jewish Identity," in Staci Boris, ed., *The New Authentics: Artists of the Post-Jewish Generation* (Chicago: Spertus Institute, 2007), 44–45.

2. Hasia R. Diner, *A Time for Gathering: The Second Migration* (Baltimore: Johns Hopkins University Press, 1992), 113.

3. Ibid., 1–5.

4. Howard B. Rock, *Haven of Liberty: New York Jews in the New World, 1654-1865* (New York: New York University Press, 2012), 5–16.

5. Ibid., 17–27.

6. Ibid., 43–45.

7. Jewish Museum of the American West website, "Kansas Exhibition Hall" and "New Mexico Exhibition Hall," accessed December 9, 2015, http://www.jmaw.org/. See also, Lee Shai Weissbach, *The Synagogues of Kentucky: Architecture and History* (Lexington, KY: University Press of Kentucky, 1995).

8. Diner, *Time for Gathering*, 21.

9. Quoted in Isaac M. Fein, *The Making of an American Jewish Community: The History of Baltimore Jewry from 1773 to 1920* (Philadelphia: Jewish Publication Society, 1971), 56–57.

10. Jonathan D. Sarna, *American Judaism: A History* (New Haven: Yale University Press, 2004), 52–57.

11. Jonathan D. Sarna, *American Judaism*, 59–60.

12. Hasia Diner, *The Jews of the United States, 1654 to 2000* (Berkeley: University of California Press, 2004), 117–34.

13. Lance J. Sussman, *Isaac Leeser and the Making of American Judaism* (Detroit: Wayne State University Press, 1995).

14. Sarna, *American Judaism*, 80–82.

15. Ibid., 110–11.

16. Ibid., 129–32, 144–45.

17. Gerald Sorin, *A Time for Building: The Third Migration* (Baltimore: Johns Hopkins University Press, 1992), 170–90. Although the term "denomination" has become common usage, see Sarna, *American Judaism*, xix–xx, for his qualifying remarks.

18. Diner, *Time for Gathering*, 100.

19. Ibid., 92–96.

20. Ibid., 103.

21. Ibid., 96.

22. Ibid., 99

23. Rock, *Haven of Liberty*, 158.

24. Ibid., 158–62; B'nai B'rith website, "About Us," October 31, 2015, accessed November 11, 2015, http://www.bnaibrith.org/about-us.html. See also, Deborah Dash Moore, *B'nai B'rith and the Challenge of Ethnic Leadership* (Albany, NY: State University of New York Press, 1981).

25. Diner, *Time for Gathering*, 87.

26. Ibid., 100–05.

27. Sorin, *Time for Building*, 162–63, and also 140–42 on Chicago.

28. Diner, *Time for Gathering*, 103.

29. Annie Polland and Daniel Soyer, *Emerging Metropolis: New York Jews in the Age of Immigration* (New York: New York University Press, 2012), 11–43, 103–35.

30. Sorin, *Time for Building*, 136–37.

31. Eric L. Goldstein, "A Different Kind of Neighborhood: Central European Jews and the Origins of Jewish East Baltimore," in Deborah R. Weiner, et al., eds., *Voices of Lombard Street: A Century of Change in East Baltimore* (Baltimore: Jewish Museum of Maryland, 2007), 22–39.

32. Elizabeth Farish , August 11, 2015; Karen Wilson, August 11, 2015; Robin Waites, November 4, 2015; telephone interviews with the author. Sorin, *A Time for Building*, 159–60.

33. Daniel Soyer, *Jewish Immigrant Associations and American Identity in New York, 1880-1939* (Cambridge, MA: Harvard University Press, 1997),

34. Sorin, *Time for Building*, 63–64; Jack Glazier, "'Transplanted from Kiev to Hoosierdom': How the Industrial Removal Office Directed Jewish Immigrants to Terre Haute," *Indiana Magazine of History*, 97(March 2001): 1–24; Carol Gendler, "The Industrial Removal Office and the Settlement of Jews in Nebraska, 1901-1917," *Nebraska History* 72 (1991): 127–34; Jack Glazier, *Dispersing the Ghetto: The Relocation of Jewish Immigrants across America* (Ithaca: Cornell University Press, 1989).

35. Jewish Encyclopedia website, "Agricultural Colonies in the United States," accessed November 6, 2015, http://www.jewishencyclopedia.com/articles/909-agricultural colonies.

36. Jonathan D. Sarna, *A Great Awakening: The Transformation That Shaped Twentieth Century American Judaism and Its implications for Today* (New York: Council for Initiatives in Jewish Education, 1995).

37. Diner, *Jews of the United States*, 189–202; Naomi W. Cohen, *Not Free to Desist: The American Jewish Committee, 1906-1966* (Philadelphia: Jewish Publication Society, 1972); *The Americanization of Zionism, 1897-1948* (Hanover, NH: University Press of New England, 2003).

38. Oscar Handlin, *A Continuing Task: The American Jewish Joint Distribution Committee, 1914-1964.* (New York: Random House, 1964), 25–26.

39. Feingold, *Time for Searching*, 1–34.

40. Ibid.; see also Howard M. Sachar, *A History of the Jews in America* (New York: Vintage, 1992), 373ff.

41. Feingold, *Time for Searching*, 62–89; Sachar, *Jews in America*, 666–67.

42. Sachar, *Jews in America*, 417–18; Hillel International website, "About Hillel," accessed October 19, 2015, http://www.hillel.org/about/hillels-around-the-world.

43. Sachar, *Jews in America*, 428–30; Feingold, *Time for Searching*, 146–49.

44. Shapiro, *Time for Healing*, chapter 2 and 64, 100–01, 108, 125, 143, 155; Sachar, *Jews in America*, 646–47.

45. Shapiro, *Time for Healing*, 133–34.

46. Ibid., 147–51.

47. Ibid., 200, 209.

48. Melissa A. Klapper, "The History of Jewish Education in America," in Raphael, ed., *Columbia History of Jews*, 207–10.

49. Riv-Ellen Prell, "Summer Camp, Postwar American Jewish Youth, and the Redemption of Judaism," *The Jewish Role in American Life* 5 (2007): 77–106; Jenna Weissman Joselit with Karen S. Mittelman, eds., *A Worthy Use of Summer: Jewish Summer Camping in America* (Philadelphia: National Museum of American Jewish History, 1993); Michael M. Lorge and Gary P. Zola, eds., *A Place of Our Own: The Rise of Reform Jewish Camping* (Tuscaloosa: University of Alabama, 2008).

50. Shapiro, *Time for Healing*, 233–41.

51. Diner, *Jews of the United States*, 350–58. See also Riv-Ellen Prell, ed., *Women Remaking American Judaism* (Detroit: Wayne State University Press, 2007); Pamela S. Nadell, "A Bright New Constellation: Feminism and American Judaism," in Marc Lee Raphael, *The Columbia History of Jews and Judaism in America* (New York: Columbia University Press, 2008), 385–405.

52. Sachar, *Jews in America*, 833. See also Riv-Ellen Prell, *Prayer and Community: The Havurah in American Judaism* (Detroit: Wayne University Press, 1989).

53. Shapiro, *Time for Healing*, 76–86.

54. Birthright Israel website, "About Us," accessed November 8, 2015, http://www.birthright israel.com/; International March of the Living website, "About the March," accessed November 8, 2015, http://motl.org/about/.

55. Pew Research Center website, "Portrait of Jewish Americans," accessed November 11, 2015, http://www.pewforum.org/2013/10/01/jewish-american-beliefs-attitudes-culture-survey/. For a critique of Pew methodology and interpretation, see Debra Renee Kaufman (Northeastern University), Paper delivered at the "Wrestling with Jewish Peoplehood" Conference, Philadelphia, April 10, 2016.

56. See, for example, Jennifer A. Thompson, *Jewish on Their Own Terms: How Intermarried Couples Are Changing American Judaism* (Rutgers, NJ: Rutgers University Press, 2014); Theodore Sasson, et al., *Millennial Children of Intermarriage: Touchpoints and Trajectories of Jewish Engagement* (Waltham, MA: Brandeis University, 2015).

57. See, among many examples, Mash-Up Americans website, "Home Page," accessed April 11, 2016, http://www.mashupamericans.com/; One Table website, "A New Way to Friday," accessed April 11, 2016, http://onetable.org/; The Kitchen website, "Home Page," accessed April 11, 2016, http://www.thekitchensf.org.

Select Bibliography

Ferris, Marcie Cohen, and Mark I. Greenberg, eds. *Jewish Roots in Southern Soil: A New History.* Hanover, NH: University Press of New England, 2006.

Friedman, Reena Sigmund. *These Are Our Children: Jewish Orphanages in the United States, 1880-1925.* Hanover, NH: University of New England Press, 1994.

Joselit, Jenna Weissman, with Karen S. Mittelman, eds. *A Worthy Use of Summer:* Jewish *Summer Camping in America*. Philadelphia: National Museum of American Jewish History, 1993.

Kahn, Ava Fran, ed. *Jewish Life in the American West: Perspectives on Migration, Settlement, and Community.* Los Angeles: Autry Museum of Western Heritage; Seattle: University of Washington Press, 2002.

Kaufman, David. *Shul with a Pool: The "Synagogue-Center" in American Jewish History.* Hanover, NH: University Press of New England, 1999.

Morawska, Ewa. *Insecure Prosperity: Small-Town Jews in Industrial America, 1890-1940.* Princeton: Princeton University Press, 1996.

Prell, Riv-Ellen. *Prayer and Community: The Havurah in American Judaism.* Detroit: Wayne State University Press, 1989.

Prell, Riv-Ellen, ed. *Women Remaking American Judaism.* Detroit: Wayne State University Press, 2007.

Raphael, Marc Lee. *Profiles in American Judaism: The Reform, Conservative, Orthodox, and Reconstructionist Traditions in Historical Perspectives.* New York: Harper and Row, 1988.

Rogoff, Leonard. *Homelands: Southern Jewish Identity in Durham and Chapel Hill, North Carolina.* Tuscaloosa: University of Alabama Press, 2001.

Rogow, Faith. *Gone to Another Meeting: The National Council of Jewish Women, 1893-1993.* Tuscaloosa: University of Alabama Press, 1993.

Soyer, Daniel. *Jewish Immigrant Associations and American Identity in New York, 1880-1939.* Cambridge: Harvard University Press, 1997.

Tenenbaum, Shelly. *A Credit to Their Community: Jewish Loan Societies in the United States, 1880-1945.* Detroit: Wayne State University Press, 1993.

Weiner, Deborah R. *Coalfield Jews: An Appalachian History.* Urbana: University of Illinois Press, 2006.

Weissbach, Lee Shai. *Jewish Life in Small-Town America.* New Haven: Yale University Press, 2003.

CHAPTER 8

CASE STUDIES
Communal Life

AS DISCUSSED in the previous chapter, the web of Jewish communal organizations is often multiform and dense. However, as organizations devoted mainly to the welfare of Jews in a locale, these organizations tend to get limited exposure in secular history organizations, even when they help to shape the lives of multiple ethnic, religious, or cultural communities. The case studies that follow are exceptions to the usual practices, though they are only suggestive of the many kinds of Jewish communal organizations that might lend themselves to interpretation, especially in local history venues.

The first case study describes a most unusual synagogue—one that was created in a prison. The second presents an online encyclopedia developed by the Minnesota Historical Society that foregrounds a wide range of Jewish communal organizations in that state. The Joint Distribution Committee (JDC) represents a national organization that has served—and continues to serve—both Jews and non-Jews who are victims of disaster. Since many ethnic and religious communities have sponsored and organized analogous organizations, the opportunity is ripe to develop interpretive projects on communal institutions that are inclusive and comparative.

The Synagogue

Eastern State Penitentiary

Eastern State Penitentiary is the most influential prison ever built. In 1787, the members of the Philadelphia Society for Alleviating the Miseries of Public Prisons convened for the first time. Their goal: "to build a true penitentiary, a prison intended to create genuine regret and penitence in a criminal's heart." Convincing public authorities to erect a prison that would move prisoners to spiritual reflection and change took many years. Only in 1829 was Eastern State opened on a new model, one designed to be more than a holding pen where physical punishment and abuse of prisoners were commonplace. Instead, prisoners were held in solitary confinement and tasked with regular work. By separating prisoners from each other and from the corruptions of the outside world, "the proponents of the system believed strongly that the criminals, exposed, in silence, to thoughts of their behavior and the ugliness of their crimes, would become genuinely penitent. Thus the new word, penitentiary."[1]

The physical embodiment of these ideas was realized in a radical new form. Architect John Haviland laid out seven cellblocks radiating out from a central surveillance rotunda. Each cell was centrally heated and provided with running water, a flush toilet, a skylight, and a private outdoor exercise space surrounded by a ten-foot wall. The cells were aligned along central corridors with thirty-foot-high barrel-vaulted ceilings, tall arched windows, and skylights. Haviland thought of the new penitentiary as a "forced monastery," a machine for reform. Over the next century, more than three hundred prisons around the world were built on Haviland's plan.[2]

Tourists flocked to Philadelphia in the 1830s and 1840s to see the new architectural wonder. A debate ensued over the effectiveness and compassion of solitary confinement. Charles Dickens, for one, wrote that he was "persuaded that those who designed this system of Prison Discipline, and those benevolent gentlemen who carry it into execution, do not know what they are doing. . . . I hold this slow and daily tampering with the mysteries of the brain to be immeasurably worse than any torture of the body." Over time, doubts about the prison's effectiveness grew and by the 1870s prisoners were exercised together; congregate workshops were added in 1905 and by 1913 the "Pennsylvania System" was officially abandoned. Eastern State was closed in 1971.[3]

Even in its early years, Eastern State had Jewish inmates, though precisely how many is not known. By 1845, Jewish clergy, serving as religious counselors, were visiting Jewish prisoners and in one exceptional instance (1851), a female prisoner was provided the services of a *mohel* to perform a ritual circumcision for her newborn son. In the early twentieth century, local Jewish clergy and organizations intensified their visits to inmates, and in October 1913 Jewish prisoners held their first communal worship services for the Jewish New Year. In 1917, Jewish inmates began to hold weekly Sabbath services, assisted by B'nai B'rith's Prison Aid Committee. In 1924, Alfred Fleisher, a practicing Jew, was appointed head of the Eastern State Board and was instrumental in establishing a dedicated synagogue in spaces previously occupied by workshops.[4]

The Eastern State Synagogue may be the first to be established in any American prison. The interior decor and furnishings were created by the inmates themselves and included a Torah Ark that rested on an elevated *bimah* (platform), benches along the side walls, and a reading table. In 1959, the synagogue was remodeled, with plasterwork moldings and a large plaster Star of David in the ceiling, colorful tile floors, and two electric candelabra in the form of the Hebrew word *Shalom* (Peace). Although the number of Jewish inmates was modest (thirty out of 1,398 in 1924), the Eastern State Synagogue held Sabbath and festival services into the 1960s, greatly aided by a dedicated corps of

Figure 8.1 Visitors in the restored Alfred W. Fleisher Memorial Synagogue at Eastern State Penitentiary Historic Site, Philadelphia.

Photo courtesy of Eastern State Penitentiary.

Jewish volunteers who regularly attended services, provided counsel, and assisted inmates to find work upon their release.[5]

With the abandonment of Eastern State in 1971, the synagogue—like other prison buildings—fell into a state of disrepair. Plasterwork on walls and ceilings peeled away, wood paneling and furniture rotted, fabric shredded. But starting in 2004, Eastern State Penitentiary, now a non-profit preservation and educational organization, began the long, costly process of restoring America's first documented prison synagogue. Intensive research was conducted in extant records, oral histories were collected, and the surviving architecture and ruined artifacts were recovered and studied. In 2008, the restored synagogue was reopened, accompanied by an interpretive exhibition (The William Portner Memorial Exhibit on Jewish Life at Eastern State) in the adjacent workshop space. In addition to interpretive text and historical photographs, the synagogue exhibit comprises a video interview with the last Jewish chaplain to serve at Eastern State, surviving artifacts salvaged from the ruins of the decayed synagogue, and an interactive exercise that invites visitors to describe a *mitzvah* (act of loving-kindness) they have performed.[6]

Today, Eastern State Penitentiary is nationally known for its significant history, for a series of innovative art installations, for its public programs (including "Terror Behind the Walls," an annual Halloween fundraising event), and—as a member of the Sites of Conscience Coalition—for its educational activities about the state of American imprisonment. The Eastern State Penitentiary Synagogue remains a unique feature of this National Historic Landmark, one that provides an unusual glimpse into American Jewish history and to communal efforts to assist fellow Jews incarcerated in America's most notable prison to practice and maintain their faith.

MNopedia

Minnesota Historical Society

In 2011, the Minnesota Historical Society went live with the first online encyclopedia of Minnesota history. Among its major headings, MNopedia includes Native Americans and African Americans. Jewish Minnesotans, a mere 1 percent of the state's population, concentrated in the Twin Cities of Minneapolis and St. Paul, are strongly represented in this digital encyclopedia, as befits an organization known for its inclusivity and for its history of publications and programs on Minnesota Jews.

The index to the Historical Society's journal, *Minnesota History*, lists dozens of references and articles dating back to the journal's third volume (1919/1920). Among these was a pointed article by Laura Weber titled "Gentiles Preferred: Minneapolis Jews and Employment, 1920-1950."[7] The Minnesota Historical Society was also the sponsor of the exhibition titled *Unpacking on the Prairie* (1996), which is discussed in the previous series of case studies on domestic life (see chapter 6), and a related book written by Linda Mack Schloff, *"And Prairie Dogs Weren't Kosher": Jewish Women in the Upper Midwest Since 1855.*[8] Subsequently, the Minnesota Historical Society published *Jews in Minnesota* by Hyman Berman and Linda Mack Schloff as part of its People of Minnesota series.[9]

Shortly after MNopedia debuted, Katherine Tane, then the executive director of the Jewish Historical Society of the Upper Midwest, applied for grants with which to commission a series of articles on Jewish history to be incorporated into the new digital encyclopedia. With funding from the Minnesota Historical and Cultural Heritage ("Legacy") grants program, the Jewish Historical Society commissioned thirty articles on Minnesota Jewish history, focused mostly on the stories of communal institutions—synagogues, schools, and welfare organizations, as well as an overview essay on Minnesota Jewish history with a bibliography and a timeline.[10] The current list of organizations and institutions comprises the following:

Mikro Kodesh Synagogue, Minneapolis
Adath Jeshurun Congregation, Minnetonka
B'nai Emet Synagogue, St. Louis Park
B'nai Abraham Congregation, Minneapolis
Temple of Aaron, St. Paul
Beth Jacob Congregation, Mendota Heights
Temple Israel, Minneapolis
Mount Zion Temple, St. Paul
Shir Tikvah Congregation, Minneapolis

Beth El Synagogue, St. Louis Park
Kenesseth Israel Congregation, St. Louis Park
Sharei Chesed Congregation, Minnetonka
Tifereth B'nai Jacob Congregation, Minneapolis
Bet Shalom Congregation, Minnetonka
Adas Israel Congregation, Duluth
Temple Israel, Duluth
Jewish Religious Life on the Iron Range
Jewish Community Relations Council of Minnesota and the Dakotas
Jewish Community Center of St. Paul
American Jewish World Newspaper
Sabes Jewish Community Center, Minneapolis
Mayim Rabim Congregation, Minneapolis
Sholom Home, St. Paul and St. Louis Park
B'nai Israel Synagogue, Rochester
Jewish Roots of Neighborhood House, St. Paul
Mount Sinai Hospital and Foundation, Minneapolis
Talmud Torah, St. Paul
Labor Lyceum and Workmen's Circle
Talmud Torah, Minneapolis
Jewish Sheltering Home for Children, Minneapolis
Jewish Youth Camping in Minnesota
Jewish Social Welfare Groups, 1871–2012

The earliest Jewish settlers in Minnesota Territory were traders, peddlers, and merchants, mostly from German-speaking central Europe. Even before they established formal organizations, Jewish settlers had begun to convene informal services. By 1856, eight St. Paul Jewish families were able to establish Mount Zion Temple, the first Jewish institution in Minnesota and to hire a *hazzan* [cantor], who was also a *shohet* (ritual slaughterer). The new group also purchased a burying ground, the first Jewish cemetery in Minnesota. Surprisingly, even before the infant congregation could secure a charter, a rift occurred, with the dissidents organizing a second congregation.[11]

The Jews of St. Paul began to establish other communal organizations in the 1870s. In 1871, Jewish women organized the Hebrew Ladies Benevolent Society. In the same year, Jewish men obtained a charter for a B'nai B'rith lodge, becoming the first Minnesota outpost of the national Jewish fraternal organization. A few years later, St. Paul's well-established "German" leaders organized a Hebrew Social Club (formally the Standard Club) with restricted membership, which hosted balls, dinners, parties, and weddings.[12] Around the same time, Jews living in Minneapolis founded the Montefiore Burial Association (1876) and two years later, their own synagogue, Shaarai Tov (later Temple Israel). And by 1885, a third synagogue was organized in Duluth (Adas Israel Congregation).

The influx of eastern European Jews from Russia, Austro-Hungary, and Romania greatly expanded both the number of resident Jews and of communal organizations. By the end of World War I, Jews in the Twin Cities had organized homes for the aged and for orphaned children, synagogues and schools, Workman's Circle chapters and a Labor Lyceum, and even a weekly newspaper. By 1920, the largest Jewish communities—in Minneapolis, St. Paul, and Duluth—featured substantial residential enclaves; smaller Jewish communities were scattered over 145 towns across the state.[13]

During the 1920s and 1930s, however, antisemitic discrimination intensified in Minnesota. Jews experienced "discrimination in employment, housing and public accommodations." An antisemitic political campaign in 1938 galvanized the formation of the Anti-Defamation Council of Minnesota (later the Jewish Community Relations Council). In Minneapolis, the epicenter of antisemitism in the state, the Jewish community opened Mount Sinai Hospital in 1951 as a direct response to the exclusion of Jewish physicians from the staffs of local private hospitals. In 1946, journalist Carey McWilliams described Minneapolis as "the capital of anti-Semitism in the United States." The unfavorable publicity that followed prompted local and state officials to enact anti-discrimination ordinances; overt acts of antisemitism declined in the postwar period.[14]

The overview provided in "From Exclusion to Integration" is richly detailed in the more than thirty entries cited previously. Mini-timelines and first-person quotes bring to life a variety of organizations that have served Minnesota Jewry for more than a century and a half. MNopedia offers a model for how a local, state, or regional history organization can acknowledge and make accessible the history of small and scattered Jewish populations, directly and cost-effectively.

I Live. Send Help.

New-York Historical Society and American Jewish Joint Distribution Committee

At the outbreak of war in 1914, nine million Jews were still living in eastern Europe—two million of their brethren having migrated to America since 1870. Their growing numbers and occupational restrictions had impoverished many eastern European Jews; Oscar Handlin notes that in Odessa in 1900, 63 percent of those who died received pauper's funerals and a third of the living received some form of communal charity. When fighting began in 1914, many Jews, especially those in the combat zones of Galicia and Bukovina, were displaced, their lives disrupted and further impoverished. The Jewish residents of Palestine, then under Turkish rule, were also in distress. Both Palestinian and eastern European Jews appealed to their compatriots living in America to send immediate aid.[15]

Their appeals met with prompt responses. In October 1914, leaders of the American Jewish Committee convened a meeting with representatives of forty national organizations; a group of one hundred leaders were appointed to act as the American Jewish Relief Committee. That same month, Orthodox Jews established the Central Committee for the Relief of Jews Suffering Through the War. A few months later, American Jewish labor groups founded yet another effort, the People's Relief Committee. Clearly an organization was needed to coordinate the work of national and local organizations and of individuals, and to serve as a central disbursing agency for American Jewish relief efforts.

Figure 8.2 A World War I poster appealing for help in the campaign for Jewish relief in war-torn Europe. Note the monumental figure holding a tray of foodstuffs and the skyline of New York City in the background, with the Statue of Liberty shown prominently to the right.

Courtesy of Prints and Photographs Division, Library of Congress.

At the end of November 1914, such an agency came into being: the Joint Distribution Committee of American Funds for the Relief of Jewish War Sufferers, later known as the American Jewish JDC or, even more simply, the Joint. Over the next century, the JDC "would become the premier global Jewish humanitarian organization by playing a pivotal role in rescuing and sustaining individuals and entire communities," both Jewish and non-Jewish.[16]

Mindful of its own distinguished history, the JDC launched a number of initiatives to mark its centennial year in 2014. The JDC published a book on its century of humanitarian service titled *I Live. Send Help: 100 Years of Jewish History in Images from the JDC Archives*, which appeared in 2014. In 2012, the JDC Archives launched a new website to showcase the treasures of its archives and to make them accessible to scholars and the public. The website includes open access to a searchable database of the organization's historical text and photograph collections, which have been digitized.

Using digitized photos and documents as a base, the JDC staff developed online photo galleries and curated online exhibits and an interactive timeline. In addition, JDC planned for a major centennial exhibition in partnership with the New-York Historical Society (NYHS). Research for the exhibition was carried out by JDC Archives staff, working in tandem with a NYHS curator; once the JDC staff had identified promising material (which amounted to several times the number of photos and objects that could be displayed), the NYHS curator asked the JDC staff to "give me a story" for each time period and, based on this key criterion, the project team was able to winnow down to a manageable number of documents, photos, sound recordings, and film clips. Once selections were made, JDC staff wrote the interpretive texts, giving the exhibition its curatorial voice.[17]

The centennial exhibition, *I Live. Send Help.*, was designed by NYHS staff and displayed at the society from June through September 2014. It proved to be a popular success. In addition to one hundred original photos, documents, and objects, the exhibition featured three video monitors, each showing from one to five film or video clips, and two audio stations, each featuring a 1949 speech about JDC rescue efforts (one about programs to assist displaced persons in European displaced persons camps and the other about the airlift of Yemenite Jews to Israel). The exhibition highlighted the full spectrum of JDC's humanitarian relief efforts—non-sectarian work with the American Relief Administration in 1920–1923 to fight hunger in Poland, Russia, and Ukraine; JDC's central role in funding the War Refugee Board (1944) and helping to evacuate Jews from Nazi-occupied Europe; resettling Holocaust survivors all over the world; helping at-risk Jews emigrate to Israel; reconnecting Soviet Jews to their heritage; and delivering non-sectarian relief and rehabilitation in disaster situations ranging from the Armenian earthquake (1988) to the 2013 Philippine typhoon.[18]

As might be expected in a show dedicated to helping those suffering from human and natural disasters, the exhibition highlights a variety of moving stories. Co-curator Marilyn Kushner of the NYHS describes one such instance:

> There is a June 7, 1941 letter in the exhibition from Morris Troper, the JDC representative in Lisbon, Portugal, during World War II, to Eleanor Roosevelt. Troper

told her how JDC was helping to get Jewish children out of Occupied France. The parents of these children knew they weren't going to survive so they placed their children in orphanages in hopes that someone would be able to find safe haven for them. Eventually the children were put on a train bound for Lisbon and then on a ship to the United States. A number of their parents were being held in Drancy, a holding camp on the outskirts of Paris—their next stop would be extermination camps in the East. This children's train actually passed through Drancy and their parents were allowed to come to the train and say good-bye. Troper told Roosevelt her how the children no longer knew how to laugh, play, or even smile because they had experienced such terror. When this train stopped in Drancy, some of the children were able to visit with their parents for [fifteen] minutes and they all held each other and cried. Troper wrote that some of these children couldn't even speak the language of their parents because they had been apart from them for so long and so they just held each other. The scene must have been unbelievably heartbreaking.[19]

The success of the exhibition project was due to an effective collaboration of the NYHS staff with the staff at JDC. Each organization brought to the initiative its own in-house expertise: the JDC Archives staff brought their familiarity with the historical stories and the primary sources, whereas the NYHS staff deployed its strengths in exhibition planning and design. The result was a project that "drives home the epochal shifts in communication, and how they've changed the nature of humanitarian work—from telegrams, letters and postcards of the last century to the Tweets, posts and messaging of ours."[20] Like the companion book, the exhibition provides a "visual testament to how one organization carries out the Jewish tradition of 'All Israel is responsible one for the other,'" writes Esther Nussbaum.[21] Or, as Susan Elefant, an exhibition visitor, remarked, "I never knew the extent of [JDC's] work. . . . This exhibit makes it all come to life. I see how important it is to carry on the tradition."[22]

Notes

1. Eastern State Penitentiary website, "General Overview," accessed February 25, 2016, http://www.easternstate.org/learn/research-library/history. See also Norman Johnston (ed.), *Eastern State Penitentiary: Crucible of Good Intentions* (Philadelphia, Philadelphia Museum of Art, 1994); Paul Kahan, *Eastern State Penitentiary: A History* (Charleston, SC: History Press, 2008).

2. Eastern State Penitentiary website, "General Overview."

3. Ibid.

4. Eastern State Penitentiary, "Synagogue Exhibit" text, accessed February 28, 2016.

5. Ibid.

6. Eastern State Penitentiary website, "Alfred W. Fleisher Memorial Synagogue," accessed February 29, 2016, http://www.easternstate.org/support/completed-projects/alfred-w-fleisher -memorial-synagogue. See also Laura A. Mass, "The Synagogue at Eastern State Penitentiary: History and Interpretation," Master's Thesis, 2004.

7. *Minnesota History* (Spring 1991).

8. St. Paul, MN: Minnesota Historical Society Press, 1996.

9. St. Paul, MN: Minnesota Historical Society Press, 2002.

10. MNopedia website, "From Exclusion to Integration: The Story of Jews in Minnesota," accessed March 14, 2016, http://www.mnopedia.org/exclusion-integration-story-jews-minnesota.

11. W. Gunther Plaut, *The Jews in Minnesota: The First Seventy-Five* Years (New York: American Jewish Historical Society, 1959), 30–31.

12. Ibid., 58-59.

13. MNopedia website, "From Exclusion to Integration."

14. Ibid.

15. Oscar Handlin, *A Continuing Task: The American Jewish Joint Distribution Committee, 1914-1964* (New York: Random House, 1964), 5–24.

16. Ibid. See also Yehuda Bauer, *My Brother's Keeper: A History of the American Jewish Joint Distribution Committee, 1929-1939* (Philadelphia, Jewish Publication Society, 1974), 6–9; *I Live. Send Help.* exhibition text, introductory panel.

17. Linda Levi, telephone interview with the author, May 11, 2015; Marilyn Kushner, telephone interview with the author, May 13, 2015.

18. *I Live. Send Help.* exhibition texts.

19. Marilyn Kushner interview posted on the Leslie Rankow website, June 4, 2015, accessed March 1, 2016, https://leslierankow.wordpress.com/tag/i-live-send-help/.

20. Michael Kaminer, *The Forward*, June 26, 2014, accessed March 1, 2016, http://forward.com/the-assimilator/200776/100-years-of-the-joint/

21 Esther Nussbaum, Jewish Book Council book review, 2014, accessed March 1, 2016, http://www.jewishbookcouncil.org/book/i-live-send-help-100-years-of-jewish-history-in-images-from-the-jdc-archives.

22. Algemeiner website, July 21, 2014, accessed March 1, 2016, http://www.algemeiner.com/2014/07/31/turning-back-the-clock-jdc-exhibit-depicts-a-century-of-jewish-humanitarian-work/.

CHAPTER 9

COMMERCE AND CULTURE
Shaping American Culture

I N 1879, a fourteen-year-old Lithuanian Jewish boy named Jacob Epstein arrived in Baltimore. There, Epstein was outfitted by a wholesaler who supplied goods on credit, then hit the road as an itinerant peddler. "After two years of tramping through Maryland, West Virginia, and Pennsylvania, he had saved up enough money to return to Baltimore and open his own store," writes Deborah Weiner. From the outset, Epstein began recruiting and supplying immigrant Jewish peddlers; over time, his Baltimore Bargain House provided goods and guidance to thousands of peddlers, storekeepers, and merchants across the South. By 1920, Epstein's Baltimore Bargain House was the nation's fourth largest wholesaler.[1]

Epstein's success was no accident, but rather the product of his marketing strategies. From his own experience, Epstein knew both *his* customers and *their* customers. He also thought ahead, identifying regions along new transportation routes with growing market potential. He maintained personal contact with his customers, offered advice, and gave them presents to mark occasions such as bar mitzvahs and weddings. He also invited merchants to his showrooms to look over his merchandise, to travel by chartered steamship to Baltimore at his expense (and without obligation to buy), and to make themselves "perfectly at home" when they came. Epstein systematized the relationship between wholesaler and retailer by establishing a "one-price" policy, and in the 1890s he began distributing catalogs directly to retailers, dispensing with salesmen and undercutting his competitors. By the 1910s, he was distributing 160,000 catalogs a year.[2]

The Baltimore Bargain House catalogs advertised an array of merchandise, not only the sundries and notions carried by peddlers, but also clothing, dry goods, jewelry, furniture, and appliances. "The catalogues did not just hawk the products," Weiner writes, "they offered information and advice on how to be a successful retailer. . . . Catalogue articles encouraged small-town merchants to respond to the fashions of the times and provided tips on how to do so. One 1906 catalogue urged: 'No matter how small your town may be—no matter how modest your business—it will pay you well, to . . . touch the limit of up-to-dateness. Modern folks are not content with the sort of stores that served their parents and grandparents. People nowadays . . . keep abreast of the times; they know what is going on outside their own communities.' . . . 'Any clerk can sell what is asked for if he has it in stock. Selling what is not asked for is where *real salesmanship* comes in.'" Epstein was "in the vanguard of the modernization of American consumer culture," Weiner argues. By connecting America's industrial cities to rural areas, he "exemplified the networks that created southern Jewish communities and enabled Jews to have a marked impact on American consumerism."[3]

If we are looking for Jewish cultural expressions that shape vernacular culture at the local level, then we need to look carefully at commerce. Here, de Toqueville points us in a useful direction: "In democratic societies nothing is greater or more brilliant than commerce," he wrote. Expanding on this theme, Stephen Whitfield writes, "Jewish immigrants encountered and adapted to a culture fixated on the notion of personal happiness," and they quickly embraced "the sensibility of the national culture: happiness as a right and expectation." From the itinerant peddler through the department store owner, the movie mogul, and the museum trustee, "the Jew, too, could believe that desires could be satisfied."[4] Over 250 years, from the eighteenth century to the present day, Jewish peddlers, merchants, and manufacturers have fed Americans' aspirations for material goods. The primary argument of this chapter is that at local, regional, and national levels, Jews have been agents of modernity, not only in entertainment, the arts, literature, and learning, not only in developing the mass media, but also by promoting the consumer revolution in America.

The Consumer Revolution Begins

From the outset, the American colonies were market-oriented—outposts of merchant capitalism whose very survival, as Ronald Seavoy claims, "depended upon maritime commerce." Although subsistence farming persisted in the New World, most settlers aimed to produce marketable commodities—tobacco, wheat, livestock, timber, and so on—and to transport them to local and international customers. The multiplication of roadways and the growing number of wagons and carts are signifiers of the impulse to participate in the market economy. This commercial outlook fueled the first stirrings of what we now term the consumer revolution. In fact, consumer culture began to take effect as early as the eighteenth century. Recent studies by scholars such as Christina Hodge and others suggest that aspirations for material goods were not confined to the wealthy elite, but that middling consumers were early adopters of genteel material practices.[5]

The material advances of the eighteenth century provided unprecedented access to novel things, both in England and in its colonies. Ownership of new fashions "extended far down the social scale," argues John Styles, "to the small farmers, day laborers, and petty tradespeople." These transactions were not just a matter of getting and spending, but also included the ways in which acquisitions were understood. In addition to physical comfort, durable and semi-durable goods were also stores of wealth, "emblems of self-advancement, markers of social distinction, or badges of personal identity." Clothing was the focus of much plebeian consumption: "I made shift . . . and a little credit to raise a genteel suit of clothes, fully adequate to the sphere in which I moved," a clerk reminisced about his youth in 1741. "The girls eyed me with some attention; nay, I eyed myself as much as any of them." Ownership of best and working clothes began to pervade the life practices of the middling sort, and clothing of the better sort was starting to be sourced commercially.[6]

In the American colonies, cities were the centers of the emergent consumer culture. They were the entrepôts of commerce, the places where cloth and clothing, furniture and furnishings, tablewares and cookwares, jewelry and finery, spices, herbs, books, newspapers, and information circulated to the growing seaboard markets. Scattered Jewish storekeepers and traders lived in the backwoods of Pennsylvania, New York, Virginia, and the Carolinas, but most of the small number of Jews in the colonies were drawn to the cities—Newport, New York, Philadelphia, Charleston, and Savannah—where they were merchants, shopkeepers, artisans, and traders, and where their ethnic networks could support their commercial ventures. They "traded throughout the Atlantic world, linking North America with Europe and the Indies," as Hasia Diner puts it. "Trade made the colonies and Jews made trade."[7] By the mid-eighteenth century, a few hundred Jews "accounted for possibly 15 percent of the colonies' import-export firms, dealing largely in cocoa, rum, wine, fur and textiles."[8]

Foot Soldiers in the Army of Commerce

The outsize success of a few Jewish merchant princes and the predominance of petty traders in the colonial period obscures the presence of Jewish peddlers, whose commercial activity became significant in American culture in the nineteenth and early twentieth centuries. Before then, the Jewish peddler was a stock character in the European commercial landscape. Mostly on foot, occasionally driving a cart or wagon, these itinerants acted as middlemen between Christian peasants (and other Jews) and the marketplace. Peddlers, almost exclusively men, carried their stock of goods and information from farm to farm, where their customers were mostly women purchasing cloth and sundries. In Europe, peddling was a family trade, passed down from one generation to the next; in America, peddling became a path to economic and social advancement for thousands of immigrant Jewish men.[9]

Until the 1820s, Jewish migration to America remained quite small: the total Jewish population was only around 3,000 in 1820. But over the next sixty years, nearly a quarter million Jews immigrated to the United States, pushed by conditions in Europe and pulled by the lure of growing economic opportunity. Throughout the nineteenth century, settlement in the South, the Midwest, and the West opened up new fields of commerce. Industrial manufactures grew rapidly, despite panics and depressions, and American commerce expanded as roads, canals, and railroads created regional and then national markets. In turn, these expanded markets fed a growing appetite for consumer

Figure 9.1 An itinerant peddler shows off his household goods to a country family. "The Peddler's Wagon," in *Harper's Weekly*, June 20, 1868.

Courtesy of the Prints and Photographs Division, Library of Congress.

items. In rural areas, with dispersed populations and limited access to urban markets, Jewish peddlers played a key role in connecting isolated households to the products of urban, industrial culture.[10]

Peddling was sometimes dangerous and always demanding. Besides the exhaustion of lugging a 160-pound sack of goods across rough roads, peddlers had to meet the challenge of connecting with their customers. Unlike storekeepers, street vendors, and sales agents, peddlers had to enter their Christian customers' homes, to communicate, and to win their customers' confidence. For new immigrants from central and eastern Europe, language barriers intensified the challenge. To succeed, the newcomers had to develop the skills required to win over their customers, since most Jewish immigrants were not experienced peddlers in their former lands. They did, however, come from a culture where trade and commerce were mainstays of the ethnic economy; many were literate and numerate; and most were able to secure an initial stock of goods from a Jewish supplier or storekeeper. The peddler's willingness to haggle over price, to undersell local retailers, and to sell their goods on an installment plan benefitted them in their new trade.[11]

Thomas D. Clark of Winston County, Mississippi, recalled the arrival of the Jewish peddler, opening his pack so that "all the wonders of the commercial world seemed to pop up before our eyes." According to Diner, Jewish peddlers "tapped into and cultivated new standards of consumption," transforming the material life of rural America.

"From the depths of his pack he brought out for display sheets and pillowcases, pictures and picture frames, clothing and cloth, needles, threads, buttons, lace, bedspreads and tablecloths, eyeglasses, suspenders. The list went on and on, as this paradigmatic peddler moved up the ladder and managed to acquire a horse and wagon. Then the goods got bigger and heavier, stoves and bathtubs, still representing the cosmopolitan standard of consumption, associated with cities, modernity, and the lifestyles of the better-off classes." As middlemen, Jewish peddlers made available city-made and imported goods to millions of scattered customers, cultivating new aspirations for comfort and luxury and new modes of consumption.[12]

At the Crossroads and Along Main Street

Peddling was in many cases only the initial step for new immigrants to grow their commercial opportunities. Peddlers not only sold but also bought rags, scrap metals, and second-hand clothes, resulting in ownership of used-clothing shops and scrap yards. Some who succeeded as peddlers, like Jacob Epstein, became suppliers of peddler's wares to other newcomers. And many peddlers were able to accumulate enough cash, credit, and experience to establish their own stores, often specializing in the goods they were used to peddling—cloth, clothing, jewelry, and sundries. They were joined by thousands of other Jewish immigrants who had prepared themselves for shop ownership as clerks, traders, salesmen, and dealers, either in Europe or in America. By the Civil War, hundreds of American communities featured Jewish-owned stores, and this number expanded rapidly after 1880 with the influx of Jews from eastern Europe and the rapid growth of the American economy.[13]

A look at Jewish commercial activity in a single community is instructive. As the online *Encyclopedia of Southern Jewish Communities* reports, at the outset of the Civil War, only seven Jewish families, most of them shopkeepers, lived in Knoxville, Tennessee, among 3,000 gentiles. In the late nineteenth century, a growing number of Jews settled in town, among them new immigrants from eastern Europe. Peddlers sponsored by the Baltimore Bargain House used Knoxville as their base of operations and several opened small stores. Some of the most successful newcomers erected landmark buildings, including the M. B. Arnstein department store and the Finklestein Building. For a long time, most Knoxville Jews were merchants, and Jewish-owned clothing, hardware, and jewelry stores lined the downtown. As late as 1971, merchant families still constituted about two-thirds of the Jewish community.[14]

The range of Jewish-owned businesses was wide. Dry goods and general stores were common in villages and small towns; specialty stores—clothing, shoes, hardware, furniture, sundries, jewelry, appliances, and the like—were opened in larger towns and cities. In keeping with their role as promoters of the new and fashionable, even modest establishments advertised themselves in terms that evoked the modern, the urbane, and the sophisticated. Stores named after Paris or New York were common; so were names like the Palace, the Grand, and the Globe. When Thomas Wolfe of Asheville, North Carolina, went to Paris, he joked that the Bon Marche must have been named after the one in

Figure 9.2 A retail store that sells "Everything and Anything" promises "death to high prices" in this amusing trade card publicizing E. Wineburgh & Co. in Portland, Oregon.

Courtesy of The Arnold and Deanne Kaplan Collection of Early American Judaica. Library at the Herbert D. Katz Center for Advanced Judaic Studies, Kislak Center for Special Collections, Rare Books and Manuscripts, University of Pennsylvania.

Asheville. And, after the Civil War, a new phenomenon—the department store—came into being as a "museum of merchandise," thanks in large measure to the midwifery of Jewish merchants.

Cathedrals of Commerce

The department store is a relatively new institution. Before the Civil War, small general stores were characteristic of the country towns, while larger specialty stores were typical of the cities. No one store provided both great variety and great scale under a single roof. Gradually, "cathedrals of commerce" and "museums of merchandise" emerged in the largest cities—New York, Chicago, and Philadelphia. Mass production made it possible for large stores to stock a wide range of items, which were organized in various "departments." The department stores employed new marketing strategies that emphasized modest cost and high volume. They fixed and marked their prices and encouraged shoppers to browse freely without making a purchase. And by the 1880s, department stores were well-established as a kind of "universal provider."[15]

Commercial success in America, from the 1870s into the post–World War II era, was epitomized by Jewish-owned department stores, whose names became synonymous with the growth of cities. Some of the best-known are those along the northeastern seaboard: Filene's in Boston; Macy's, Bergdorf Goodman, Saks Fifth Avenue, Abraham & Straus, and Bloomingdale's in New York; Gimbel's and Lit Brothers in Philadelphia; Hutzler's, Hecht's, and Hochschild Kohn's in Baltimore. But leading department stores were a national phenomenon. Stephen Whitfield provides a list of Jewish-owned department stores across the South, which included Garfinckel's in Washington, DC, Thalheimer's in Richmond, Goldsmith's in Memphis, Neiman-Marcus in Dallas, Sakowitz's in Houston, Godchaux's in New Orleans, Cohen Bros. in Jacksonville, and Rich's in Atlanta. The presence of these palaces of consumption runs across the country, from Nachman's in Newport News, Virginia, through Miller's in Chattanooga, Tennessee, to Goldwater's in Phoenix, Arizona, and on to I. Magnin in San Francisco, not to mention regional chains like the Hess Stores in Tennessee, Virginia, Kentucky, and Georgia, or the Lazarus Stores in Ohio, Indiana, and West Virginia. And in many smaller communities, there were stand-alone department stores like Pushin Brothers in Bowling Green, Kentucky, or Herpolsheimer's in Grand Rapids, Michigan.[16]

The department stores were typically housed in grand buildings designed in fashionable styles, and they incorporated reception areas, lavatories, changing rooms, beauty salons, restaurants, and tea rooms. New technologies—the elevator and escalator, electric lighting, plate glass display windows, ventilating systems, the telephone, and the pneumatic tube—were used to increase efficiency and to enhance service. Large staffs of buyers (who ran the departments), floorwalkers (who provided on-the-scene-supervision), salespeople, and service staff catered to customer needs and desires. The grand stores pioneered new advertising methods such as full-page ads in the daily newspapers. They ran seasonal and special sales. They sponsored parades, programs, events, and celebrations. And they promoted the idea of fashion. In the consumer economy, the market for luxuries

Figure 9.3 The women's department of Korrick's New York Department Store in Phoenix, Arizona, 1913.

Courtesy of the Pearl and Cecil Newmark Memorial Archives, Arizona Jewish Historical Society.

expanded and new markets were created for the latest fads, fashions, and innovations. Customers were encouraged to believe that by purchasing the right clothes, furniture, accessories, and foods, they could achieve status, success, and satisfaction, respectability, self-confidence, and even character. The great department stores became tastemakers and educators for the expanding middle class in communities across the country.

By the twentieth century, department stores had become icons of the new consumer culture that emphasized acquisition and personal gratification. They were also key features of the modern city, markers of urban health and dynamism. They made downtown a destination and shopping an experience. Before the closing decades of the nineteenth century, shopping had been a chore, undertaken for necessity rather than for pleasure. Until then, most stores were specialty shops, selections were limited, and customers were expected to buy if they entered the store. When department stores inaugurated a new era of display, browsing, and service, the shopping experience and women shoppers were elevated to a new plane. Previously, downtown had been a bastion of male culture and social life: the department store made downtown a cleaner, safer, and more inviting venue for women, feminizing the city's commercial center. This had a profound impact on the downtown in towns and cities, large and small.

Chains of Consumption

By the 1920s, department stores had begun to expand into chains—among them Gimbel's, the May Company, Allied, and Interstate. But the most prominent retail chain was Sears Roebuck. Sears was not founded by Jews, but in 1895 Julius Rosenwald (1862–1932), the son of a one-time peddler and clothing store owner, who was himself a successful clothing manufacturer, bought into the company. Rosenwald became Sears's de facto marketing director. "He brought to the company a rational management philosophy and diversified product lines: dry goods, consumer durables, drugs, hardware, furniture, and nearly anything else a household could desire. From 1895 to 1907, under Rosenwald's leadership as Vice President and Treasurer, annual sales of the company climbed from $750,000 to upwards of $50 million."[17] He also "set about establishing a new standard of quality control that significantly enhanced the firm's reputation and profitability. . . . By the time of Rosenwald's retirement as chairman in 1932 . . . the name Sears Roebuck had become perhaps the most respected in American business." It had also become the single largest retail chain in the world.[18]

Jews also led the way in promoting discount shopping. As *Business Day* reports, in the 1950s Eugene Ferkauf (1920–2012), the founder of E. J. Korvette, "was one of the first businessmen to grasp the emergence of a new breed of postwar consumer. Seeing a population of Americans financially better off, impatient to get on with their lives after World War II and susceptible to the advertising shown on the latest new thing, their television sets, he concluded that victory belonged to the very bold. Mr. Ferkauf would not only discount, he would discount more deeply than anyone ever had. Seeing people streaming to the suburbs, he imagined the sort of sprawling, free-standing, conveniently situated, no-frills variety store that came to define American retailing. After he built it, Sam Walton came to New York to pick his brain; two years later, Mr. Walton founded Wal-Mart. By the mid-1960s, the Korvette chain had dozens of stores, including one on Fifth Avenue in Manhattan, and scores of imitators had followed Mr. Ferkauf's model."[19]

When Ferkauf got started, discounting was limited by federal law. Korvettes got around this by offering free memberships to its customers and styling itself a "retail cooperative." Korvettes passed along discounts to its customers, despite fair trade suits from Gimbel's and Macy's, none of which was successful. The chain also adopted a low-price, low-service model similar to those of five-and-dime stores. At a time when most department stores were still located in central business districts, Korvettes focused on selling in strip malls in the suburbs, easily accessed by its rapidly growing population of suburban customers; larger stores incorporated supermarkets, tire centers, pharmacies, and pet stores, all attractive to suburbanites. And when it expanded into states with Blue Laws prohibiting sales on Sunday, Korvettes successfully challenged those laws. Although the business failed in the 1970s, Ferkauf's strategy of low prices, quick turnover, and high volume helped shape today's retail landscape, setting the stage for later discount chains such as Walmart and warehouse clubs such as Costco.[20]

Manufacturing American Style

Jewish success in commerce led directly to another well-known niche of ethnic entrepreneurship, the manufacture of ready-made clothing. Jewish involvement in the garment industry began with the *shmatte* (rag) and old clothes business, tailoring, and dry goods. But by the mid-nineteenth century, the manufacture of men's ready-to-wear started to assume industrial proportions and a small number of successful Jewish merchants had begun to enter the business. The Civil War, with its demand for millions of uniforms, hats, and shoes, vastly expanded the market, creating important opportunities for Jewish entrepreneurship. By the end of the nineteenth century, stitching and selling garments cut to standard sizes played a key role in the Jewish economy, becoming the most common occupation for new Jewish immigrants. By 1910, Jews accounted for a quarter of all those employed in the garment industry nationally, and an even larger share of those who cut and sewed cloaks, coats, suits, and shirtwaists.[21]

Coupled with innovative ways of marketing, such as grand emporia and mail-order catalogues, Jewish leadership, first in menswear and then in womenswear, had a profound effect on Americans' aspirations, taste, and style. Adam Mendelsohn writes that "As manufacturers began to churn out ever-larger quantities of ready-made garments in the second half of the nineteenth century, the producers and purveyors of clothing played a pivotal role in refashioning Americans into mass consumers."[22] Also, in a period of mass immigration, adoption of "American" clothing was the fastest and surest signifier of presenting an American image. "I was forever watching and striving to imitate the dress and the ways of the well-bred American merchants," said one man who arrived from eastern Europe, where his wardrobe featured coarse pants and rough textured shirts. "A whole book could be written on the influence of a starched collar and a necktie on a man who was brought up as I was."[23] As the clothing industry helped to make the Jews in America, their central role in parts of the modern clothing industry made Jews important players in American consumer culture.

Jewish makers of clothing have had a significant impact on American fashion and taste since the nineteenth century. Levi Strauss (1829–1902), an immigrant from Bavaria, won fame during the California Gold Rush by producing denim trousers reinforced with rivets (in partnership with Latvian immigrant Jacob Davis, who actually invented the riveted trousers). Blue jeans remain a staple of American fashion today. Latvian immigrant Moses Phillips began selling hand-sewn flannel shirts from a pushcart in Pottsville, Pennsylvania, in 1881; by the 1920s, he was partnered with John van Heusen and marketing the innovative soft-folding collar "that captured the stiff-collar look of the era while affording the wearer a more comfortable fit," becoming the top dress-shirt seller in America.[24] Ida Cohen Rosenthal (1886–1973), an immigrant from Russia, patented the modern bra (1926) and co-founded the world's leading bra manufacturer, the Maiden Form Brassiere Company in 1930, literally changing the shape of American women.[25] And Israel Myers created London Fog raincoats whose "design and pioneering use of

Compliments of

COHEN & KOENIGHEIM.

Figure 9.4 Trade card distributed by Cohen & Koenigheim, "The Stylish Clothiers," merchant tailors of San Antonio, Texas.

Courtesy of The Arnold and Deanne Kaplan Collection of Early American Judaica. Library at the Herbert D. Katz Center for Advanced Judaic Studies, Kislak Center for Special Collections, Rare Books and Manuscripts, University of Pennsylvania.

polyester blends helped Londontown become the dominant maker of men's coats in the United States in the 1960's and 70's," according to *The New York Times*.[26]

Jewish clothing designers have also come to the fore in the postwar period. Anne Klein (1923–1974; born Hannah Golofski) founded Junior Sophisticates—a clothing company that transformed the clothing styles, choices, and attitudes of young American women, making them "look more stylish, more polished, and, above all, more grown up."[27] Ralph Lauren (born Ralph Lipshitz in 1939) won a Coty Award in 1970 for his menswear line and soon after produced a full line of women's clothing; his company remains a leader in luxury clothing design under a variety of brand labels.[28] Calvin Klein (b. 1942) launched his own company in 1968. In 1974, he was the first designer to receive the Council of Fashion Designers of America award for outstanding design in both men's and women's wear.[29] Donna Karan (b. 1948) started her own business in 1984 "to design modern clothes for modern people" and was honored by the Council of Fashion Designers of America for her men's wear design (1992), women's wear design (1990 and 1996), and lifetime achievement (2004).[30] Jewish leadership in clothing design continues with figures such as Michael Kors, Isaac Mizrachi, Zac Posen, Charlotte Ronson, and Tamara Mimran. Parallel narratives can be constructed for Jews in cosmetics, footwear, and accessories. Meanwhile, Jews have retained leadership in the retailing of clothing. Leslie Wexner, owner of The Limited, Express, and Victoria's Secret, and Donald and Doris Fisher, owners of The Gap, Banana Republic, and Old Navy, are just two of the more prominent examples. [31]

The Soundscape of Our Lives

By the beginning of the twentieth century, the expansion of consumer culture and the development of new consumer-oriented industries opened doors for Jewish entrepreneurship, especially in the entertainment business. Popular music and the movies, to take just two examples, were fields where attentiveness to customer expectations, sensitivity to changing styles, and "networks that interconnected producers, distributors, and purveyors" helped to transform these new fields into Jewish ethnic niches. As Adam Mendelsohn remarks, "It was perhaps no accident that several Hollywood moguls and sheet music publishers started as salesmen in the clothing trade."[32] The outlook of these entertainment entrepreneurs, strikingly similar to their counterparts in commerce, is epitomized in the credo of Samuel L. "Roxy" Rothapfel (1882–1936): "Don't 'give the people what they want'—give 'em something better."[33]

As hard-headed businessmen, songwriters, sheet music publishers, theater owners, movie producers, and distributors tended to downplay narrowly ethnic content. They aimed instead to please as many as they could while off-putting as few as possible. As a result, generations of Jews in the entertainment world tended to underplay overtly Jewish content (including the Jewish identities of many popular stars). Rather than portray Jewish life—or even American life—as it is, it was "far more common for the Jews of Hollywood to imagine what the Gentile world has wanted to see of itself," Stephen Whitfield remarks.[34] This tendency can be seen in the work of Russian immigrant Irving Berlin (1888–1989), born Israel Isidore Balin, probably the most prolific and successful American songwriter. Berlin aimed to "reach the heart of the average American," which he did conspicuously in songs such as "Alexander's Ragtime Band," "White Christmas," "Easter Parade," "There's No Business Like Show Business," and "God Bless America."[35] From "Yonkle the Cowboy Jew" (sheet music published in 1908) through Bob Dylan (born Robert Zimmerman) and Steven Sondheim, Jewish songwriters have transcended cultural boundaries and adapted a wide range of styles. Even when a song was written in Yiddish with eastern European overtones, it could be translated into a mainstream vernacular. One classic example is "Bei Mir Bis Du Schein" (1932), written in Yiddish by Jacob Jacobs (lyricist) and Sholom Secunda (composer), transposed into English by Sammy Cahn, and sung in swing rhythm by the Greek-American Andrews Sisters—the first gold record by a female vocal group (1937).[36]

Similarly, Jewish pioneers and leaders in mass media—the movies, radio, and television—have helped to shape the forms and content of cultural consumption in America. (Jews have also been key figures in American literature, music, dance, the theater, the visual arts, and intellectual life, especially notable for injecting both wit and moral seriousness into these cultural forms. But here we are concerned primarily with popular and mass culture, the background and the enduring images of everyday American life.) We could almost say that "the soundtrack of our lives" and the shared imagery of American vernacular culture (mentalités) over the past century have been inflected, even in many instances composed, by Jews.[37]

These cultural expressions manifest concretely in our own communities, affecting our lives and those of our families, friends, and neighbors as a look at local cultural venues suggests. In many places, the vaudeville theater, opera house, or movie theater was owned or managed by Jews. In Alabama, for example, Polish immigrant Louis Rosenbaum opened a number of grand movie theaters, including the Princess and the Majestic in Florence, as well as theaters in Tuscaloosa, Sheffield, and Athens.[38] From the 1890s into the 1930s, Jews were powers in the regional vaudeville circuits. Morris Meyerfield, Jr., known as "the Rockefeller of Vaudeville," was a principal organizer of the Orpheum Circuit, which for many years dominated vaudeville bookings from Cincinnati west to the coast. Likewise, when local theaters presented the hit plays and musicals of the day, the source was most often one of the Broadway theater chains dominated by a handful of Jewish theater owners and producers such as Abraham Lincoln Erlanger, Charles Frohman, the Shubert brothers, and the Nederlander family.[39] Both the local venues and the content of popular culture reflect the outsize influence of Jews in show biz.

For Sale: A New Way of Life

Advertising and marketing are key elements of modern consumer culture, powerful forces for shaping our aspirations and acquisitions. Throughout the twentieth century, Jews have been pioneers and leaders in promoting ways to sell everything from shampoo to television shows, politicians to suburban developments. Edward Bernays (1891–1995), an Austrian Jewish immigrant, set up shop in 1919 as a public relations counsel. Today he is recognized as "the father of public relations" and a pioneer in what he termed "the engineering of consent." In addition to refining and promoting the use of press releases and making use of the social sciences, Bernays was known for orchestrating elaborate corporate advertising campaigns and multimedia consumer spectacles on behalf of clients such as Proctor & Gamble, General Electric, and the American Tobacco Company. In 1924, Benjamin Sonnenberg (1901–1978), a Russian Jewish immigrant, opened his public relations firm, describing himself as "a cabinetmaker who fashioned large pedestals for small statues." Among his clients were CBS, Lever Brothers, and Pan American World Airways. Carl R. Byoir (1886–1957), a Polish Jewish immigrant, went into business in 1930; in time, his public relations firm became one of the largest in the country. Among his notable campaigns was one to establish the March of Dimes; another—on behalf of the Great Atlantic and Pacific Tea Company (aka A&P), then one of the largest retailers in the world—was designed to protect chain stores from restrictive federal legislation.[40] The work of these public relations pioneers was complemented by Albert Lasker and William Bernbach in advertising, Ernest Dichter in market research, and Paul Lazarsfeld in applied psychology.[41]

Through the first half of the twentieth century, the marketing of consumer culture continued apace, despite the crises of depression and war. By the end of World War II, William J. Levitt (1907–1994) could set out to create and market a whole new community and way of life in Levittown, Long Island (1947). Neither suburbs nor planned communities were novelties in America. But what distinguished Levittown was its scale and methods. Levitt's innovation in creating this planned community was to "build the houses in the manner of an assembly line, where specialized workers with a specific task moved from house to house as they were constructed en masse." Priced modestly, the houses of Levittown were affordable for returning veterans and their families—and the timing was perfect to meet the demand for new homes that was pent-up throughout World War II as production was concentrated on military needs. Responding to rising levels of aspiration, each house was landscaped and equipped with appliances. Ultimately Levittown grew to seventeen thousand homes, earning Levitt the title of "father of modern American suburbia" and recognition from *Time* magazine as one of the "100 Most Influential People of the 20th Century."[42]

Shaping the American Dream

Throughout the twentieth century, Jewish writers and intellectuals have been instrumental in shaping our national vision as an inclusive society. Jews have coined and popularized the lexicon of American pluralism. Israel Zangwell (1864–1926) popularized the metaphorical phrase "the melting pot" in his 1909 play of the same name, which "celebrated America"s capacity to absorb and grow from the contributions of its immigrants." Starting in 1915, philosopher Horace M. Kallen (1882–1974) championed "cultural pluralism," "the ideal that cultural diversity and national pride were compatible with each other and that ethnic and racial diversity strengthened America." Another popular formulation of pluralism, this time in religious terms, was offered by Will Herberg in his 1955 best-selling book, *Protestant, Catholic, Jew: An Essay in American Religious Sociology*. In recent decades, a number of Jewish academics have been proponents of multiculturalism as a paradigm for American society.[43]

As we have seen, Jewish efforts to shape our views of the world have been more than abstract or conceptual. In hundreds of locales across the continent, we can see concrete reminders of Jewish cultural expression in stores, theaters, suburban tract developments, and community organizations. In Florence, Alabama, Louis Rosenbaum and his son, Samuel, donated $40,000 to fund the first public library, while the Rauh Memorial Library in Indianapolis honors a pioneer industrialist. In Helena, Arkansas, the declining Jewish community donated its synagogue to the state for use as a community arts center; the Strauss Theater Center (1961) in Monroe, Louisiana, honors a local philanthropist and civic leader. The Masur Museum of Art (1964), also in Monroe, the Levine Museum of the New South in Charlotte, North Carolina, and the Museum of Science and Industry in Chicago (originally the Rosenwald Museum of Science and Industry) are among the many public museums founded or supported by Jewish cultural patrons. Other civic-minded Jews have been honored by the naming of public parks and gardens, including the Goldberg and Joseph Memorial Park in Wilburton, Oklahoma, Herz Park in Terre Haute, Indiana, and Brand Park in San Fernando, California.[44]

As the writer Jill Robinson put it (exaggerating a bit), "The American Dream is a Jewish invention."[45] Robinson was referring to the world projected by Hollywood movies in the heyday of the studio system. But it is certainly fair to say that Jews have been instrumental in promoting our intellectual, literary, and artistic life, our media of mass communication, and our modern consumer culture, with its aspirations for personal realization and the comforts of communal affluence.

Notes

1. Deborah R. Weiner, "Filling the Peddler's Pack: Southern Jews and Jacob Epstein's Baltimore Bargain House." Paper delivered at the Southern Jewish Historical Society Annual Conference, Baltimore, November 5, 2005.

2. Ibid.

3. Ibid.

4. Stephen J. Whitfield, "American Jewish Culture," in *The Meaning of the American Jewish Experience: A Joint Conference of the American Jewish Committee and Brandeis University* (Waltham: Brandeis University Press, 2004), 12.

5. Ronald E. Seavoy, *An Economic History of the United States from 1607 to the Present* (New York: Routledge, 2008), 7, 32, 37, 55. See also Christina J. Hodge, *Consumerism and the Emergence of the Middle Class in Colonial America* (New York: Cambridge University Press, 2014); T. H. Breen, *The Marketplace of Revolution: How Consumer Politics Shaped American Independence* (New York: Oxford University Press, 2004); Jan de Vries, *The Industrious Revolution: Consumer behavior and the Household Economy, 1650 to the Present* (New York: Cambridge University Press, 2008); Cary Carson, Ronald Hoffman, and Peter J. Albert, eds., *Of Consuming Interests: The Style of Life in the Eighteenth* Century (Charlottesville: University Press of Virginia, 1994).

6. John Styles, *The Dress of the People: Everyday Fashion in Eighteenth Century England* (New Haven: Yale University Press, 2007), 1, 321ff.

7. Hasia Diner, *The Jews of the United States, 1654 to 2000* (Berkeley: University of California Press, 2004), 20–29.

8. Howard M. Sachar, *A History of the Jews in America* (Vintage Books: New York, 1993), 21.

9. Hasia Diner, *Roads Taken: The Great Jewish Migrations to the New World and the Peddlers Who Forged the* Way (New Haven: Yale University Press, 2015), 40f., 65, *passim*.

10. Ibid., 99, 159.

11. Ibid., 65, 86, 164–65.

12. Ibid., quote 111, 4, and 112.

13. Ibid., 61, 164–65. Sachar, *History of the Jews*, 53–61.

14. *Encyclopedia of Southern Jewish Communities* website, s.v. "Knoxville, Tennessee," accessed December 22, 2015, http://www.isjl.org/tennessee-knoxville-encyclopedia.html. A few outstanding community studies confirm the key role Jews played as middlemen in the local economy, among them Deborah R. Weiner, *Coalfield Jews: An Appalachian History* (Urbana: University of

Illinois Press, 2008) and Ewa Morawska, *Insecure Prosperity: Small-Town Jews in Industrial America, 1890-1940* (Princeton: Princeton University Press, 1999).

15. Avi Y. Decter, "Introduction: Memory and Meaning in Baltimore's Jewish-Owned Department Stores," in *Enterprising Emporiums: The Jewish Department Stores of Downtown Baltimore*, eds. Avi Y. Decter and Juliana Ochs Dweck (Baltimore: Jewish Museum of Maryland, 2001), 4–5.

16. Stephen J. Whitfield, *American Space, Jewish Time* (Hamden, CT: Archon Books, 1988), 233; *Wikipedia*, s.v. "Hess's," accessed December 22, 2015, https://en.wikipedia.org/wiki/Hess's; *Wikipedia*, s.v. "Lazarus (department store)," accessed December 22, 2015, https://en.wikipedia.org/wiki/Lazarus_%28department_store%29.

17. *Wikipedia*, s.v. "Julius Rosenwald," accessed December 23, 2015, https://en.wikipedia.org/wiki/Julius_Rosenwald.

18. Sachar, *History of the Jews*, 336.

19. *New York Times* online, "Eugene Ferkauf," accessed December 23, 2015, http://www.nytimes.com/2012/06/07/business/eugene-ferkauf-founder-of-e-j-korvette-chain-dies-at-91.html?_r=0.

20. *Wikipedia*, s.v. "E.J. Korvette," accessed December 23, 2015, https://en.wikipedia.org/wiki/E._J._Korvette.

21. Adam D. Mendelsohn, *The Rag Race: How Jews Sewed their Way to Success in America and the British Empire* (New York: New York University Press, 2015).

22. Mendelsohn, *Rag Race*, 7.

23. Johanna Neumann, "From Ghetto to Glamour—How Jews Redesigned the Fashion Business," Jewish Virtual Library website, accessed January 4, 2016, http://www.jewishvirtuallibrary.org/jsource/History/NeumanFashion.html.

24. Ibid.

25. *JWA Encyclopedia* website, s.v., "Ida Cohen Rosenthal," accessed January 4, 2016, jwa.org/encyclopedia/article/rosenthal-ida-cohen.

26. *New York Times* online, "Israel Myers," accessed December 23, 2015, http://www.nytimes.com/1999/12/31/business/israel-myers-is-dead-at-93-originated-london-fog-coat.html.

27. *Wikipedia*, s.v., "Anne Klein," accessed January 4, 2016, https://en.wikipedia.org/wiki/Anne_Klein.

28. *Wikipedia*, s.v., "Ralph Lauren," accessed January 4, 2016, https://en.wikipedia.org/wiki/Ralph_Lauren.

29. *Wikipedia*, s.v., "Calvin Klein," accessed December 23, 2015, https://en.wikipedia.org/wiki/Calvin_Klein.

30. *Wikipedia*, s.v., "Donna Karan," accessed December 23, 2015, https://en.wikipedia.org/wiki/Donna_Karan.

31. See, for example, *Wikipedia*, s.v., accessed January 4, 2016, "Helena Rubenstein," http://jwa.org/encyclopedia/article/rubinstein-helena; "Estee Lauder," https://en.wikipedia.org/wiki/Est%C3%A9e_Lauder_%28businesswoman%29; "Kenneth Cole," https://en.wikipedia.org/wiki/Kenneth_Cole_%28designer%29; and "Marc Jacobs," https://en.wikipedia.org/wiki/Marc_Jacobs.

32. Mendelsohn, *Rag Race*, 222.

33. Quoted in Robert Sklar, *Movie-Made America: A Cultural History of American Movies* (New York: Vintage Books, 1975), 41. See also *Wikipedia*, "Samuel Lionel 'Roxy' Rothafel," accessed January 4, 2016, https://en.wikipedia.org/wiki/Samuel_Roxy_Rothafel; Ross Melnick, *American Showman: Samuel "Roxy" Rothafel and the Birth of the Entertainment Industry, 1908-1935* (New York: Columbia University Press, 2012).

34. Stephen J. Whitfield, *Voices of Jacob, Hands of Esau: Jews in American Life and Thought* (Hamden, CT: Archon Books, 1984), 69. See also David Zurawik, *The Jews of Prime Time* (Hanover, NH: University Press of New England, 2005); David Lehman, *A Fine Romance: Jewish*

Songwriters, American Songs (New York: Nextbook, 2009).

35. *Wikipedia*, s.v., "Irving Berlin," accessed January 4, 2016, https://en.wikipedia.org/wiki/Irving_Berlin.

36. *Wikipedia*, s.v., accessed December 23, 2015, "Alexander's Ragtime Band," https://en.wikipedia.org/wiki/Alexander's_Ragtime_Band; "Strange Fruit," https://en.wikipedia.org/wiki/Strange_Fruit; and "Bei Mir Bistu Shein [*sic*]," https://en.wikipedia.org/wiki/Bei_Mir_Bistu_Shein.

37. This also links to the complex interactions of African Americans and Jews in popular culture. See Jeffrey Melnick, *A Right to Sing the Blues: African-Americans, Jews, and American Popular Song* (Cambridge, MA: Harvard University Press, 1999); Michael Rogin, *Blackface, White Noise: Jewish Immigrants in the Hollywood Melting Pot* (Berkeley: University of California Press, 1996).

38. Louis Rosenbaum's son and daughter-in-law, Stanley and Mildred Rosenbaum, commissioned Frank Lloyd Wright to design their home (which is discussed in chapter 5); their son, Jonathan Rosenbaum, grew up in Florence, Alabama, and became a leading film critic.

39. Howard Sachar, *History of Jews*, 353ff.; *Encyclopedia of Southern Jewish Communities* website, s.v., "Florence, Alabama," accessed December 22, 2015, http://www.isjl.org/alabama-florence-encyclopedia.html; *Wikipedia*, s.v., "Morris Meyerfield," accessed December 22, 2015, https://en.wikipedia.org/wiki/Morris_Meyerfield,_Jr.; *Wikipedia*, s.v., "Orpheum Circuit," accessed December 22, 2015, https://en.wikipedia.org/wiki/Orpheum_Circuit.

40. *Wikipedia*, s.v., accessed January 5, 2016, "Edward Bernays," https://en.wikipedia.org/wiki/Edward_Bernays; "Benjamin Sonnenberg," https://en.wikipedia.org/wiki/Benjamin_Sonnenberg; and "Carl R. Byoir," https://en.wikipedia.org/wiki/Carl_R._Byoir.

41 *Wikipedia*, s.v., accessed January 5, 2016, "Albert Lasker," https://en.wikipedia.org/wiki/Albert_Lasker; "William Bernbach," https://en.wikipedia.org/wiki/William_Bernbach; "Ernest Dichter," https://en.wikipedia.org/wiki/Ernest_Dichter; "Paul Lazarsfeld," https://en.wikipedia.org/wiki/Paul_Lazarsfeld.

42. *Wikipedia*, s.v., "William Levitt,"" accessed December 23, 2015, https://en.wikipedia.org/wiki/William_Levitt.

43. Joe Kraus, "How The Melting Pot Stirred America: The Reception of Zangwill's Play and Theater's Role in the American Assimilation Experience," *MELUS*, 24, no. 3, "Varieties of Ethnic Criticism" (Autumn 1999): 3–19; *Wikipedia*, s.v., "Horace Kallen," accessed December 21, 2015, https://en.wikipedia.org/wiki/Horace_Kallen; Sachar, *History of Jews*, 425ff,

44. *Encyclopedia of Jewish Communities* website, s.v., accessed December 21, 2015, "Florence, Alabama," http://www.isjl.org/alabama-florence-encyclopedia.html; "Helena, Arkansas," http://www.isjl.org/arkansas-helena-encyclopedia.html; "Monroe, Louisiana," http://www.isjl.org/louisiana-monroe-encyclopedia.html. Bernard Postal and Lionel Koppman, *A Jewish Tourist's Guide to the U.S.* (Philadelphia: Jewish Publication Society, 1954), 55, 151, 167, 169.

45. Quoted in Kenneth Turan, "Letting Jews Be Jews," in *Jews in the Los Angeles Mosaic*, ed. Karen S. Wilson (Los Angeles: Autry Center of the American West, 2013), 47.

Select Bibliography

Diner, Hasia R. *Roads Taken: The Great Jewish Migrations to the New World and the Peddlers Who Forged the Way.* New Haven: Yale University Press, 2015.

Hoberman, J., and Jeffrey Shandler, eds. *Entertaining America: Jews, Movies, and Broadcasting.* New York: The Jewish Museum, 2003.

Joselit, Jenna Weissman. *A Perfect Fit: Clothes, Character, and the Promise of America.* New York: Metropolitan Books, 2001.

Lehman, David. *A Fine Romance: Jewish Songwriters, American Songs*. New York: Nextbook, 2009.

Martens, Melissa, and Avi Y. Decter, eds. *Enterprising Emporiums: The Jewish Department Stores of Downtown Baltimore*. Baltimore: Jewish Museum of Maryland, 2001.

Melnick, Jeffery. *A Right to Sing the Blues: African Americans, Jews, and American Popular Song*. Cambridge: Harvard University Press, 1999.

Mendelsohn, Adam D. *The Rag Race: How Jews Sewed Their Way to Success in America and the British Empire*. New York: New York University Press, 2015.

Rogin, Michael, *Blackface, White Noise: Jewish Immigrants in the Hollywood Melting Pot*. Berkeley: University of California Press, 1996.

Schrerer, Barbara A. *Becoming American Women: Clothing and the Jewish Immigrant Experience, 1880-1920*. Chicago: Chicago Historical Society, 1994.

Whitfield, Stephen J. *American Space, Jewish Time*. Hamden, CT: Archon Books, 1988.

Whitfield, Stephen J. *In Search of American Jewish Culture*. Hanover, NH: University Press of New England, 1999.

Whitfield, Stephen J. *Voices of Jacob, Hands of Esau: Jews in American Life and Thought*. Hamden, CT: Archon Books, 1984.

Zurawik, David. *The Jews of Prime Time*. Hanover, NH: University Press of New England, 2003.

CHAPTER 10

CASE STUDIES

Shaping American Culture

IN THE PREVIOUS chapter, emphasis has been put on expressions of Jewish culture that are readily found in communities large and small across the continent, especially the Jewish role in shaping American consumer culture. The case studies that follow, on the other hand, constitute a kind of counterpoint to that chapter, focusing on expressions of Jewish culture that have had an influence on more conventional categories of culture—the performing and visual arts. Here the disproportionate concentration of Jews in large urban centers—New York and Los Angeles, in particular—is strongly felt.

The first case study is of a Judaic Art Gallery in Raleigh, North Carolina, which presents masterpieces of Judaica, or ceremonial art. The second study describes a video on a living klezmer musician that was produced by the Philadelphia Folklore Project, which involved a reconsideration of standard accounts of that genre of Jewish music. Jumping back in time, the new Crystal Bridges Museum of American Art in Bentonville, Arkansas, interprets a suite of early American family portraits. The Museum of the City of New York just recently mounted a major exhibition on New York's Yiddish theater, while the American Library Association and dozens of local libraries have presented the story of Jewish composers and songwriters whose work has shaped the American Songbook. Despite their variety of subject and approaches, these initiatives suggest some of the many possibilities for presenting and interpreting the important role of Jews in the shaping of American culture.

Judaic Art Gallery

North Carolina Museum of Art

In 1971, Abram Kanof, a retired physician, moved from New York City to Raleigh, North Carolina. Dr. Kanof was not only a physician but also a collector and expert on

Jewish ceremonial art (Judaica). He had served as the president of the American Jewish Historical Society and as a board member of The Jewish Museum in New York, where he and his wife established the Tobe Pascher Workshop for Modern Jewish Art. Passionate about his avocation, Kanof gravitated to the North Carolina Museum of Art (NCMA). And in 1975 he convinced the NCMA director, Moussa Domit (a Lebanese American), to mount an exhibition of "Ceremonial Art in the Judaic Tradition."[1]

The exhibition proved to be both a critical and popular success. Building on that, Dr. Kanof convinced the NCMA to establish a permanent Judaic Art Gallery, seeding it with select objects from his personal collection. Initially, the Judaic Art Gallery occupied a modest "jewel-box" gallery in the NCMA's 1983 building. But when the NCMA opened its new and vastly larger West Building in 2010, the Judaic Art Gallery was given a larger dedicated space. Less than five years later, the Judaic Art Gallery was expanded yet again. Today it occupies around 1,700 square feet of space, with about sixty works of ceremonial art showcased in new custom vitrines and featured on public and school tours and "art encounters."

For many years, Dr. Kanof led efforts to promote the display and interpretation of Judaica at NCMA, first as an adjunct curator and then as a popular docent. Working closely with John Coffey, the museum's curator of American and modern art and later deputy director for art (and a self-described "lapsed Presbyterian"), Kanof was able to add new items to the display. "From the beginning the Judaic Art Gallery expressed Abe Kanof's ecumenical vision," writes Coffey. "He knew that his audience was predominantly not Jewish. What he hoped to create was a place accessible to all where the spiritual and cultural life of the Jewish people could be both celebrated and shared through memorable works of art."[2]

Kanof and Coffey reinstalled the gallery in 1996 and published the first *Guide to the Judaic Art Collection of the North Carolina Museum of Art*, with an essay by Dr. Kanof. In 2001, two years after Dr. Kanof's demise, Coffey worked with Kanof's friends and family to establish the statewide Friends of the Judaic Art Gallery, with the aim of supporting the gallery's mission and role at NCMA. The Friends group has funded an ongoing and ambitious program of acquisitions and underwritten gallery improvements, curatorial research, object conservation, long-term loans from New York's Jewish Museum, and a variety of educational initiatives.

Today, the Judaic Art Gallery "celebrates the spiritual and cultural life of the Jewish people through the splendor and artistry of ceremonial objects."[3] The gallery comprises an introduction with highlights of the collection, decorative ornaments for the Torah and synagogue use, and objects for celebration of the Sabbath, festivals, and life cycle events in the Jewish home. While much of the collection features objects from Europe, the Middle East, and Asia, the gallery also displays masterpieces by such modernists as Ludwig Yehuda Wolpert and Moshe Zabari, both of whom were active at the Tobe Pascher Workshop in New York starting in the 1950s. Gabriel Goldstein, former deputy director of the Yeshiva University Museum and a leading consultant on Judaica, describes the NCMA space as "a major gallery with beautiful art exhibited in an elegant and exciting way."[4] "The Judaica has been selected for its beauty, aesthetic and historical resonance,

Figure 10.1 Visitors at the Judaic Art Gallery, North Carolina Museum of Art, viewing *Standing Hanukkah Lamp*, designed c. 1926 by Ze'ev Raban of the Bezalel Workshop, Jerusalem (2005.8).

Photo by Karen Malinofski. Courtesy of the North Carolina Museum of Art.

and masterful craftsmanship, along with its spiritual and religious significance," he says. "The objects hold their own among the NCMA's art treasures."[5]

"The Judaic Art Gallery is one of the true gems of the North Carolina Museum of Art," says Lawrence Wheeler, the museum's director. "First-time visitors are surprised, then delighted to find a gallery devoted to Jewish ceremonial art. It is one of the things that gives the museum its distinctive character."[6] "Our collection is driven by so much Christian subject matter," he says, "to have another perspective on celebrating faith is interesting to people."[7] "We endeavor not only to preserve and display these beautifully crafted objects, but also to serve as a forum for religious and cultural understanding."[8] As plans mature and resources allow, the Judaic Art Gallery will continue to grow its role as a site of cross-cultural discourse.

"The problem with Judaica, until recently, was that it was an amateur calling," says John Coffey, the curator who has overseen the Judaic Art Gallery since Kanof's death. "It was a hobby without rigorous scholarship attached to it, like other decorative arts. I'd like to raise the level of quality to the same as the Old Masters we have. And that is what we are doing."[9] But approaches on how to organize these efforts differ. The NCMA Judaic Art Gallery is one of just three permanent displays of Judaica in North American art museums; the others are at the Minneapolis Institute of Arts and the Royal Ontario

Museum in Toronto. In each of these three museums, Judaica is shown in discrete clusters. But at the Museum of Fine Arts in Boston, Judaica is dispersed alongside art of various places and periods. Torah finials on loan from the Touro Synagogue in Newport, Rhode Island, are displayed in the Museum of Fine Arts's American Wing amid a collection of Newport furniture and a Miriam's Cup crafted by Cynthia Eid is shown in the Farago Gallery of contemporary craft and decorative arts.[10]

Approaches to the interpretation of Judaica in mainstream—especially encyclopedic—art museums are likely to follow divergent paths for years to come. Dr. Vivian Mann, former chair of Judaica at the Jewish Museum, favors integrating Judaica rather than isolating it in its own space. "Since there are few restrictions on the forms of ceremonial art in Jewish law," she says, "Judaica reflects the style of the surrounding culture." Curators from the Columbus Museum of Art in Ohio are thinking about the museum's Jewish collections in a way "that talks about Jewish life," says Nannette Maciejunes, the museum's director. "We're on an exploratory road. It's a journey to see what's possible." Placement of Jewish art is one dimension of the larger issue of how best to integrate American Jewish history into the larger American narrative.[11]

Eatala

Philadelphia Folklore Project

In 1954, Elaine Hoffman Watts graduated from the prestigious Curtis Institute of Music in Philadelphia, the first woman percussionist to be accepted at Curtis. For more than forty years, she performed and taught percussion with symphonies, theaters, and schools. But her most important achievement and greatest fame comes as a third-generation klezmer musician who has sustained a Jewish cultural tradition that goes back for centuries in eastern Europe and for more than 150 years in Philadelphia. Her musical artistry and cultural knowledge have made her a national treasure: in 2007, she received the National Heritage Award from the National Endowment for the Arts, one of only six Jewish artists to be so honored over three decades. Hoffman is also the subject of a documentary video, *Eatala*, produced by the Philadelphia Folklore Project in 2011.[12]

Klezmer music traces its history to the late sixteenth and early seventeenth centuries, when Jewish musicians organized guilds in Bohemia, Poland, and Lithuania. In these areas, where Gypsies (Roma) were not numerous, klezmorim were the majority of professional musicians. They constituted an occupational caste, with their own professional jargon, musical styles, and lineages. Klezmer ensembles were exclusively male, composed of strings, hammered dulcimer, wooden flute, and, after 1800, clarinets, brass, and a frame drum. By the end of the nineteenth century, their distinctive style and repertoire, which included light classical and peasant folk music, came to dominate the cities and towns of Ukraine, Moldavia, and Lithuania. Moreover, klezmorim played for non-Jews as well as Jews, ranging from Polish magnates to peasant weddings. By 1900, klezmer music incorporated a mixture of Western, Ashkenazic, Near Eastern, and Baltic elements.[13]

"Within Jewish society, the main venue for klezmer bands and the primary opportunity for performance and for paying work was the wedding." Traditional weddings could go on for days, commencing with meditative music prior to the wedding, moving on to various forms of dance, and special display numbers or concerts on request. Most klezmorim, however, did not make a living out of their music and resorted to other vocations, especially barbering. Only a few of the leading European klezmorim immigrated to America, notably the Lemisch family from Romania, who came to Philadelphia in the 1850s.[14]

Jewish Philadelphia, as it happens, was heavily populated by immigrants from southern Ukraine and Moldavia, heartlands of klezmer music. About 75 percent of Philadelphia Jews came from these two regions, which were characterized by an ethnic rather than a religious approach to life. By 1920, there were 240,000 Jews in Philadelphia, the largest immigrant group in the city. Among the newcomers was Joseph Hoffman (1869–1939), a virtuoso trumpet player and leading klezmer composer, who arrived in Philadelphia—by accident—in 1905. Several of Joseph Hoffman's children became professional musicians, notably his conservatory-trained son Jacob (father of Elaine Hoffman Watts), but they struggled to earn a living as klezmorim since klezmer was seen by the 1920s as a vestige of the Old World culture Jewish immigrants were trying to shed. However, Philadelphia Jewry was relatively conservative, and by the 1930s a Jewish wedding sequence had emerged, moving from quiet background music, through the "Star-Spangled Banner" and "Hatikvah," to dance numbers and special requests.[15]

Elaine Hoffman Watts, born in 1932, grew up in a family suffused with music and musicians. Aside from her father Jacob, a virtuoso xylophonist who played on the Keith Vaudeville Circuit and with the Philadelphia Orchestra, several of her uncles and aunts were also professional performers. While teaching and performing in a variety of venues, Elaine Hoffman Watts continued to play klezmer music, drawing on her grandfather's 1927 folio of compositions and scores. Despite the decline in klezmer music and the narrowing of professional opportunities after World War II, a younger generation of musicologists and musicians propelled a klezmer revival in the closing decades of the twentieth century. Elaine Hoffman's unique history and style—musicologist Hankus Netsky describes her as "playing the tunes on the drum, not just the beat"—has made her a nationally known klezmer musician.[16]

When she came to prominence, the Philadelphia Folklore Project sponsored a concert with Elaine Hoffman, followed by production of a feature-length documentary video. The Folklore Project produces exhibitions, publications, and public programs that focus attention on traditional folk arts that are in danger, with special attention to folk arts that are in service to social justice causes. As both a woman in a male-dominated profession and a leading practitioner of klezmer, Elaine Hoffman fit perfectly into the Philadelphia Folklore Project's mission. Moreover, Hoffman and the *Eatala* video project fall into Philadelphia Folklore Project's process of ethnographic inquiry, which employs multiple lenses and multiple voices to capture both the nuances of the story and its catalytic moments. The result is a collaborative process of cultural documentation, a collaboration that engages the artist, the folk tradition, and the community in a lively conversation that crosses ethnic, gender, and generational lines.[17]

Portraits of the Levy-Franks Family

Crystal Bridges Museum of American Art

In 2006, Crystal Bridges Museum of American Art acquired a suite of six colonial portraits for its new museum in Bentonville, Arkansas. The portraits, attributed to the New York limner Gerardus Duyckinck (1695–1746), represent members of the Levy and Franks family. Both Moses Levy and his son-in-law Jacob Franks were prominent Jewish merchants, resident in New York City, with family and business connections in London. As "the largest intact group of family portraits painted in colonial North America," the paintings occupy a place of honor in the Crystal Bridges Museum. The label text that accompanies the portraits reads as follows:

> These six works form the largest intact group of family portraits painted in colonial North America. Stylistic and technical analyses suggest that they are all by Gerardus Duyckinck I, who followed his father into the family business of painting tavern and shop signs, carriages, household objects, and the occasional portrait. The Levy-Franks family held a prominent place in New York's Jewish and mercantile communities. German-born Moses Levy and his family, including eldest daughter Abigaill, immigrated to New York around 1704. Abigaill married Jacob Franks, scion of another important German-Jewish family. Abigaill and Jacob had nine children, five of whom are represented here. Duyckinck's repeated use of blue, red, and brown in rendering costume and drapery as well as his repetition of poses and gestures throughout the canvasses unify the group. The works are further connected by their stylistic origins in contemporary portraits of the British aristocracy, which colonial artists knew from imported engravings. Duyckinck's reliance on prints may account for the flat quality of his figures.

Moses Levy (1665–1728) was admitted as a freeman of New York City in 1695, giving him the right to engage in retail trade. His daughter Abigaill was born in London in 1696, suggesting that Moses was a visiting trader in New York, rather than a permanent resident. He appears to have settled in New York around 1704, though he traveled to London on business. A leading Ashkenazi merchant, Moses Levy traded distilled rum and manufactured soap in the West Indies, and speculated in land. At the time of his death, his estate was valued at six thousand pounds. He was also a leader in New York's Jewish community, one of the financial mainstays of the small congregation.[18]

In 1706, Jacob Franks (1688–1769), the son of Abraham Naphtali Franks, a "Jew broker" in London, arrived in New York. In 1708 or 1709, Jacob boarded in the home of Moses Levy, and in 1711 he contracted with a marriage broker to arrange a marriage with Abigaill Levy (1688–1746). The couple was married in 1712, and their first child, Naphtali, was born in 1715. Jacob Franks was a leading merchant of his era, trading a wide variety of commodities in London and the West Indies. Franks and his family also served as a purveyor of foodstuffs and materiel to British forces during both King George's War and the French and Indian War. Government contracts with the Franks family totaled more than a million pounds sterling, making the Franks clan the richest colonial Jewish family. Jacob and Abigaill Franks moved comfortably in the highest social circles of colonial New York, were tended by slaves and servants, and owned a country house on Long Island.

Jacob Franks was a learned Jew and the *parnas* (president) of Shearith Israel Congregation. When the congregation built its first synagogue in 1730, Franks was the leading contributor and one of four men to lay the cornerstone of the new building. Abigaill was also Jewishly educated and managed a kosher home. She was also well-read in the secular literature of her day: among her favorite authors were Pope, Fielding, Smolett, Dryden, Montesquieu, and Addison. Abigaill's surviving letters to her son Naphtali, in the years 1733–1746, provide a lively portrait of contemporary family, political, and social life. "Her letters also shed extraordinary insight into the efforts of colonial American Jews to establish a functional equilibrium between being Jewish and being part of the larger colonial Christian society."[19]

Abigaill's letters to Naphtali shed important light on the genesis and significance of the Levy-Franks portraits. In July 1733, Abigaill sends thanks to her husband's older brother Isaac for sending his portrait: "I think it a very handsome picture though everyone that knows him [Isaac] tells me it falls short of the original." Then in June 1734, Abigaill shipped a portrait of her son Moses to Naphtali: "Moses' picture Capt. Smith will deliver. I must tell you it's not flattered. My mother [that is her stepmother, Grace Mears Levy] would not have me send it, being she does not think it well done." She also references portraits of herself and her daughter Rycha, which she does not intend to ship to Naphtali. In the same letter, Abigaill encourages Naphtali to take possession of her portrait, then in the hands of Asher Levy, Abigaill's brother, who was resident in London. Then in 1739, Naphtali sent to his family in New York a portrait of himself together with portraits of his aunt and cousins, the family of Isaac Franks. Abigaill responds to the gift as follows:

> Your pictures are quite an acceptable present. . . . The whole family was in raptures. Your father walks about the parlour with such pleasure a-viewing of them as is not to be expressed. Most of your acquaintance knew your picture but I will ingeniously [ingenuously] own I don't find that likeness but it was designed for you & that pleases me to have it.

Abigaill's letters suggest a sequence. In 1733, the receipt of Isaac Franks' portrait pleased Jacob and Abigaill Franks. A year later, Abigaill and her husband seem to have commissioned at least three portraits—of Abigaill, her son Moses, and her daughter Rycha. And in 1739, several more portraits were sent from London. As Paul Needham suggests, "we see the purpose in sending and displaying portraits: to give pleasure to the family. Most commonly in Abigail's letters her husband is referred to as worn down and irritable by the pressure of business, but here his pleasure is inexpressible."[20]

The surviving suite of Levy-Franks family portraits includes a portrait of Moses Levy. But Moses Levy had died in 1728. It appears that Abigaill and her husband commissioned a copy of an earlier life portrait of Moses Levy, one of a pair of portraits depicting Moses and his second wife, Grace Mears Levy. Abigaill disliked her stepmother, who was only two years older than she, so she had no incentive to reproduce her stepmother's portrait, only her father's. Needham suggests that the Franks daughter shown holding a basket of flowers is Rycha Franks rather than her younger sister Phila, the traditional identification.

The prominence of the Levy-Franks family and the context provided for them by Abigaill Franks' letters invest the Levy-Franks portraits with a high level of historical as well as artistic significance. Crystal Bridges Museum of American Art has made a point of identifying the sitters as colonial American Jews in its label copy and guided tours, giving renewed prominence to a colonial Jewish family.

New York's Yiddish Theater: From the Bowery to Broadway

Museum of the City of New York

From the early 1900s, New York City was the world capital of the Yiddish stage. Melodramas, operettas, revues, and sophisticated dramas played to large crowds of Yiddish-speaking first- and second-generation immigrants. In 1925, a peak year, the city's fourteen Yiddish theaters catered to more than a million spectators. Yiddish theaters sprang up in Manhattan, the Bronx, and Brooklyn, ranging from grand palaces to intimate houses. Second Avenue between Houston and Fourteenth Streets, known as "the Jewish Rialto," was a smaller Yiddish version of Broadway. Its four flagship playhouses, lavish structures built especially for the Yiddish stage, offered the best, most professional Yiddish productions. "Second Avenue" became a brand name, much like "Broadway show." Stars of the Yiddish theater, especially matinee idol Boris Thomashefsky and the great tragedian Jacob P. Adler, were lionized, their private lives providing a rich source for gossip and empathy.

To evoke, examine, and celebrate this remarkable combination of high art and popular entertainment, the Museum of the City of New York organized a major exhibition titled *New York's Yiddish Theater: From the Bowery to Broadway*, curated by Edna Nahshon, a professor of theater at the Jewish Theological Seminary. The exhibition is accompanied by a substantial and richly illustrated catalog and a series of public and educational programs. The exhibition presents some 250 artifacts—posters and playbills, photos and film clips, costumes and stage designs—to describe the varieties of Yiddish theater, profile its major writers, stars, and designers, and tease out its influences and its legacies.[21]

On entering the exhibition, visitors encounter a wall-mural photo of the palatial 1,700-seat Grand Street Theatre in 1905, the first playhouse built specifically as a Yiddish theater. The photo shows its magnificent facade covered with terra-cotta detail and a marquee advertising Jacob P. Adler playing his signature role as the "Yiddish King Lear" in Jacob Gordin's drama of the same name. This was Yiddish theater at its most glamorous and elegant, with strong writing, lavish sets and venue, and compelling acting. Originally, in the 1880s and 1890s, much of the Yiddish theater project in New York was less sophisticated. Many plays were quasi-plagiarisms from German or Romanian, transposed to a Jewish setting. Scripts were often honored in the breach, with actors ad-libbing or breaking into unrelated songs and jokes. The audiences, mostly working class, were loud

Figure 10.2 One of the Yiddish theater's most famous stars, David Kessler (1860–1920), as Yankel Shapshovitz in Sholem Asch's sensational play, *God of Vengeance*, c. 1912.

Courtesy of the Museum of the City of New York. MCNY F2012.63.255.

and boisterous, and the melodramas and operettas they adored were dismissed by high-brow critics as *shund* (trash).[22]

The first Yiddish theatrical production in New York (1882) was put on by a troupe comprised, like their audiences, of recent immigrants from Russia. They presented *The Witch*, an operetta by Abraham Goldfaden, the "father of the Yiddish theater," who had established the first professional Yiddish theatrical troupe in Jassy, Romania, in 1876. His operettas, popular to this day, were soon imitated, establishing musical theater as the most popular genre of the Yiddish stage. In 1891, when the Russified intellectual Jacob Gordin attended his first Yiddish play in New York, he was appalled: "Everything I saw and heard was far from real Jewish life. All was vulgar and coarse." Gordin set out to change the folksy culture of the Yiddish stage, instituting a more natural language, banning ad-libs, and demanding a faithful rendition of the playwright's text. His plays, notably *Mirele Efros*, *The Kreutzer Sonata*, *The Jewish King Lear*, *God, Man, and the Devil*—all written in America—proved tremendous star-vehicles and are the cornerstone of the Yiddish drama canon.

Vaudeville, with its musical numbers, skits, dance, and comedy routines, was immensely popular, but "it was frowned upon by the intellectual elite, as well as the operators of legitimate theaters, who feared the low-cost competition. Yiddish actors also looked down on vaudevillians, with the result that only a few vaudeville performers were able to cross over to the legitimate stage. Likewise, the Hebrew Actors Union rejected them, and the vaudevillians had to form a union of their own."[23] Even the many legitimate theater productions, however, were in business to draw large crowds, contain costs, and turn a profit. "This was the theater that boasted contributors with business cards reading: 'Tailor, actor and playwright. Author of the Spanish Inquisition. Pants altered and pressed.'"[24]

In the early twentieth century, however, Yiddish theater of a more literary and serious sort came to the fore. Several experimental theater companies emerged, determined to go beyond star culture and folksy amusement. The most prominent and enduring of these was the Yiddish Art Theatre, established in 1918 by Maurice Schwarz, a leading figure in New York's Yiddish theater. The Yiddish Art Theatre's repertoire "combined world drama by writers like George Bernard Shaw, Henrik Ibsen, and Anton Checkhov, with works by major Yiddish playwrights, including Sholem Aleichem, H. Levick, Sholem Asch, and others."[25] The Yiddish Art Theatre survived until 1950. Nearly all its productions were directed by and starred Schwartz, one of the last actor-managers of the American theater.

The great figures of the Yiddish theater, however, remained its actors. Its stars "were considered the 'royalty' of the immigrant Jewish quarter; their lifestyle, clothing, and amorous affairs were closely followed by an adoring public. . . . Megastars of the pre-World War I period included the dominating tragedian Jacob P. Adler; his rival David Kessler; the versatile, German-trained Rudolph Schildkraut; matinee idol Boris Thomashevsky; the brilliant comic Zigmund Mogulesco; as well as the fiery Keni Liptzin and the regal Bertha Kalich."[26] Stars of subsequent generations included Molly Picon, Paul Muni, Menasha Skulnik, Stella and Luther Adler, and others, many of whom developed careers on the English-language stage and in film.

During the 1930s, Yiddish theater in New York introduced modernist stage design to America. Set designer Boris Aronson, for example, "helped bring the groundbreaking scenographic innovations of the Russian theater to the local American scene. His bold designs redefined the relationship between actor and space and often used the new, non-representational visual language of modern art." In the 1920s and 1930s, the Yiddish stage became a crucible for political theater. Among the leading companies was the Artef (1925–1940), a Yiddish workers' art theater sponsored by the Communist newspaper, the *Freiheit*. The Yiddish stage could even boast a puppet theater, Modicut, that parodied popular songs and stage productions, while satirizing politics and culture.[27]

Why did the Yiddish theater become the immigrant community's most beloved pastime? "Adding glamour and excitement to a sometimes drab existence, it helped new arrivals bridge their old-world past and their new American reality. Everyone went to the theater: young and old, male and female, workers and bosses, shopkeepers, socialists, communists, intellectuals, rabbis, and freethinkers."[28] Moreover, Yiddish theater was not an isolated phenomenon. It flourished amidst a burgeoning Yiddish culture of newspapers and magazines, lecture halls, political societies, sheet music, and recordings. Yiddish theater also participated in a creative dialogue with Broadway theater, introducing European modernism while adapting American themes and genres.

By the 1930s, however, Yiddish culture and the Yiddish theater were beginning to fade, as immigration had practically ended and a new generation of American-born Jews were coming of age.[29] Yet the influence of Yiddish theater did not abate. It inflected classic borscht-belt shtick, producing a generation of postwar performers. It influenced American film and theater through projects like the Stella Alder School of Acting (which trained some of the country's leading actors), Boris Aronson's much-admired stage design, and productions like *Fiddler on the Roof*, which was based on Sholem Aleichem's "Tevye" stories, published in Yiddish in the 1890s. Indeed, several contemporary playwrights, including Tony Kushner, Donald Margulies, and Paula Vogel, have written works based on classics of the Yiddish theater—or on its rich history.

New York's Yiddish Theater is an expansive, often compelling exploration of an important chapter in American Jewish history and in the history of American theater. Its use of set design and embedded film clips, in particular, help to evoke the power and popularity of Yiddish theater, while the catalog, edited by Edna Nahshon, curator of the exhibition, provides context, analysis, and detail. In this project, the lost world of Yiddish theater returns, engaging a new generation in its variety and thick culture. Given that touring companies traveled to many locales across the continent, this project may serve as a model and guide for many history organizations interested in local expressions of American Jewish culture.

A Fine Romance: Jewish Songwriters, American Songs, 1915–1965

American Library Association, Nextbook, Inc., and the Bainbridge Library

On New Year's Day 2013, David Hyde Pierce opened up a PBS Great Performances presentation with a lively patter song about the challenge of creating a Broadway musical:

> You may have butch men by the score, whom the audience adore.
> You may have some animals from zoos.
> Though you've Poles and Krauts instead, you may have unleavened bread,
> But I tell you, you are dead, if you don't have any Jews!

The Peabody Award–winning documentary, *Broadway Musicals: A Jewish Legacy*, was telling it like it is: Broadway musicals were grounded in *Yiddishkeit* (Jewish culture) and the work of Jewish songwriters in the twentieth century fills the American songbook.[30]

Just two years earlier, in 2011, the American Library Association, in collaboration with Nextbooks, Inc., picked up on the same theme, circulating a banner exhibit on American Jewish songwriters, 1915–1965, to fifty-five libraries across the continent. The

American Library Association exhibit was based on a book by David Lehman, *A Fine Romance: Jewish Songwriters, American Songs, 1915-1970*,[31] who served as the exhibit curator and scriptwriter. The American Library Association show comprised eight light-weight, free-standing, double-sided banners with text and illustrations, which could be installed in a variety of configurations conforming to the varied facilities of host institutions. The Bainbridge Library, a branch of the Geauga County Public Library in Bainbridge, Ohio, cleared space in its central area and organized the banner show in a zig-zag fashion. Fiction and nonfiction books, DVDs, and CDs related to the subject were prominently displayed nearby.[32]

Like all the hosts of *A Fine Romance*, the Bainbridge Library was responsible for additional fundraising and planning of complementary public programs. The Bainbridge Library sponsored an impressive five-week series of programs. To kick off the exhibition, Bill Rudman, host of the Cleveland weekly radio show *Footlight Parade* and manager of the Musical Theater Project, which documents and celebrates the American musical experience, spoke on "Jewish Songwriters United: Their Impact on the American Musical." A local high school varsity jazz band performed a variety of American standards at the exhibition opening. On four successive Friday afternoons, the Bainbridge Library screened classic American musicals—*Swing Time* (music by Jerome Kern, lyrics by Dorothy Fields), *Carousel* (music by Richard Rodgers, book and lyrics by Oscar Hammerstein), *Pal Joey* (music by Richard Rodgers, lyrics by Lorenz Hart), and *Annie Get Your Gun* (music and lyrics by Irving Berlin, book by Dorothy Fields and Herbert Fields). The program series concluded with a presentation by cantorial soloist Larry Sheir, "From Tin Pan Alley to Broadway." The Bainbridge Library also collaborated with three other local institutions in developing public programs: the Beachwood Library, the Maltz Museum of Jewish Heritage, and the Shaker Heights Public Library, which hosted the traveling exhibition right after the Bainbridge.[33]

A Fine Romance drives home its key point: A remarkably large proportion of the "jazz standards, ballads, torch songs, up-tempo dance numbers, and show stoppers that make up the American songbook" were created by songwriters who were "Jewish by birth and heritage." These classics of American music were popular for their "optimism no less than [their] wit and sophistication, passion and verve, . . . they beguiled multitudes and prove, in their enduring appeal, that the goals of popular culture and high artistic achievement can happily coincide." That enduring appeal was epitomized in President Barack Obama's first inaugural address in 2009, when he declared, "We must pick ourselves up, dust ourselves off, and begin again the work of remaking America," a paraphrase of Dorothy Fields and Jerome Kern's lyric in *Swing Time*: "Pick yourself up, dust yourself off, start all over again."[34]

Mostly first- and second-generation newcomers, American Jewish songwriters arrived on the music scene at a propitious time. Exciting new technologies—radio, the microphone, the talking movie, and the long-play record—were boosting popular culture to new heights. Sheet music had become big business by 1900, and the music publishing firms had concentrated along West Twenty-Eighth Street in New York, an area that became known as "Tin Pan Alley," though it quickly spread uptown toward Times Square. At a time when Jews constituted the largest number of its residents, New York was the vibrant center of the music industry. "There," writes Stephen Whitfield, "were the biggest booking agencies, the radio networks, the recording studios and labels, and the theaters and emporia that showcased the performers."[35]

Jewish songwriters "put the spirit of their Judaism into their creative work," inflecting their music with traditional Jewish motifs and qualities. "The opening chords of George Gershwin's 'It Ain't Necessarily So' come straight from a benediction over the Torah," writes David Lehman. The songwriters created a new art form in the thirty-two-bar song with a "Jewish" quality that favors the minor key, bent notes, and altered chords. "Even happy songs sound a little mournful," Lehman says. "Sweetness mixes with sadness, a plaintive undertow emerges, and you feel the melancholy of future loss in the very instant of present happiness." Masters of the mixed mood like Lorenz Hart ("glad to be unhappy"), these mostly first- and second-generation songwriters laced their compositions with tremendous verve and wit.[36]

Jewish American songwriters also pioneered the "integrated musical," starting with Jerome Kern and Oscar Hammerstein's 1927 classic, *Show Boat* (based on the novel by the Jewish writer Edna Ferber). In this new departure, the songs advanced the dramatic narrative and were integral to the story being told. The development of the American musical continued in *Oklahoma!*, the 1943 Broadway hit by Hammerstein and Richard Rodgers. Written in the midst of World War II, *Oklahoma!* evoked "the bright golden haze on the meadow" and declared that "We know we belong to the land, / And the land we belong to is grand."[37]

In their myriad compositions, generations of Jewish songwriters fashioned a romantic, generous view of America, the country that had taken them in, given them a home, and offered them the opportunity to express their ideas. Songwriters like Irving Berlin (born Israel Baline) expressed their love for America in anthems such as *God Bless America*. Yet they also saw America with clear eyes. Despite the optimism of their lyrics and the joy of their tunes, American Jewish songwriters also addressed serious issues such as racial prejudice (*South Pacific*) and gender (*Annie Get Your Gun*). They also engaged in a musical dialogue with African American idioms such as ragtime, blues, jazz, and spirituals. In George Gershwin's *Porgy and Bess*, for example, the wail of a clarinet (which comes right out of the Klezmer tradition) counterpoints the bluesy numbers.

A Fine Romance shows that "the soundtrack of the American romance . . . was largely the product of a Jewish imagination." The exhibition also demonstrates the value of a core project or springboard, from which collaborating organizations can develop a spectrum of public interpretive programs—performances and lectures, displays and screenings. The project suggests the utility of sharing interpretive resources for subjects that transcend a single locale or region, as is the case with the great American songbook.[38]

Notes

1. Margaret Kanof Norden, "Dr. Abram Kanof, 1903-1996," *American Jewish History* 87, no. 1 (March 1999): 95–96.

2. John Coffey, "Our Own Dr. Kanof," *Circa: The NCMA Blog*, September 29, 2010, accessed January 13, 2016, http://ncartmuseum.org/blog/view/our_own_dr_kanof.

3. "The Friends of the Judaic Art Gallery" (brochure), North Carolina Museum of Art, n.d.

4. Quoted in Craig Jarvis, "Sacred Space," *Our State: Down Home in North Carolina*. March 2011, 141–47.

5. Quoted in Michael Kaminer, "New Visibility for Carolina Judaica Collection," *The Jewish Week*, April 20, 2010.

6. Ibid.

7. Quoted in Robin Cembalest, "Out of the Ghetto," *Tablet*, May 25, 2011.

8. "North Carolina Museum of ArtJudaic Art Gallery Reopens After Expansion Project," [press release], June 29, 2015.

9. Kaminer, "New Visibility."

10. Cembalest, "Out of the Ghetto."

11. Ibid.

12. KlezmerQuerque website, February 2013, accessed March 1, 2016, http://www.nahalat-shalom.org/klezmer-music-dance/archives/klezmerquerque-2013.html; Hankus Netsky, "The Klezmer in Jewish Philadelphia, 1915-70," in Mark Slobin, *American Klezmer: Its Roots and Off-shoots* (Berkelely: University of California Press, 2002), 52–72.

13. YIVO Encyclopedia, "Music," accessed March 1, 2016, http://www.yivoencyclopedia .org/article.aspx/Music/Traditional_and_Instrumental_.

14. YIVO Encyclopedia, "Music""; Hankus Netsky, "The Klezmer in Jewish Philadelphia," 69, note 8.

15. Hankus Netsky, "The Klezmer in Jewish Philadelphia," 52–72.

16. Ibid. See also *Eatala* (Philadelphia: Philadelphia Folklore Project, 2011).

17. Selina Morales, interview with the author, August 14, 2015.

18. Paul Needham, "The Franks Family and Portraits," draft text of a pamphlet commissioned by the Walton Family Foundation, c. 2006; Howard B. Rock, *Haven of Liberty: New York Jews in the New World, 1654-1865* (New York: New York University Press, 2012), 29. For more on the family's commercial networks, see Eli Faber, *A Time for Planting: The First Migration* (Baltimore: Johns Hopkins Press, 1992), 45–46, 64–66.

19. Edith B. Gelles, ed., *The Letters of Abigaill Levy Franks, 1733-1748* (New Haven: Yale University Press, 2004); Needham, "The Franks Family"; Rock, *Haven of Liberty*, 33–35; Ellen Smith, "Bilah Abigail Levy Franks, 1688-1746," in *Jewish Women's Archive Encyclopedia*, accessed January 28, 2016, http://jwa.org/encyclopedia/article/franks-bilhah-abigail-levy. See also Faber, *Time to Plant*, 84–89.

20. Needham, "The Franks Family."

21. Edna Nahshon, ed., *New York's Yiddish Theater: From the Bowery to Broadway* (New York: Columbia University Press, 2016).

22. Annie Polland and Daniel Soyer, *Emerging Metropolis: New York Jews in the Age of Immigration, 1840-1920* (New York: New York University Press, 2012), 219–20.

23. *New York's Yiddish Theater* exhibition script, written by Edna Nahshon, guest curator, for the Museum of the City of New York.

24. Ezra Glinter, "The Life, Death and Rebirth of Yiddish Theater," *Forward*, April 1, 2016, 28.

25. *New York's Yiddish Theater* exhibition script.

26. Ibid.

27. Ibid.

28. Ibid.

29. On the fading of "Second Avenue," see Jeffrey S. Gurock, *Jews in Gotham: New York Jews in a Changing City, 1920-2010* (New York: New York University Press, 2012), 21–22.

30. *Broadway Musicals: A Jewish Legacy* was written, directed, and produced by Michael Kantor and narrated by Joel Grey. The documentary featured interviews with leading songwriters, critics, and historians, with performances by stars such as Zero Mostel, Matthew Broderick, and Barbra Streisand.

31. David Lehman, *A Fine Romance: Jewish Songwriters, American Song, 1915-1970* (New York: Schocken Books, 2009).

32. Donna Fried and Brigid Novak, telephone interview with the author, March 9, 2016. Thanks also to Lori Weber and Therese Feicht for providing critical information.

33. Geauga County Public Library *Lines & Links* newsletter, "'June is Bustin' Out All Over' at Bainbridge," Summer 2011 courtesy of Therese Feicht.

34. David Lehman, *A Fine Romance* exhibition script, "Introduction."

35. Stephen J. Whitfield, *In Search of American Jewish Culture* (Waltham, MA: Brandeis University Press, 1999), 94; David Lehman, *A Fine Romance*, 4, *passim*; Lehman, *A Fine Romance* exhibition script, "That's Entertainment."

36. David Lehman, *A Fine Romance* exhibition script, "I'll Write Jewish Tunes."

37. Lehman, *A Fine Romance* exhibition script, "Jerome Kern" and "Rodgers and Hammerstein."

38. Lehman, exhibition script, "Introduction."

CHAPTER 11

THE JEWISH ENCOUNTER WITH DISCRIMINATION, TOLERANCE, AND PLURALISM IN THE UNITED STATES

Zev Eleff

IN 1911, Rabbi Henry Schneeberger of Baltimore's Chizuk Amuno Congregation delivered a resounding Thanksgiving sermon. "In no other land under the sun can Israel fulfill its glorious mission, to be a ray of light unto the nations, as in this country." To the cleric, Judaism fit very comfortably into the core principles of the United States. "Let us as American Israelites," concluded Schneeberger, "transmit to our descendants, the precious heirloom of our fathers, pure and unsullied, and so educate our children, that they will honor their faith and grow up as law-abiding citizens of our beloved country."[1] Many speeches delivered by Jewish clergymen and laypeople echoed similar sentiments to the ones expressed by the Orthodox preacher, especially on the occasion of national holidays. The attempts to "synthesize" Judaism and Americanism were evident in the writings of American Jews from the time that they first arrived in large numbers in the middle decades of the nineteenth century until our own time.

However, these ideas were particularly detectable at the turn of the twentieth century. There were several reasons for this. First, mass migration of Jews from eastern Europe transformed the religious group's population and its social dynamic in the New World. In 1880, Jews numbered about 250,000 women and men. At the turn of the century, that figure increased to one million Jews. By 1930, Jews totaled more than four million American residents. The unprecedented numbers of primarily Yiddish-speaking Polish and Russian Jews compelled the established Jewish community to convince the newcomers and their non-Jewish neighbors that the millions of "Hebrew" immigrants could be acculturated to American norms. The second reason was that by this time the

American Jewish community had gained a sturdier foothold in the United States and could, with confidence, challenge the sense that its members were merely second-class citizens in Protestant America. This did not come easy. American Jews required all the poise and self-confidence they could muster to flourish in an oftentimes uneasy and sometimes prejudiced century. In the face of rising antisemitism in Europe, many contemporary Jews championed the idea that "America is different." No doubt, it was. Yet, the exceptional nature of the Jewish sojourn in the United States is just as much a result of this community's struggle to persevere in changing times as it is the consequence of the democratic and pluralistic character of America. This subject extends beyond Rabbi Schneeberger's time. It is a theme that must be explored in all epochs of Jewish life in the United States.

Paving Roads to Tolerance

The Jewish encounter with tolerance—and intolerance—began in the colonial period. In 1654, about two dozen Jews aboard the *St. Charles* arrived in New Amsterdam. It is not clear whether this group was the first band of Jews to touch down on North America, but it was certainly among the earliest. Their presence irked some of the leaders of the Dutch colony. Director-General Petrus Stuyvesant and Rev. Dominie Johannes Megapolensis of the local Reformed Church were hardly pleased by the appearance of the Jewish newcomers. Despite attempts to remove them, the Jewish residents remained in New Amsterdam, thanks to the timely intervention of their coreligionists in the Netherlands. The episode was hardly exceptional. In actuality, Stuyvesant reacted more harshly in his attempts to keep Quakers and Lutherans out of New Amsterdam. Ten years later, the British captured the colony and renamed it New York. The English were kind to their Jewish subjects and permitted them to more or less police themselves in religious matters as long as they abided by the regulations of the British colony.

The emergence of the United States and its founding principles did much to secure a significant place for Jews in the new nation. Written and ratified in the late 1780s, the U.S. Constitution (Article Six and the First Amendment) offered Jews equal rights in the American legal system. The small number of Jews—probably around one thousand—were quite pleased with this. In 1790, the Jews of Newport, Rhode Island, wrote to President George Washington, hailing the new government for "generously affording to all liberty of conscience and immunities of citizenship." In turn, Washington affirmed the Constitution's promise, informing Rhode Island's Jews that the United States "gives to bigotry no sanction" and "to persecution no assistance."

This proved true for the Jews of Newport. However, Jewish citizens in other locales found cause for concern. For the first several decades of the nineteenth century, for instance, the Jews of Maryland were in principle barred from holding public office because all public oaths were sworn in affirmation with Christian doctrine. The Maryland matter caused much debate and tested the limits of religious tolerance. In 1826, after years of debate, the state passed the so-called Jew Bill that "extend[ed] to the sect of people professing the Jewish religion, the same rights and privileges enjoyed by Christians."[2] Later episodes revealed that Jews retained a degree of caution about American tolerance during the first decades of the new republic. In 1844, the governor of South Carolina invited "all Christian nations" to observe a "day of Thanksgiving, Humiliation and Prayer." The exclusion of South Carolina's one thousand Jews irked the very visible minority group. More than a hundred Jewish Charlestonians signed a letter to the governor that reminded the Governor of the U.S. Constitution's protection of people of all religious faiths.[3]

Notwithstanding these episodes, Jews appreciated their unparalleled status in the United States. On February 1, 1860, Rabbi Morris Raphall of New York's Congregation B'nai Jeshurun delivered a prayer to open the morning session at the House of Representatives in Washington, DC. This was a first for a Jew in the United States. Of course, American Jews delighted in this recognition of the revered clergyman. Just as important, however, was the attention paid by other American observers. For instance, a month after Raphall's address, Frank Leslie's popular newspaper offered readers an illustration of a sagacious and bespectacled Raphall. The handsome portrait was accompanied by an article that celebrated Raphall's career and recent visit to Congress.[4] Consider also the case of Mordecai Manual Noah, the noted journalist, politician, and probably the most well-known Jew in the United States in this period. Noah's political rivals referred to him as the "lineal descendant of the monsters who nailed Jesus to the cross" and as a "Shylock [who] will have his flesh at any cost."[5] Nonetheless, Noah continually preached a message of religious tolerance. On one occasion, he begged his audience at a New York synagogue to "respect and assist all religions which acknowledge God, and whose principles are justice and mercy."[6] Accordingly, most American Jews permitted the "Shylock" insults to pass without comment. After all, they realized, Jews in the United States were free to establish synagogues and could participate in all trades and professions, unlike the case in Europe. What is more, in the first half of the nineteenth century, Jews ranked well ahead of other non-Protestant religious groups like Catholics and Mormons.

The second-half of the nineteenth century was different, however. In this period, Jews in America were challenged to defend their place in American society. The wave of native anti-Jewish sentiment was unanticipated. In the late 1850s, Jews formed the Board of Delegates of American Israelites in response to rising anti-Jewish activity overseas. It did not occur to its founders that the Board of Delegates might be useful to combat bigotry in the United States. Unfortunately, however, Jewish leaders were soon called upon to defend their people in America.

The Civil War occasioned cause for concern. On December 17, 1862, General Ulysses S. Grant issued General Orders No. 11. The decree called for the expulsion of all Jews from Grant's war zone: "The Jews, as a class violating every regulation of trade established by the Treasury Department and also department orders, are hereby expelled from the department within twenty-four hours from the receipt of this order." It is unclear how many Jews were impacted by the anti-Jewish proclamation. The vast majority of the 150,000 Jews in the United States were unaffected. But it soon became a moot point as Jewish leaders voiced their concerns to the president. The "obnoxious order," as Grant's wife later described it, was quickly revoked. "If such an order has been issued," wrote

IKEY

We know him by his nose,
His disgusting airs and flashy clothes,
We know him by the way he cheats
The poor, needy victims of life's shady streets;
His heart (if he has one) is a case-hardened shell;
Perhaps it will soften a little in h——

Figure 11.1 Caricature of "Ikey," a dealer in second-hand clothes. "We know him by the way he cheats / The poor, needy victims of life's shady streets."

President Abraham Lincoln to Grant, "it will be immediately revoked."[7] Lincoln was kind to Jews and went so far as to ensure that Jewish chaplains be introduced into the Union army. Yet, General Orders No. 11 represented a growing nativism and anti-Jewish animus during the Civil War. Northern newspapers used the words "Israelite" to describe disloyalty to the Union. The same was true in the South. Confederates used "Jew" as a shorthand to describe dishonest people. Worst, still, was that a number of Jews feared that Lincoln's Emancipation Proclamation would simultaneously raise the state of African Americans and endanger Jews by placing this "ethnic class"—Jews were not yet considered part of White America—at the bottom of the social ladder.

The fears and "Judaeophobia" did not, in fact, expand into the major social problems that they threatened to become. In fact, General Grant had something to do with this. In 1868, Grant was elected president, despite opposition from leading American Jews who very much resented General Orders No. 11. Actually, President Grant treated Jews far better than did General Grant. In his two terms as president, Grant appointed a number of Jews to public office, far more than any previous U.S. president. He also was swift to act when American Jews beseeched the president to intercede on behalf of persecuted Jewish masses in Romania. And, at the conclusion of his presidency, Grant was also the first American head of state to visit Jerusalem. Of course, the stature of the Jew in American society chiefly benefited from the activities of the Board of Israelites and other groups that sought to assuage their non-Jewish neighbors. Men like Rabbi Max Lilienthal of Cincinnati exerted much effort to reach out to Protestant leaders and to ensure that Christians properly understood the intentions of their Hebrew neighbors and their fondness for American values. On one occasion, Lilienthal stressed that "the immortal signers of the Declaration of Independence knew of no bigotry and of no political prejudices, they knew man merely as man, and as such adjusted to every one's equal rights and enjoyment."[8]

The Jewish position was also helped along by newfound wealth. A number of Jewish families prospered through the manufacturing and distribution of clothing. For example, the garment industry elevated the Seligman family to a rarified position among America's affluent elites. Joseph Seligman eventually moved into finance, as did other successful German-born Jewish émigrés. Of course, not every Jew "made it" in America. Many did not. Yet, it is also true that larger numbers of Jews used their social networks and ethnic ties to work with one another and to aid their coreligionists. This quality of the Jewish community in the United States enabled Jews to become particularly mobile and to benefit from one another's successes.

Jewish wealth and status also had drawbacks. Some non-Jewish elites resented the appearance of Israelites in their circles. One Jew noted that the "higher you ascend in the scale of intellect and officers of the public service, the more bigotry and prejudice do you find."[9] Perhaps the most well-publicized instance of this sort involved the prominent Joseph Seligman. In 1877, Judge Henry Hilton turned away Seligman from the former's Grand Union Hotel in Saratoga, New York. The newspapers reported that Hilton instructed the manager of the hotel to inform the Seligmans that "Mr. Hilton has given instructions that no Israelites shall be permitted in future to stop at this hotel."[10] The

Figure 11.2 Caricature of over-dressed, nouveau riche Jews drawn by Rose O'Neill. Cover of *Puck* magazine, October 16, 1901.

Courtesy of National Museum of American Jewish History, Philadelphia. NMAJH 1985.50.136.

affair received great attention due to Seligman's public stature. Hilton did not relent. Instead, he slandered Seligman, claiming that the banker was disliked—"is distasteful"—among his non-Jewish Wall Street colleagues. The claim was enough for a number of Seligman's business partners to write the following in a letter to the *New York Times*: "Judge Hilton is under a misapprehension as to the relations of the Messrs. Seligman with their associates, which always have been and are of the most satisfactory character."[11] In addition, the revered Rev. Henry Ward Beecher viewed the event as an opportunity to preach tolerance to his Brooklyn congregation: "When I heard of the unnecessary offense that has been cast upon Mr. Seligman, I felt that no other person could have been singled out that would have brought home to me the injustice more sensibly than he."[12]

Unfortunately, the Seligman-Hilton affair was not an isolated incident. Two years later, the president of the Manhattan Beach Corporation in Coney Island, New York, also barred Jews from his hotel. His rationale conjured up the caricature of the miserly Jew:

> Personally I am opposed to Jews. They are a pretentious class who expect three times as much for their money as other people. They give us more trouble on our road and in our hotel than we can stand. Another thing is that they are driving away the class of people who are beginning to make Coney Island the most fashionable and magnificent watering place in the world.[13]

Yet, these episodes seemed to only encourage Jews and non-Jews to push for greater tolerance. In the final decades of the nineteenth century, Jews in the United States made a particularly strong effort to preach pluralism and argue for Judaism's role to achieve that goal. In 1885, a group of leading Reform rabbis that met in Pittsburgh to establish a set of principles for their congregations resolved to include the following plank among its "Declaration of Views:"

> We recognize in Judaism a progressive religion, ever striving to be in accord with the postulates of reason. We are convinced of the utmost necessity of preserving the historical identity with our great past. Christianity and Islam, being daughter religions of Judaism, we appreciate their providential mission, to aid in the spreading of monotheistic and moral truth. We acknowledge that the spirit of broad humanity of our age is our ally in the fulfillment of our mission, and therefore we extend the hand of fellowship to all who cooperate with us in the establishment of the reign of truth and righteousness among men.[14]

In other words, Jewish leaders recognized the crucial task of appealing to the larger set of American values and principles. In the 1880s, this meant ensuring that Judaism moved its adherents to the "establishment of the reign of truth and righteousness among men." For others, it meant forming educational programs for the massive wave of eastern European Jewish immigrants to learn English and speedily obtain skills that could help the newcomers find suitable employment in the United States. Both enterprises served as firm statements by American Jews that they too belonged and would do everything possible to make sure that their community somehow fit within the elusive but essential borderlines of American pluralism.

Pushing for Pluralism

The emphasis on social inclusion was a concern shared by Jews, Catholics, and other non-Protestants in the United States, especially due to the mass migration that took place around the turn of the twentieth century. In 1880, the Jewish population totaled around 250,000. These were by and large Jews of German descent who had worked hard to learn English and Americanize any way they could. Forty years later, migration was near an end and Jews numbered more than three million women and men in the United States. The throngs of immigrants hailed from eastern Europe and spoke with thick Yiddish accents. To the great consternation of the established American Jewish communities, the newcomers seemed to dress and behave in all the ways that antisemitic invective had alleged. Whether this was true or not is beside the point. It reinforced an unfortunate image. In a very real sense, the new character and appearance of the Jew in American life posed a greater threat to American Jewry than did Judge Hilton.

The most egregious scene of anti-Jewish violence in this period occurred near Marietta, Georgia. In 1913, twenty-nine-year-old Leo Frank, the administrator of the National Pencil Company in Atlanta, was convicted of the murder of thirteen-year-old Mary Phagan. Many believed the evidence against Frank was not sufficient to determine the Jewish man's guilt, an argument taken up by his lawyer in appeals. Two years later, Georgia's governor commuted Frank's death sentence to life imprisonment. The affair generated a great deal of commotion in the local and national press, much of the discussion centering on Frank's Jewishness. In June 1915, one rather militant journalist who had provoked a great deal of antisemitism went so far as to call for Frank's lynching. That is exactly what transpired. Two months later, a mob of well-to-do men from Mary Phagan's hometown of Marietta abducted Frank from prison. On August 16, 1915, the men drove him to the outskirts of Marietta and hanged Frank early the next morning.

To be sure, the barbarism of the Leo Frank lynching was something of an aberration in American Jewish life. It paled in comparison to the horrific treatment of African Americans in the Jim Crow South, but the antisemitic sentiment bespoke a renewed feeling that Jews were "outsiders" in Protestant America. Of course, the situation hardly compared to the anti-Jewish violence in some sectors of Europe. Yet some Jews refused to concede that there was a difference. In 1907, Rabbi Charles Fleischer of Boston cautioned that "they are after us again." He referred to an outbreak of missionary work in his area that refused to permit Jews to worship their religion in peace. "Even in America," he warned, "there must be a Jew-hunt." The renowned and enraged Reform rabbi compared American missions to Jews to the situation overseas where, Fleischer contended, "the good Christians like, now and then, to slay the bodies of a few Jews."[15]

Most Jews did not speak with such hyperbole. Still, a number of them were angered by actions that appeared prejudicial. In 1915, months before the Frank lynching, Rabbi David Philipson wrote to the superintendent of the Cincinnati public schools. He was

Figure 11.3 The lynching of Leo Frank (1884–1915) in Marietta, Georgia, August 17, 1915. The Frank case aroused attention in the national press, but also incited antisemitism within Georgia.

livid that his children were forced to sit through an eighth-grade performance of Shakespeare's *Merchant of Venice*. Philipson explained to the administrator that while he understood that the play was a "classic," he nevertheless wished the schools to select other "classics" that could better promote tolerance among Jews and Christians:

> I denounce it as a libel against my people, a "classic" though the play may be. I mean, classics, too, may err. The classics, too, have sinned as much as they have been sinned against. Classic or no classic, the reading or the performance of the play in the preparatory school (I am inclined to think even in the High School) is heinous in its effect upon the Jewish children, as you may perceive from the experience of my boy and girl, pupils in the fourth and fifth grades, respectively, of the Clifton School.[16]

Other Jews adopted a very different tactic in reacting to antisemitism. This type of civic freedom fighter stood up to discrimination against Jews in the workplace (banking, medicine, and teaching, for instance) and in housing (restrictive covenants). On the latter score, Jews were barred from a third of the more "desirable" homes and apartments in

Manhattan. Jews fought well into the 1960s to gain access to suburban neighborhoods. They were pleased with the 1916 appointment of Louis Brandeis as the first Jew to the U.S. Supreme Court, but they yearned for more pervasive change as well. In the 1920s, Harvard College placed severe quotas on admission of Jews. "Where Jews become numerous they drive off other people and then leave themselves," stated a fearful President Abbott Lawrence Lowell in 1922. Harvard's leader was unsure of whether the predicament he observed resulted from Jewish "clannishness" or a Jewish tendency to "form a distinct body, and cling, or are driven, together, apart from the great mass of undergraduates."[17] What he did claim, though, was that "segregation by groups" was wholly undesirable at his school. Jews at this time made up 22 percent of the Harvard undergraduate population, having more than tripled in size since 1908. Sensing a "Jewish problem" at Harvard, Lowell put a limit on the number of Jews to be accepted at his college in order to maintain the school's "character as a democratic, national university, drawing from all classes of the community and promoting a sympathetic understand among them."[18] To dodge the quota, Arnold Horwitz changed his very "Jewish sounding" surname to "Horween." In all likelihood, the All-American fullback and captain of Harvard's undefeated football squad was less than honest when he penciled in an answer to the question on the Harvard College application that asked: "Has there been any change in your family name?"[19]

Horween's decision to conceal his Jewish identity was not an uncommon strategy of many prospective Jewish undergraduates in the United States. Once Harvard imposed restrictions on Jewish admission, many private American colleges followed. It is important to note that many of these restrictive policies applied equally to Jews as they did to Catholics and other minority groups, and carried on into graduate programs as well. Adelphi, Barnard, Brown, Columbia, Cornell, Duke, Johns Hopkins, Northwestern, New York University, Princeton, Washington and Lee, and Yale all instituted Jewish quotas. Although Jewish quotas were less common at public universities, there were exceptions. Qualified Jews faced strong prejudice when applying to Ohio State, Penn State, Rutgers, and the Universities of Cincinnati, Illinois, Kansas, Minnesota, Texas, Virginia, and Washington.

In most cases, young Jewish women and men who desired to attend these universities chose to follow some variation of Horween's route rather than combat the intolerance head on. There was at least one exception, but not of a teenager vying for undergraduate admission. In 1922, Rabbi Louis Newman proposed a plan to establish Menorah University, a school that would welcome Jewish and non-Jewish undergraduates. Newman's plan never materialized. Jewish communal leaders were concerned that a Jewish-sponsored college would engender a level of parochialism that would work against their attempts to move into the more comfortable category of "American insiders." For instance, a well-heeled Jewish lay leader in Cleveland cautioned against the Newman plan. "The training which the student receives in the small world of the college is only preparatory to his contacts and activities in the larger world outside," commented Alfred Benesch, "and more democratic and universal his associations in the smaller world of the college, the better and more useful citizen will he become."[20] The influential lawyer, Louis Marshall, offered a similar criticism of a proposal to establish a college under Orthodox Jewish auspices. "If one's loyalty to Judaism cannot survive contact with the outside world, then there must be something wrong with the individual," wrote Marshall of Yeshiva College.[21]

For Marshall, the importance of acculturating was hugely important. Yet, he did not mean that Jews should accept second-class status in the face of virulent antisemitism. Marshall and others were constantly on guard to oppose bigots like radio personality Father Charles Coughlin, who routinely linked Jews to Bolshevism and other movements that Americans considered nefarious. Most importantly, Marshall exerted incalculable energy combatting Henry Ford and the automaker's antisemitic propaganda. First published in 1919, Ford's *Dearborn Independent* frequently contained outrageous claims about Jews, much of them borrowed from the infamous *Protocols of the Elders of Zion*. Published in Michigan, the newspaper was distributed in many of Ford's dealerships and thereby gained a national audience. In 1927, Marshall took the fight into the courtroom. Faced with legal challenges and a formidable opponent, Ford issued a public apology to Marshall that "to my great regret I have learned that Jews generally, and particularly those of this country, not only resent these publications as promoting anti-Semitism, but regard me as their enemy." Ford vowed that "henceforth The Dearborn Independent will be conducted under such auspices that articles reflecting upon the Jews will never again appear in its columns."[22]

To be sure, most Americans did not hold Ford's opinion of Jews. Still, it is also true that a tide of nativist attitudes washed over the United States in the decades that followed the Great War. Particularly in small towns where the Jewish population tended to be composed of immigrant families, Jews felt "unease." What is more, without the support of large Jewish community centers and synagogues, the Jews in these locations lacked the wherewithal to educate and network with more hostile non-Jews. In subsequent years, Americans voiced fears over increased interactions with foreigners who might express their "Bolshevism" and "un-American" views with their children and other impressionable groups. Accordingly, Jews were blamed for bootlegging liquor after the Prohibition Act in 1919 forbade the sale of alcohol. Jews were involved in this illegal trade but not in the proportion with which they were blamed. Perhaps, though, anti-Jewish nativism can be best illustrated in the realm of immigration. In 1921, the federal government passed an emergency quota act that was meant to temporarily restrict the flow of migration from overseas. Lawmakers had Jews—among other populations—in mind when they were drafting the law. In December 1920, the Committee on Immigration of the U.S. House of Representatives warned of "Russian Poles or Polish Jews of the usual ghetto type." This lot, alleged politicians, were "filthy, un-American and often dangerous in their habits."[23] Along with legitimate economic and political fears, these bigoted sentiments—trumpeted by the racist Ku Klux Klan, among others—were manifested in the Immigration Act of 1924. The so-called Johnson-Reed Act revised the temporary order as a permanent law that virtually halted migration from "undesirable" nations in eastern and southern Europe. Henceforth, a small number of Jews managed to resettle in the United States as "illegals"—another illicit trade for which Jews received outsized blame—but far more were turned away due to the new legislation.

Just as important, American Jews were hardly of one mind on immigration restriction. Some opposed the new immigration standards as antisemitic policy (they typically

Christian

Vigilantes

Arise!

BUY
GENTILE

EMPLOY
GENTILE

VOTE
GENTILE

Boycott the Movies!

HOLLYWOOD is the Sodom and Gomorrha
WHERE
INTERNATIONAL JEWRY
CONTROLS
VICE - DOPE - GAMBLING
where
YOUNG GENTILE GIRLS ARE RAPED
by
JEWISH PRODUCERS, DIRECTORS, CASTING DIRECTORS
WHO GO UNPUNISHED
✦✦✦✦✦✦✦✦✦✦✦✦✦✦✦✦✦✦✦✦
THE JEWISH HOLLYWOOD ANTI-NAZI LEAGUE CONTROLS
COMMUNISM
IN THE MOTION PICTURE INDUSTRY
STARS, WRITERS AND ARTISTS ARE COMPELLED TO PAY FOR COMMUNISTIC
ACTIVITIES

Figure 11.4 A c. 1937 antisemitic flier called for Americans to "Boycott the Movies!" claiming that international Jewry controlled vice, dope, and gambling and that the Hollywood Anti-Nazi League controlled "Communism in the Motion Picture Industry." Boycott the Movies! Jewish Federation Council of Greater Los Angeles, Community Relations Committee Collection, Part II.

Courtesy of Special Collections and Archives, Oviatt Library, California State University, Northridge.

ignored the fact that migration from Asia had long been curtailed in the final decades of the nineteenth century). This group spoke up about America's responsibility to take in the downtrodden and rehabilitate them. In like manner, American Jewish leaders also wrote about the Jewish contributions to the United States, insinuating that there was no reason to think that Jewish newcomers would be any less valuable to the country. However, there were also some Jews in the United States who felt obliged to fall in line and accept the legislation. They pleaded with their coreligionists to understand that continued mass migration would amount to a major burden to rank-and-file Americans who could ill-afford to lose their jobs to Europeans.

In a sense, the Jewish community in the United States was torn over their dual allegiances—to their "Jewishness" as well as to their "Americanism." Nonetheless, even the most indignant sorts were forced to relent in the face of the newer and stricter (and, for some, anti-Jewish) immigration laws. Moreover, the myriad of these insider-outsider challenges facing American Jews moved them to establish organizations that could properly lobby and represent their interests. Accordingly, the Anti-Defamation League (1913), the American Jewish Committee (1916), the American Jewish Congress (1918), and the National Conference of Christians and Jews (1924) were all founded with some intention of protecting and pushing for Jewish interests in America. All of these groups understood that their existence were credits to the culture of goodwill and freedoms provided to them in the United States. At the same time, organizational leaders—on local and national levels—also recognized that it was their shared mission to move the nation closer to a more just state of religious and ethnic pluralism.

The Rise and Fall of Judeo-Christian America

In the early morning of February 3, 1943, a German submarine fired missiles at the *USS Dorchester*. The cruise ship had been headed up the northeast coast of Canada en route to Europe to aid the ally cause against the Nazis in World War II. The ship was badly damaged and the nine hundred military personnel onboard were ordered into lifeboats and secure lifejackets. Unfortunately, not everyone could escape the sinking vessel. Four selfless chaplains—one Jewish rabbi, one Catholic priest, and two Protestant ministers—offered their lifejackets to their flock. Then, the chaplains helped others reach lifeboats and linked arms in prayer as they perished along with the ship. The clergymen were heroes, celebrated for their sacrifice and ecumenical brotherhood. The tale was retold through newspaper, book, art, and film. In 1948, the faces of the "immortal chaplains" were produced on a postage stamp. In short order, Americans looked at the martyrdom as a symbol of their "Tri-Faith" nation.

The emergence of a Tri-Faith America was due to more than one or a series of heroic actions. The seeds for it were planted in a previous epoch, as was explored earlier, even as most Americans were resistant to the idea. Yet it can be argued that the spectacular rise of this idea was catalyzed by a shared disgust for Nazism and its Japanese allies. The National Conference of Christians and Jews led the campaign. In 1942, it brought together well-known clergymen to write and sign a Declaration of Fundamental Religious Beliefs Held in Common by Catholics, Protestants and Jews. The organization heralded the achievement as an effort of the "three faiths" to perpetuate the "Judeo-Christian tradition" that allegedly was settled firmly on the bedrock of the United States.[24]

In subsequent decades, the Cold War and a more trenchant enemy in the Soviet Union did much to cement that sentiment in the United States. The image of an America held up by Christian and Jewish "values" was ubiquitous. For an increasing number of Americans, their Judeo-Christian culture represented the best of Western society, democracy, and other notions that could be said to be diametrically opposed to Communism. It could be found in newspapers, popular literature, the professions, college campuses, and at the center of commercial advertisements. It was manifested in campaigns for Brotherhood Week and social work on behalf of "United America." All this had a good deal to do with anti-Communist feelings but was also the result of a more religiously conscious American public that had come of age in the postwar era. In 1955, the sociologist Will Herberg summed up the feelings of many American religionists in his highly influential (and highly profitable) *Protestant-Catholic-Jew*. "For being a Protestant, a Catholic, or a Jew is understood as the specific way, and increasingly perhaps the only way, of being an American and locating oneself in American society. It is something that does not in itself necessarily imply actual affiliation with a particular church, participation in religious activities, or even the affirmation of any definite creed or belief; it implies merely identification and social location." In other words, concluded Herberg of his "Triple Melting Pot," "Not to be a Catholic, a Protestant, or a Jew today is, for increasing numbers of American people, not to be anything, not to have a *name*."[25]

The presumed ideological coherence of Judaism and Christianity was also one of the important factors that brought Catholic and Jewish religious views closer together. In 1965, the Catholic Church's Second Vatican Council officially removed Jewish culpability for the death of Jesus from its theology. The decision was hailed by American Jews as a watershed moment in Jewish-Christian dialogue. One year after the Vatican proclamation, Rabbi Abraham Joshua Heschel delivered an important address at Union Theological Seminary in New York that stressed that "No Religion is an Island." In that lecture, the distinguished theologian marveled at the religious pluralism on display in the major discourses of religious leaders. "I cannot forget that when Paul Tillich (Protestant), Gustave Weigel (Catholic), and myself were invited by the Ford Foundation to speak from the same platform on the religious situation in America, we not only found ourselves in deep accord in disclosing what ails us, but above all without prior consultation, the three of us confessed that our guides in this critical age are the prophets of Israel, not Aristotle, not Karl Marx, but Amos and Isaiah."[26]

Antisemitism did not come to a halt, of course. From time to time, Jews were accused of supporting Communism and other radical groups. Jews reacted to these allegations, despite recommendations that efforts to combat these associations and bigotry were unnecessary. The American Jewish Committee and Anti-Defamation League launched programs to disassociate Jews from the new postwar "enemies" of the American people.[27] Justified or not, Jewish groups feared the return of prejudice; stability, they recognized, was a fleeting notion. In 1953, the Orthodox National Council of Young Israel thought it advisable to take steps to decry the actions of American (Jewish) traitors Julius and Ethel Rosenberg. The synagogue organization passed a resolution that affirmed that "loyalty to the Government is a principle of Traditional Judaism" and that the "Soviet Union has always advocated atheism and opposed religious practices." Most Jews, however, were optimistic and ignored the lingering occasions of antisemitism.[28]

What is more, for a goodly number of Jews, this spirit of pluralism extended well beyond ecumenical matters. In the 1940s, a number of Jews took important parts in the civil rights causes of African Americans. In truth, back in the early twentieth century a handful of affluent Jews supported upstart groups like the National Association for the Advancement of Colored People. However, it was in the post–World War II period that an earnest coterie of Jewish leaders rose up to help out African Americans. This was particularly true of leaders within Reform Judaism and its Central Conference of American Rabbis. Reform religious leaders and laypeople offered more than just funds and rhetoric. They joined with Freedom Riders and picketed with protestors (and faced the wrath of white supremacists). Founded in 1961, the Religious Action Center of the Reform Jewish Movement rallied behind Martin Luther King, Jr., and other African American leaders. More traditional-minded Jews also took part in the movement. Each effort was made with some hesitation, but undertaken nonetheless. Once again, it seems appropriate to quote Rabbi Heschel. In January 1963, he delivered the opening speech at the National Conference on Religion and Race in Chicago. There, Heschel opined that "the concern for the dignity of the Negro must be an explicit tenet of our creeds. He who offends a Negro, whether as a landowner or employer, whether as waiter or salesgirl, is guilty of offending the majesty of God."[29]

These mutual feelings did not last. The 1970s and 1980s gave way to an "Age of Fracture" that divided groups in America along new lines. A number of factors placed social wedges between Jews and non-Jews. Foremost, after years of ignoring the issue, Jewish leaders started to respond to the challenges of intermarriage. In 1971, the National Jewish Population Survey found that more than 30 percent of recently married Jews chose a non-Jew as a spouse. The figure surprised many and left a bitter taste in the mouths of those who had lost their optimism for Jewish survival in the United States. After considerable angst, the leaders of Reform Judaism opted to take official steps to embrace the non-Jewish spouses of its members while Orthodox and Conservative Judaism repudiated such an approach. In any case, intermarriage once again compelled Jews to review their relationship with their Christian neighbors and their shared beliefs in a Judeo-Christian America.

Other issues revealed further cracks in the short-lived bond that Jews and Christians formed in the middle decades of the twentieth century. Controversial matters like abortion rights, church-state relations, the Equal Rights Amendment (for women), and the Vietnam War crippled the "vital center" of American religion and repositioned its constituents on the Left or the Right. The latter gained unprecedented influence in the final decades of the 1900s. Furthermore, the new configuration alienated the most pluralistically inclined liberal Jews, who wondered aloud whether their "own conception of religion is at fault."[30]

This period also witnessed a decline in Jewish-Black relations. In 1968, the protracted Ocean Hill-Brownsville teachers strikes pitted the newly established and primarily black community-controlled school boards in Brooklyn against a heavily Jewish teachers union. A new generation of African American leaders started to include a noticeably antisemitic trope in their civil rights rhetoric. And on the other side, the Ocean Hill-Brownsville episode provided Jewish New Yorkers an excuse to "ignore black New York's anguish, and turn toward unambiguous expressions of white identity."[31] In coming years, the relationship between Jews and African Americans was further strained by opposing views on affirmative action legislation. The director of the American Jewish Congress' Commission on Law and Social Action testified at a Senate hearing: "We believe that there is a need for a fundamental reevaluation of what is meant by affirmative action, for that concept, which originally called for going beyond mere non-discrimination, has been perverted into a new form of discrimination."[32]

Of course, not everyone agreed with Jewish organizations' stance on affirmative action. Consider a letter to the editor submitted to a Jewish newspaper on Long Island:

> As a Jewish woman, I do not share the aversion which the organized community feels toward affirmative action quotas. Yes, I do oppose quotas, but I think many in the Jewish community feel quotas are much more dangerous than they actually are. Many people involved in this area agree that quotas have hurt Jewish men a lot less than they have helped Jewish women. So doesn't that mean there's been a net gain for Jews?[33]

The woman's letter bespoke the internally fractured nature of the Jewish community. On the one hand, the letter-writer admitted that hers was the minority view, one that was perceived as out of sync with the history of Jews and American pluralism. Yet she appealed to her coreligionists to consider her other role as a woman, a group that had benefited greatly from quotas—albeit not the racial variety—that permitted greater access to male-dominated sectors in higher education and the workforce. The same sort of challenges faced others with dual and oft-times competing loyalties. Around the turn of the twenty-first century, then, the quest for pluralism for many women and men did not center on their religion so much as other markers of identity.

Owing to all this reshuffling, American Jews concluded the twentieth century with a large measure of uncertainty about their place in the United States. To boot, this came along with renewed concerns over local antisemitism. Despite decades of goodwill between Jews and other Americans, parents and grandparents transmitted their memories of anti-Jewish action and sentiment to their descendants. "My parents," recalled one Jew in the 1980s, "often spoke of the [Leo] Frank case and I recall my mother saying: 'A *shtikle* anti-Semitism,' a bit of anti-Semitism."[34] This revival of Jewish insecurity took some by surprise, particularly young people who did not grow up with it. One Jewish teenager related her sad experiences while acting in a play about anti-Jewish rhetoric and free speech for local public school audiences. During her performance, the young woman recalled how the audiences hurled slurs at her cast mates and typically sided with the antisemitic villains rather than the would-be more sympathetic protagonists: "I suppose I shouldn't have been so shocked and overwhelmed, since I had heard stories for the longest time, but I was. The first time I personally experienced anti-semitism, but still, at the age of seventeen, I remained untouched by that reality."[35] Finally, the matter was further confounded by the establishment of the State of Israel in 1948 and the constant attention paid to it by journalists in the final quarter of the century. Jews and Christians alike wondered aloud whether "Anti-Zionism had become a new form of Anti-Semitism."[36]

Invariably, the present is the most difficult period to evaluate. Happily, Jews hold public office, are not excluded at any American university, and are free to purchase any home that fits their needs and budget. They are encouraged to build synagogues and celebrate religion openly. However, fears of being cast aside as outsiders linger in the consciousness of Jews in the United States. Much of this is revealed in times of great tension between the United States and Israel. In time, historians will be able to better understand the Jewish engagement with American pluralism in our current century. For now, we must assume that the trends will remain cyclical, interdependent upon the attitudes of Jews and non-Jews alike.

Notes

1. Henry W. Schneeberger, sermon delivered on November 29, 1911, Chizuk Amuno Congregation Archives, Baltimore, Maryland.

2. See Edward Eitches, "Maryland's 'Jew Bill,'" *American Jewish Historical Quarterly* 60 (March 1971): 258–71.

3. See Jonathan D. Sarna, "Christians and Non-Christians in the Marketplace of American Religion," in *American Christianities: A History of Dominance and Diversity*, eds. Catherine A. Brekus and W. Clark Gilpin (Chapel Hill: University of North Carolina Press, 2011), 119–32.

4. "Morris Jacob Raphall, Chief Rabbi of the New York Jews," *Frank Leslie's Illustrated Newspaper* (March 3, 1860): 219.

5. See Louis Ruchames, "The Abolitionists and the Jews: Some Further Thoughts," in *A Bicentennial Festschrift for Jacob Rader Marcus*, ed. Bertram Wallace Korn (Waltham: American Jewish Historical Society, 1976), 508.

6. Mordecai M. Noah, *Discourse, Delivered at the Consecration of the Synagogue of K.K. Shearith Israel in the City of New York, on Friday, the 10th of Nisan, 5578, Corresponding with the 17th of April, 1818* (New York: C.S. Van Winkle, 1818), 28.

7. See Jonathan D. Sarna, *When General Grant Expelled the Jews* (New York: Nextbook, 2012), 3–23.

8. M. Lilienthal, "Oration," *The Israelite* (December 22, 1865): 196.

9. S. Wolf, "A Defence of the Jewish Race," *The Evening Post* (November 22, 1864): 1.

10. "A Sensation at Saratoga," *New York Times* (June 19, 1877): 1.

11. "Mr. Seligman's Friends," *New York Times* (June 21, 1877): 8.

12. See Stephen Birmingham, *"Our Crowd": The Great Jewish Families of New York* (New York: Harper & Row, 1967), 146.

13. "Revising a Prejudice," *New York Herald* (July 22, 1879): 5.

14. See *The Changing World of Reform Judaism: The Pittsburgh Platform in Retrospect*, ed. Walter Jacob (Pittsburgh: Rodef Shalom Congregation, 1985), 108.

15. Charles Fleischer, "On 'Converting the Jews,'" *Boston Advocate* (January 11, 1907): 1.

16. David Philipson to Randall J. Condon, March 19, 1915, Box 1, Folder 2, MS-35, American Jewish Archives, Cincinnati, Ohio.

17. Harold S. Wechsler, "An Academic Gresham's Law: Group Repulsion as a Theme in American Higher Education," *Teachers College Record* 82 (1981): 575–76.

18. See Henry Aaron Yeomans, *Abbot Lawrence Lowell, 1856-1943* (Cambridge: Harvard University Press, 1948), 212.

19. See Louis I. Newman, "Is a Jewish University in American Desirable?: A Thorough Discussion of One of the Most Burning Problems of Our Day," *Jewish Tribune* (October 27, 1922): 8.

20. See "A Jewish University in America?: More Statements on This Subject," *Jewish Tribune* (November 17, 1922): 2.

21. "The Proposed 'Hebrew' College Detrimental," *American Israelite* (April 30, 1925): 4.

22. See *Statement by Henry Ford* (New York: American Jewish Committee, 1927).

23. See Libby Garland, *After They Closed the Gates: Jewish Illegal Immigration to the United States, 1921-1965* (Chicago: University of Chicago Press, 2014), 38.

24. See Kevin M. Schultz, *Tri-Faith America: How Catholics and Jews Held Postwar America to Its Protestant Promise* (Oxford: Oxford University Press, 2011), 60.

25. Will Herberg, *Protestant-Catholic-Jew: An Essay in American Religious Sociology* (Garden City: Doubleday, 1955), 53.

26. *No Religion is an Island: Abraham Joshua Heschel and Interreligious Dialogue*, eds. Harold Kasimow and Bryon L. Sherwin (Maryknoll: Orbis, 1991), 10.

27. See Stuart Svonkin, *Jews Against Prejudice: American Jews and the Fight for Civil Liberties* (New York: Columbia University Press, 1997), 116.

28. "The Rosenberg Case," *Young Israel Viewpoint* (September-October 1953): 48.

29. Abraham Joshua Heschel, *The Insecurity of Man: Essays on Human Existence* (New York: Farrar, Straus & Giroux, 1967), 98.

30. See Alexander Schindler, *Consultation of Conscience* (Washington, DC: Washington Hebrew Congregation, 1985), 5.

31. See Jerald E. Podair, *The Strike that Changed New York: Blacks, Whites, and the Ocean Hill-Brownsville Crisis* (New Haven: Yale University Press, 2002), 209.

32. William Bole, "Affirmative Action: Jews Fight Quotas and Preferential Treatment but Many Fear Backlash," *Long Island Jewish World* (July 24, 1981): 1.

33. Susan Gold, Letter to the Editor, *Long Island Jewish World* (August 7, 1981): 2.

34. Daniel Friedman, "The Case of Leo Frank," *Jewish Press* (May 3, 1985): 50.

35. Neshama Carlebach, "The Truth," *Community of Hebrew Academy of Toronto Yearbook (Metamorphosis)* (1992): 51.

36. See, for example, David Myers, "Anti-Zionism: A New Form of Anti-Semitism," *Long Island Jewish World* (January 23, 1991): 14.

Select Bibliography

Baldwin, Neil. *Henry Ford and the Jews: The Mass Production of Hate.* New York: Public Affairs, 2002.

Cohen, Naomi W. *Encounter with Emancipation: The German Jews in the United States, 1830-1914.* Philadelphia: Jewish Publication Society, 1984.

Dinnerstein, Leonard. *Antisemitism in America.* New York: Oxford University Press, 1994.

Garland, Libby. *After They Closed the Gates: Jewish Illegal Immigration to the United States, 1921-1965.* Chicago: Chicago University Press, 2014.

Sarna, Jonathan D. *When General Grant Expelled the Jews.* New York: Nextbook, 2012.

Schultz, Kevin M. *Tri-Faith America: How Catholics and Jews Held Postwar America to Its Protestant Promise.* Oxford: Oxford University Press, 2011.

Wechsler, Harold S. *The Qualified Student: A History of Selective College Admission in America.* New York: Wiley, 1977.

CHAPTER 12

CASE STUDIES
Discrimination and Tolerance

ISSUES OF prejudice and discrimination are common currency in our society, both in the past and the present. Throughout American history, Jews have been stereotyped and caricatured, as enemies of Christianity, as avaricious, as inbred and secretive—in short, as the Other. Social, economic, and political discrimination, in varying degrees, have been features of the American Jewish experience from colonial times to present, even though Jews have never been the group most disparaged in America. Today, American Jews are generally seen as part of the White establishment, ironically at the very moment that American Jews are increasingly intermarried and multiracial.

The four case studies presented here cover a range of antisemitic expressions, coupled with an interesting case study of philo-semitism—that of President Abraham Lincoln. The first project focuses on a Jewish vacation retreat along the Maryland shore during a time when access to the Chesapeake was restricted. The second examines in detail President Lincoln's relationships with Jews. The third project looks at Jewish contributions to American culture from the colonial period to the Civil War, which included vigorous defenses of Jews and Jewish rights. The fourth project, sponsored by Emory University, documents a period of discrimination in that institution's dental school and the university's effort to confront a "shameful chapter" in its history.

For Fishing, Family, and Fun

Shady Side Rural Heritage Society

In 1924, a group of young men from the Washington, DC, area purchased the former home of Captain Salem Avery in Shady Side, Maryland, about thirty-five miles from Washington on the shores of the Chesapeake Bay. The buyers were members of the National Lodge of Masons—and they were mostly the sons of immigrant Jews. Within

I'm cutting
quite a figure

Figure 12.1   Postcard of a caricatured Jewish man skating on ice, whose tracks make a dollar sign, Twin Bluffs, Wisconsin, 1908.

Courtesy of National Museum of American Jewish History, Philadelphia. Peter H. Schweitzer Collection of Jewish Americana. NMAJH 2006.1.6381.

a few years, they had torn down the old kitchen wing, built a new addition with a large meeting room and sleeping quarters upstairs, and had opened their clubhouse to members of other Masonic lodges.[1]

At the time, many beaches along the Chesapeake Bay were restricted, so Jews interested in gaining access to bathing and fishing resorted to leasing or purchasing property.[2] "Especially in more rural areas, discrimination against Blacks, Jews, and other 'undesirables' such as Southern Europeans persisted into the 1960s," writes Jeffrey T. Coster. "Many hotels and vacation spots refused service to Jews. The lack of access to beaches and accommodations often forced Jews to rely on their own resources. If anti-Semitism only occasionally revealed itself within Freemasonry, in the wider society in the 1920s it could be more overt and pervasive."[3]

The Fishing Club at Shady Side reflected the strivings of second-generation Jews to acculturate, to be accepted as full participants in American society, and to have their own spaces. The Club also exemplifies 1920s trends in leisure and recreational culture. But most of all, the Fishing Club was an experience of relaxing with family and friends in a rustic setting. As Ilana Abramovitch writes, "Neither fancy equipment nor well-appointed accommodations were required. What was central was a spirit of community, comfort, and ease among people of similar background."[4] Originally a retreat for a "fraternity of men that liked to be together," the Fishing Club combined several new forms of recreation

Figure 12.2 "Gentiles Only" sign at a restricted beach, Beverly Beach, Maryland, 1948–1958.

Photo by Rudolph Torovsky. Courtesy of the Maryland State Archives. MSA SC3571-1-256.

in a unique blend, "with aspects of a summer camp, a country club, a Masonic fellowship, a destination for auto-camping, a fishing lodge, a shore house, an ethnic haven."[5]

The Fishing Club at Shady Side operated as a communal living space for more than sixty years and multiple generations of Washington-area Jewish families. In the 1970s, interest waned, and eventually the Fishing Club was sold to the Shady Side Rural Heritage Society for use as the Society's headquarters. The sale was made with the understanding that the Heritage Society would preserve the history and memory of the Fishing Club, and with the hiring of the Society's first professional director, Janet Surrett, the story of this unusual venture was interpreted to the public in an ambitious set of public programs based on extensive research and documentation.[6]

Surrett raised money from federal and state agencies and hired consultant Barry Kessler as project director. Kessler mobilized interest among the Fishing Club families, especially the older generation (many of whom have since died). In 2006, the Heritage Society sponsored a reunion of Fishing Club families, leading to the collection of photos and memorabilia, plus more than twenty video histories, which were archived; copies were also sent to the Maryland Historical Society to ensure their preservation. Based on this trove of resources, Barry Kessler organized a major exhibition and a book-length catalog featuring the full text of the exhibition script, essays by two scholars, and a reminiscence by Paul Foer, a member of one of the early Fishing Club families.[7] Although the exhibition focused primarily on the experience of communal living and the recreational aspects of what the families affectionately called "Our Place," the catalog explicitly addressed the context and challenges of antisemitism as a key part of the story.

For Fishing, Family, and Fun: Seven Decades of Communal Living by the Chesapeake Bay is a model of how a small, local heritage organization can successfully tackle an unusual story, big themes, and an ambitious project, one that continues to inform and enrich interpretation of the site.

Lincoln and the Jews

New-York Historical Society and Shapell Manuscript Foundation

In sharp contrast to Shady Side's ambitious local project is a major exhibition on *Lincoln and the Jews* (2015) organized by the New-York Historical Society in cooperation with the Shapell Manuscript Foundation.[8] Based on a book by Jonathan Sarna and Benjamin Shapell,[9] the exhibition focuses on Lincoln's friendships with Jews, his acceptance of Jews as full and equal citizens, and several well-known instances of his interventions on behalf of American Jews in the face of persistent antisemitism. At a time when many Americans had little or no personal contact with Jews, Lincoln "interacted with many individual Jews during his lifetime: as friends, associates, supporters, acquaintances and people he pardoned or appointed."[10]

This large-scale project by one of America's preeminent historical organizations, which included one hundred original artifacts, an audio tour, and an interpretive brochure, followed hard on the heels of *Passages Through the Fire: Jews and the Civil War* (2013), organized by the American Jewish Historical Society and Yeshiva University Museum in New York, which touches on related themes.[11] The earlier exhibition looked "at the ways in which the Civil War was a crucible for American Jewish identity . . . establishing a framework for the full participation of Jews in American life—militarily, politically, economically and socially."[12] In addition to important objects, documents, and images, *Passages Through the Fire* included three short videos by award-winning filmmaker Oren Rudavsky on Jews and slavery, Grant's General Orders No. 11 expelling Jews from his military district, and the Civil War's legacy for American Jewry. The exhibition was accompanied by a book of the same title.[13]

Lincoln and the Jews emphasizes the key role played by the president in resisting the challenge of antisemitism and ensuring the full participation of Jews in American life. Although the number of Jews in America grew rapidly in the first decades of the nineteenth century, in 1860 Jews numbered only 150,000 in a population of thirty-one million. Jews' outsized role in peddling and retail, however, made them a conspicuous minority, in the countryside and small communities as well as the larger urban centers. Jewish concentration in commerce, and their reliance on kin networks, reinforced popular stereotypes of Jews as people who "have bent all their energies to the accumulation of money,"[14] a view that was shared by many leaders in government and in the army. Among those whose stereotyping or outright antisemitism is documented were Vice President Andrew Johnson and prominent Generals William T. Sherman, Benjamin F. Butler, and George B. McClellan.[15]

The standard account of Jews in the Civil War period is Bertram W. Korn's book, *American Jewry and the Civil War*.[16] Korn gives special attention to two incidents of Federal discrimination against Jews, in both of which Lincoln played an important role. The first stemmed from Congressional legislation establishing commissions for military chaplains; these commissions, however, were restricted to "regularly ordained minister[s] of some Christian denomination." Korn characterizes this measure as "the first instance of outright discrimination [against Jews] and legal inequity in a Congressional enactment." American Jewish leaders and the Jewish press began a public campaign to secure equal treatment before the law, arguing that "the said Acts are oppressive, inasmuch as they establish a prejudicial discrimination against a particular class of citizens, on account of their religious belief."[17] *Lincoln and the Jews* addresses this incident directly and succinctly. Here is the panel text relating to the chaplaincy controversy:

> With the buildup of troops in the Civil War, Congress moved to provide military chaplains, whom both active and wounded soldiers could look to for spiritual comfort. By law they had to be "ordained ministers of a Christian denomination." The Cameron Dragoons, a largely Jewish regiment, elected Michael Allen, a Jew, as their chaplain. When Allen was forced to resign (being neither Christian nor ordained), they courageously elected Rev. Arnold Fischel, of Congregation Shearith Israel. When Fischel's appointment was rejected, he, representing the Board of Delegates of American Israelites, successfully petitioned the president. Thanks largely to Lincoln's intervention, the law was changed.[18]

Shortly after the chaplaincy issue was resolved by new legislation (July 1862), a second antisemitic controversy erupted in December 1862. General Grant, commanding a vast military district, was determined to stop illegal smuggling between Northern and Southern merchants, many of whom were Jews. To do so, Grant issued General Orders No. 11, expelling all Jews then resident in his military district. Grant's measure, mostly unfounded in fact (and motivated in part by anger at his own father, who had asked General Grant for special consideration for him and his two Jewish partners) created a wave of reaction.[19] General Orders No. 11 was characterized as an "enormous outrage on all law and humanity" and demands for their repeal were immediate and insistent.[20] Representations were made directly to Lincoln, who promptly countermanded Grant's order. *Lincoln and the Jews* describes the incident as follows:

> General Ulysses S. Grant, faced with an influx of cotton speculators and smugglers in the area under his command—the huge swath of territory stretching from Mississippi to southern Illinois—blamed the Jews for this profiteering. In July 1862, he ordered his soldiers to examine the baggage of all speculators coming south, adding,

"Jews should receive special attention." In early November, he ordered that Israelites "should be kept out." On December 17, 1862, he issued his General Orders No. 11, expelling "Jews as a class" from his territory within twenty-four hours. When Lincoln learned of Grant's order, he made sure it was quickly revoked.[21]

In the face of widespread antisemitism, Lincoln's response to the chaplaincy crisis and Grant's orders would be quite enough to confirm his reputation for broadmindedness, fairness, and good judgment. But as *Lincoln and the Jews* demonstrates, the president also had many personal encounters with individual Jews. While many of these were perfunctory or incidental, Lincoln did maintain close ties to two Jewish allies, his chiropodist, Dr. Isachar Zacharie, and one of his Illinois supporters, the lawyer Abraham Jonas, whom Lincoln characterized as "one of my most valued friends."[22] The New-York Historical Society exhibition presents a number of original documents that show the depth and duration of the Lincoln-Jonas friendship. And his relationship with Dr. Zacharie—whom Lincoln treated as a confidential agent—is shown to be consequential. In addition, Lincoln extended commissions to Jewish officers, pointing out to his Secretary of War, Edwin M. Stanton, that "I believe that we have not yet appointed a Hebrew," while confirming the commissioning of C. M. Levy, an Orthodox Jew from New York, as a quartermaster with the rank of captain.[23]

Lincoln and the Jews, then, portrays him as the first president to have Jews in his circle of acquaintance and friendship. According to Dr. Sarna, Lincoln "judged people as individuals."[24] And, says Sarna, "Lincoln played an important role in turning Jews from outsiders in America to insiders."[25] To be sure, Lincoln worked to maintain good relations with all faiths, but what distinguishes his "attitudes toward Jews [was that they] were so dramatically at odds with mainstream American opinion at the time," writes Edward Rothstein, critic at large for the *Wall Street Journal*.[26] *Lincoln and the Jews* reminds viewers of Lincoln's exceptionally humane character and underscores his remarkable affinity for the Other, even as it underscores the prevalence of antisemitic feeling in mid-nineteenth-century America.

By Dawn's Early Light

Princeton University Art Museum

In 1801, the first issue of *The Port Folio*, a Philadelphia weekly magazine, described Berlin as "An old town . . . of which a quarter part are Jews . . . distinguished by those peculiarities which mark all European towns where a large proportion of Israelites reside— . . . [its] FILTH." Another article in the same issue castigated Jewish patriotism as consisting of jealousy, rivalry, ignorance, pride, and hatred. Antisemitic comments and stereotypes such as these were commonplace in the early national period. They were buttressed by a torrent of books, articles, and meetings sponsored by Christian missionary societies bent on converting America's Jews. Jews were also buffeted by the Protestant indoctrination in public school textbooks, Christian oaths required for holding public office, and laws that restricted commercial activity on Sundays. As Thomas Jefferson observed in an 1828 letter to Mordecai Manuel Noah, sectarian prejudice was "disdained by all while feeble, and practiced by all when in power."[27]

Dismissive remarks and discrimination in public life met with continual resistance from America's small, but growing Jewish population in the decades after the Revolution. Despite being cultural outsiders and religious non-conformists, Jews enjoyed unprecedented civil rights and political liberty, security of their property, and opportunity for advancement. American Jews used these privileges to rebuff critics and missionary efforts, to assert their rights as citizens, and to shape their own religious lives and communal institutions. In short, Jews in the years before the Civil War were not only objects of others' gaze, but creators and shapers of their own culture and that of the new nation as well.[28]

The tensions and opportunities for Jewish cultural expression in the new Republic are the subjects of *By Dawn's Early Light: Jewish Contributions to American Culture from the Nation's Founding to the Civil War*, an exhibition of rare books, manuscripts, objects, photographs, paintings, and newspapers with an accompanying book of essays organized by the Princeton University Library and installed at the Princeton University Art Museum. Nearly two hundred items, many from the private collection of Leonard L. Milberg, demonstrate how "Jewish men and women adapted American and Jewish intellectual and artistic idioms to express themselves in new ways. . . . they provide a window into an era of cultural vitality and change, illuminating the extraordinary creativity of American Jews in the new Republic, as well as the birth of American Jewish culture."[29]

"The earliest instances of American Jewish religious expression emerged to combat challenges to Jewish identity and community posed by the campaigns of Christian missionaries," writes Karla Goldman. Among the earliest was a pamphlet by Jacob Nikelsburger, *Koul Jacob in Defence of the Jewish Religion: Containing the Arguments of the Rev. C. F. Frey, One of the Committee of the London Society for the Conversion of the Jews, and Answers Thereto*, which was published in New York in 1816. The Rev. Frey was a Jewish convert to Christianity who came to American expressly to head the first missionary society in the United States founded specifically to convert Jews. Frey's mission also called forth the first American Jewish periodical, *The Jew; Being a Defense of Judaism against All Adversaries, and Particularly against the Insidious Attacks of Israel's Advocate*, edited by Solomon Henry Jackson, which began publication in 1823. "In the present enlightened age, not to defend Judaism," declared the editor, "would be considered a tacit acknowledgment that it was indefensible."[30]

Jews in the new nation were even quicker to assert their rights. An entire section of the Princeton exhibition is titled "Speaking for Themselves." Among the items featured here is a letter from the Savannah congregation to the newly inaugurated President Washington. Written by Levi Sheftall, the letter "thanked Washington for his 'unexampled liberality' that had 'dispelled that cloud of bigotry and superstition' that hovered over Jews. Washington's response echoed Sheftall's sentiments, rejoicing that an enlightened spirit 'is much more prevalent than it formerly was.'" In 1798, Gershom Mendes Seixas, the *hazan* of Congregation Shearith Israel in New York, delivered an oration in response to President Adams' call for a national day of fasting and prayer. In his *Discourse*, Seixas "offered thanks to God for having 'established us in this country where we possess every advantage that other citizens of these states enjoy,'" while establishing a precedent for delivering sermons in English on national days of thanksgiving or reflection. "By the middle decades of the nineteenth century, Jews offered their views in print, in the press, and from the platform on a wide range of topics, including slavery, secession, women's rights, and numerous other subjects that engaged them as citizens and as Jews."[31]

Jewish religious and congregational life in the new Republic was another area of experimentation and adaptation. Although the American Jewish population was surging in the decades before the Civil War, congregational membership was low and interfaith marriage rates were high. To address the realities of living in a society where being a Jew was a matter of choice, "new prayer books (some in English) and translations of religious texts; new styles of worship and belief, including Reform Judaism; and the introduction of regular sermons delivered in both English and German" were introduced into congregational life. The first English translation of the traditional *siddur* (prayer book), Isaac Pinto's *Prayers for Shabbath, Rosh-Hashanah, and Kippur . . . according to the Order of the Spanish and Portuguese Jews*, was published in 1766, preceding the British publication of a comparable translation into the vernacular. The translation was necessary because the Hebrew "was imperfectly understood by many." Starting in the 1820s, efforts to reform and adapt continued apace, producing distinctly American forms of liturgy and belief.[32]

By Dawn's Early Light includes examples of Jewish contributions across the cultural spectrum—in medicine and science, visual arts and literature, reportage and polemic. Some of the items exhibited are well-known, such as the exchange of letters between the Jewish community of Newport, Rhode Island, and President Washington. Other items, especially those emanating from Jewish communities in the Caribbean (which exceeded the mainland Jews in numbers and prominence up to the early 1800s) have been ignored or undervalued, even though antebellum Jewish culture was infused with a Caribbean spirit. (One notable example of this interplay is Alexander Hamilton, whose mother married a Jewish merchant in St. Croix and who probably converted to Judaism; Hamilton himself was educated in a Jewish school and became fluent in Hebrew!) The exhibition serves as a reminder that many valuable primary sources, representing a diversity of Jewish voices, remain in the hands of individuals and families and must be sought out for pubic interpretive purposes. But most important, the exhibition underlines the need for our interpretations of Jewish history to develop narratives in which Jews, tiny minority though they were (and are), have agency. In this respect, the *By Dawn's Early Light* project provides a useful corrective.

From Silence to Recognition

Emory University

In 2006, Dr. Perry Brickman, a retired oral surgeon, attended a special event at his alma mater, Emory University. The occasion was the thirtieth anniversary of the Jewish Studies program at Emory. Part of the commemoration was an exhibition on *Jews at Emory: Faces of a Changing University*. As Dr. Brickman viewed the exhibition, he was struck by one particular section, developed by Associate Professor of History Eric Goldstein, which documented discrimination against Jewish students enrolled in the Emory University School of Dentistry during the 1950s.

As it happens, Dr. Brickman was himself a victim of that antisemitic prejudice. Early in the summer of 1952, after his first year of dental school at Emory, Brickman received a letter from the dean of the dental school informing him he had flunked out. During the course of the summer, Brickman discovered that three of his classmates had also failed, all of whom were Jewish. Swallowing his disappointment and shame, Brickman entered the University of Tennessee dental school, graduated high in his class, and enjoyed a long and distinguished career.[33]

The materials Dr. Brickman saw on display evidenced persistent bias against Jewish students by the dental school dean, John E. Buhler. From 1948 to 1961, of the thirty-nine Jewish men who enrolled, a dozen were flunked out and fifteen were forced to repeat coursework—in all, 65 percent of the Jewish students. Jewish enrollment at the dental school dropped. And the school adopted an application form which designated students as either Caucasian, Jewish, or Other.[34]

Dr. Buhler's discriminatory practices did not escape notice. In 1961, a group of students filed complaints of antisemitism, first with the Atlanta Jewish Community Relations Council (which rejected them) and then with the regional chapter of the Anti-Defamation League. The Anti-Defamation League Regional Director, Arthur Levin, took the charges seriously, conducted an investigation, and presented his findings to the Emory Dean of Faculty. Buhler left Emory that year, but the university denied that his antisemitic actions had anything to do with his leaving; he became dean of the dental school at the Medical University of South Carolina. The following year, the Anti-Defamation League published a book titled *Some of My Best Friends* that included a chapter on graduate schools and a graph showing systematic discrimination against the Emory dental students.[35]

It was this graph that caught Dr. Brickman's attention. Galvanized by the material he encountered, Brickman set out to learn more. "It was the first time I'd seen those figures of how many people had flunked," he said. "I had no idea how many there were. It was obvious that it was a systemic problem." Brickman was determined to identify the former students who had suffered from bias as individuals and to interview them about their experiences. But, to his surprise, they were reluctant to reopen bitter memories, so great was their shame and pain.

The "fraternity of silence" was finally broken when one of those dismissed by Buhler (who went on to a successful medical career) agreed to speak on the record. "It's hard for [my kids] to imagine that this really happened," said one informant. "Our parents said, 'you must not have studied enough,'" said another. Dr. Brickman tracked down others and conducted a series of videotaped interviews with them. After four years of taping, Brickman had compiled enough material to create a short documentary on his home computer. He then shared his homemade video with several prominent alumni and faculty, who brought it to the attention of Emory University officials.[36]

In response, the Emory Vice President, Gary S. Hauk, commissioned a pair of Atlanta-based documentary filmmakers, David Hughes Duke and John Duke, to create a documentary based on Dr. Brickman's video interviews. In October 2011, Emory University President

James Wagner issued a public apology to nearly thirty former dental school students and their families, saying that the actions at the dental school were "the opposite of what Emory strives to be—an ethically engaged university that celebrates its current broad diversity." President Wagner's remarks were followed by a screening of *From Silence to Recognition* and a panel discussion. More than four hundred people crowded the room to hear the university's acknowledgment of "a shameful chapter in our history," as Emory Vice President Hauk put it.[37]

Emory University's apology and its commissioning of the documentary film are unusual among the many universities that practiced discrimination during the mid-twentieth century, mostly in the form of student quotas and faculty hires. The documentary has since been screened at other sites ranging from Dallas to Hartford, but primarily at Jewish film festivals and with largely Jewish audiences. Still, Dr. Brickman's persistence and Emory's forthrightness constitute an important model of how public history can help contemporary people and community institutions to make peace with the past.

Notes

1. Barry Kessler, ed., *For Fishing, Family, and Fun: Seven Decades of Communal Living by the Chesapeake Bay.* (Shady Side, MD: Shady Side Rural Heritage Society, Inc., 2008), 3.

2. Deborah R. Weiner, "Baltimore's Backyard: Jewish Vacations in Maryland," in Avi Y. Decter and Melissa Martens, eds., *The Other Promised Land: Vacationing, Identity, and the Jewish American Dream* (Baltimore: Jewish Museum of Maryland, 2005), 33.

3. Jeffrey T. Coster, "For Fraternity and Family: Social Networks, Popular Recreation, and the Origins of the National Masonic Fishing and Country Club," in Kessler, ed., *For Fishing, Family, and Fun*, 45.

4. Ibid., 53.

5. Ibid., 49.

6. Telephone interview with Barry Kessler, March 23, 2015.

7. Telephone Interview with Barry Kessler, March 23, 2015.

8. The full title of the exhibition is *With Firmness in the Right: Lincoln and the Jews*, however, both the New-York Historical Society's website and the exhibition's interpretive brochure feature the subtitle rather than the full title.

9. Jonathan D. Sarna and Benjamin Shapell, *Lincoln and the Jews: A History* (New York: Thomas Dunne Books, 2015).

10. *With Firmness in the Right: Lincoln and the Jews*, (exhibition text), New-York Historical Society/Shapell Foundation, 1. Courtesy of the New-York Historical Society.

11. The exhibition was shown first at the Yeshiva University Museum in New York and subsequently at the Jewish Museum of Maryland in Baltimore. The exhibition was complemented by a book of the same name.

12. Jewish Museum of Maryland, accessed April 30, 2015, https://jewishmuseummd.org/single/passages-through-the-fire-jews-and-the-civil-war/.

13. Jeffrey Edelstein, ed. *Passages Through the Fire: Jews and the Civil War* (New York: American Jewish Historical Society and Yeshiva University Museum, 2013).

14. Editorial, "The Jews, as Citizens," *Washington Sentinel*, Washington, DC, May 21, 1854, quoted in *With Firmness in the Right: Lincoln and the Jews*, exhibition text, New-York Historical Society/Shapell Foundation, 3.

15. *Lincoln and the Jews* exhibition text.

16. Bertram W. Korn, *American Jewry and the Civil War*, third ed. (Philadelphia: Jewish Publication Society, 2001).

17. Petition of the Board of Delegates, December 6, 1861, quoted in full by Korn, *American Jewry*, 78–80.

18. *Lincoln and the Jews* exhibition text, 22.

19. Jonathan D. Sarna, *When General Grant Expelled the Jews* (New York: Schocken Books, 2012). See also Korn, *American Jewry*, 143–84.

20. Telegram from Cesar Kaskel, et al. to President Lincoln, December 28, 1862, quoted in Sarna, *When General Grant Expelled the Jews*, 11.

21. *Lincoln and the Jews* exhibition text, 23.

22. *With Firmness in the Right: Lincoln and the Jews* (interpretive brochure), New-York Historical Society, 2015, 5.

23. *Lincoln and the Jews* exhibition text, 27.

24. Quoted in Sandee Brawarsky, "'With Malice Toward None': Exhibit at New-York Historical Society Reveals Rich Relationship between Abraham Lincoln and the Jews," *The Jewish Week*, March 17, 2015, accessed April 30, 2015, http://www.thejewishweek.com/arts/museums/malice-toward-none.

25. Quoted in Jennifer Schuessler, "'Lincoln and the Jews' Explores Bonds With a Nation's Growing Minority," *The New York Times*, March 19, 2015, accessed April 30, 2015, http://www.nytimes.com/2015/03/20/artd/frdign/lincoln-and-the-jews.

26. Edward Rothstein, "The Unusual Relationship Between Abraham Lincoln and the Jews," *Mosaic*, April 1, 2015, accessed April 30, 2015, http://mosaicmagazine.com/observation/2015/04/the-unusual-relation.

27. Diane Ashton, "Women Writers Advance their Jewish Views," in Adam D. Mendolsohn, ed., *By Dawn's Early Light: Jewish Contributions to American Culture from the Nation's Founding to the Civil War* (Princeton: Princeton University Press, 2016), 99–100. See also Howard Rock, "The Jews and the State" in Mendelsohn, *Dawn's Early Light*, 42.

28. Mendelsohn, *Dawn's Early Light*, 3, 189, *passim*.

29. Exhibition text, "Introduction."

30. Karla Goldman, "Early American Judaism: New Forms of Religious Expression," in Mendelsohn, ed., *Dawn's Early Light*, 82. Exhibition script, September 19, 2015.

31. Exhibition script, September 19, 2016.

32. Karla Goldman, "Early American Judaism," in Mendelsohn, ed. *Dawn's Early Light*, 61–74; Exhibition text, September 19, 2015.

33. Samuel G. Freedman, "Emory Confronts a Legacy of Bias Against Jews," *New York Times*, October 6, 2012, accessed March 15, 2016, http://www.nytimes.com/2012/10/07/education/emory-confronts-legacy-of-bias-against-jews-in-dental-school.html?_r=0.

34. Judie Jacobson, "From Silence to Recognition," *Connecticut Jewish Ledger*, March 9, 2013, accessed March 15, 2016, http://www.jewishledger.com/2013/03/from-silence-to-recognition-2/; Samuel G. Freedman, "Emory Confronts a Legacy"; Lisa Derrick, "FDL Movie Night," *Shadow Proof*, November 19, 2012, accessed March 15, 2016, https://shadowproof.com/2012/11/19/fdl-movie night.

35. Judie Jacobson, "From Silence to Recognition"; Samuel G. Freedman, "Emory Confronts a Legacy"; Lisa Derrick, "FDL Movie Night."

36. Mary Loftus, "Anti-Discrimination: University confronts former dental school bias against Jewish students," *Emory Magazine*, Winter 2013, accessed March 15, 2016, http://www.emory.edu/EMORY_MAGAZINE/issues/2013/winter/of_note/dental.html.

37. Quoted in Loftus, "Anti-Discrimination."

CHAPTER 13

JEWISH ORGANIZATIONS AS INTERPRETIVE RESOURCES

Grace Cohen Grossman and Avi Y. Decter

THIS BOOK has focused on interpretive opportunities and projects carried out by secular organizations. In part, this is to highlight possibilities for inclusion that are little-known or widely ignored, and in part to encourage emulation among a wide range of history organizations. However, Jewish museums and historical organizations, individually and collectively, represent valuable resources for practitioners interested in bringing aspects of American Jewish history into their programs or more directly engaging their local Jewish constituents. The notes that follow offer an introduction to the history of American Jewish museums and historical organizations together with suggestions about resources that are likely places with which to begin an interpretive project. A list of recent exhibitions on American Jewish history mounted by American Jewish museums suggests the range of topics that might be considered.[1]

In the Beginning

The earliest official representation of the American Jewish community occurred at the 1876 Centennial Exposition in Philadelphia. Significantly, at the time of the Centennial Exposition, there were no Judaica collections in the United States that might have been used to represent Judaism in the form of an exhibition. Instead, the International Order of B'nai B'rith was invited to sponsor one of six monuments that were to be installed at the exposition representing ethnic and religious groups. B'nai B'rith selected Moses Jacob Ezekiel (1844–1917) as the artist and chose "Religious Liberty" as the theme of the sculpture. The message was a symbolic statement that Jews and Judaism occupied their rightful place in American democratic society.[2]

The success of the 1876 Centennial Exposition encouraged the development of the World's Columbian Exposition held in Chicago in 1893/1894. There, Judaism was represented in the U.S. Government Building as part of the installation of the U.S. National Museum (now the Smithsonian) within an exhibition on "Religious Ceremonials." The exhibition was the brainchild of Cyrus Adler (1863–1940), who was the prime mover behind the establishment in 1887 of a collection of Judaica at the Smithsonian and the formation of a new department of "Religious Ceremonials." He was also the driving force behind the founding of the American Jewish Historical Society in 1892, the first ethnic history organization in the United States. In 1903, Adler helped facilitate the creation of the Semitic Museum at Harvard, and in 1904 he encouraged the donation of twenty-six ceremonial objects to serve as the nucleus for a museum at the Jewish Theological Seminary in New York (later The Jewish Museum). In 1912, Adler helped broker the plan to develop a collection of Hebraica and Judaica at the Library of Congress.[3]

In the spirit of the *Wissenschaft des Judentums*, the movement for the scientific study of Judaism that originated in Germany in the 1820s, Adler's agenda was the recognition of the study of Judaism as an essential component of higher learning which should take its legitimate place in the world of secular scholarship. Through the collection at the U.S. National Museum and the exhibitions he organized, Adler openly and proudly expressed the tenets of the Jewish faith. His initial acquisitions for the U.S. National Museum included Jewish ceremonial objects, mostly of the eighteenth and nineteenth centuries. Meanwhile, the first major private collection of Jewish ceremonials, the Sonneborn Collection comprising ninety-five items, was donated to the Johns Hopkins University.

Figure 13.1 A Jewish sweatshop in Baltimore, Maryland, c. 1915, where the needle trades were cornerstones of the ethnic economy.

Courtesy of the Jewish Museum of Maryland. JMM 1991.24.3a.

Sonneborn wanted the objects to be used for research and teaching at the university, and put on display for the public.[4]

In 1913, an exhibition of special significance celebrated the cultural heritage of new immigrants. Titled *Exposition of the Jews of Many Lands*, the goal of exhibit organizer Boris Bogen, a social worker and himself an immigrant from Russia, was to help young people better understand their parents and appreciate the traditions of their homelands, thereby bridging the gap between generations. The venue was the Jewish Settlement House in Cincinnati, and the display included over five hundred artifacts borrowed from immigrants from some twenty-seven countries where Jews had lived. As noted by Jonathan Sarna, this exhibit was a polemic against "Anglo-conformity," which aimed to rob immigrants of their heritage. Also in 1913, the National Federation of Temple Sisterhoods established the Union Museum at Hebrew Union College (HUC) in Cincinnati, center of the Reform Movement in America. Thus, even before World War I, foundations had been laid for the collection, preservation, study, and interpretation of American Jewish history in both secular and specifically Jewish institutions.[5]

At Mid-Century

From the outbreak of World War I until the conclusion of World War II, growth in American organizations devoted to Jewish history was incremental and uneven. Both the Jewish Theological Seminary and the HUC projects continued to acquire important collections, mostly related to Jewish life in the Old World. The American Jewish Historical Society grew its collections as did a number of congregations led by Congregation Emanu-El in New York (1927). But one of the key developments was the move of the YIVO Institute for Jewish Research from its home in Vilna, Poland, to New York in 1940. YIVO was founded by scholars and intellectuals in 1925 to document and study eastern European Jewish life in all its aspects: language, history, religion, folkways, and material culture.

> World War Two and the Holocaust forced YIVO's relocation. Its collections in Vilna were looted by the Nazis, but with the help of the U.S. Army, YIVO was able to recover some of these materials and begin its work anew in America. . . . Today, YIVO's collections are the primary source of the documentary history of East European Jewry.[6]

In the years immediately after World War II new and re-invigorated institutions proliferated. In 1947, the Jewish Museum moved from the Jewish Theological Seminary Library to its own home in the Warburg Mansion on Fifth Avenue. Also in 1947, Jacob Rader Marcus (1896–1995) established the American Jewish Archives at HUC "to collect, preserve, and make available for research, materials on the history of Jews and Jewish communities in the Western Hemisphere, including data of a political, economic, social, cultural, and religious nature," and the next year HUC formally re-established its HUC Museum. In 1950, Temple Tifereth Israel in Cleveland, on the occasion of the congregation's centennial, formally established the first synagogue museum in America. Five years later, the Leo Baeck Institute was founded by leading German-Jewish émigré intellectuals who were determined to preserve the vibrant cultural heritage of German-speaking Jewry that was nearly destroyed in the Holocaust. And in 1957, B'nai B'rith opened a museum at its headquarters in Washington, DC.[7]

The most prominent interpretive effort of the 1950s, however, was the American Jewish Tercentenary (1954) celebrating "The Three Hundredth Anniversary of Jewish Settlement in the United States of America." The anniversary was celebrated with numerous exhibitions and events around the country, notably the national tercentenary exhibition titled *Under Freedom*, which was organized by The Jewish Museum in New York, where it opened on December 1, 1954, and traveled to the Smithsonian, where it was displayed beginning in May 1955. The introduction explains the goal of the planners:

> This exhibit seeks to tell the story of the Jews in America. It is a story of migration, of settlement, of devotion, of struggle, and of achievement. It is a record of the way in which one group of Americans, preserving their identity as they took their part in the making of our great Nation, have lived and advanced UNDER FREEDOM Inevitably, it is a tribute to the living faith of Judaism and to the living promise of America.[8]

Because the organizers sought to attract a broad audience, the exhibit described the Jewish experience as part of the fabric of American society. "It stressed the positive aspects of the social history of American Jews—the shared experience, the common denominator, the universal emotion—rather than occasional differences and controversies which are part of the life of a democracy." The American Jewish Tercentenary Committee also published a manual on exhibits as well as a "Community Manual" with various program materials, among them bibliographic references of America Jewish history developed by Jacob Rader Marcus, children's books and stories compiled by Philip Goodman (1911–2006), Executive Secretary of the Jewish Book Council, and even plans developed by Adele Gutman Nathan (1889–1986), a writer and producer of historical pageants, on "Producing Tercentenary Pageants."[9]

In honor of the tercentenary, there was another "official" major exhibition in Manhattan, which was on display at the Metropolitan Museum of Art during January and February of 1955. Though linked to the three hundredth anniversary year, the topic was not the American Jewish experience, but Judaism. As described on the book jacket of the companion volume *Jewish Ceremonial Art*, The Jewish Museum "helped the Metropolitan Museum of Art to organize an exhibit of Jewish ceremonial objects, under the title, 'Art of the Hebrew Tradition.'" The book is described as being the result of that exhibition and "like the exhibit, graphically portrays the cultural strands and the religious tradition which have united to mold and fashion the spirit of the American Jew."[10]

Tercentenary projects were sponsored by a variety of organizations. An exhibition of the works of Colonial American Jewish silversmith Myer Myers (1723–1795), was on view at the Brooklyn Museum (1954). Myers is the only Colonial American Jewish silversmith for whom a body of work is known. The American Jewish Historical Society and the Historical Society of Pennsylvania jointly sponsored an exhibition entitled *Prologue to a Tercentenary* which was displayed in Philadelphia in February to March 1954. On view were portraits, rare books, and manuscripts on Jewish participation in American life. And the Museum of Fine Arts in Boston displayed the Colonial era paintings of the Levy Franks family on loan from the American Jewish Historical Society. Altogether, the six portraits represent three generations of members of the Levy and Franks family—the earliest depictions of American Jews and the largest group of family portraits from the Colonial period (see also chapter 6).[11]

Approaching the American Bicentennial

In the generation after 1954, four major Jewish museums were established. The Magnes Museum in Berkeley, California, was opened in 1962; the Spertus Museum of Judaica in Chicago was opened in 1968; and Yeshiva University in New York formally established its museum in 1973. The fourth major museum was a bicentennial project, the Museum of American Jewish History (later the National Museum of American Jewish History) on Independence Mall in Philadelphia, two blocks from the Liberty Bell and Independence Hall. The new museum presented *The Role of the Jew in the Forging of the Nation* as its inaugural exhibition. The museum aimed "to show how Jews have participated in the development of a great nation." The exhibition, though fairly small, ranged widely with topics addressing different aspects of Jewish life from the first years of Jewish settlement through the early years of the republic.[12]

For the bicentennial, The Jewish Museum in New York presented *Americana from the Jewish Museum Collection*. In conjunction with the American Jewish Historical Society, the Rose Art Museum at Brandeis University presented *Two Hundred Years of American Synagogue Architecture* "with the intention . . . to trace the evolution of the American synagogue, and through it, develop a paradigm for the study of the history of American architecture." The Spertus Museum organized a complementary exhibition entitled *Faith and Form: Synagogue Architecture in Illinois*, which it was hoped would serve as a model for similar surveys in other states. Meanwhile, the Jewish Federation of Metropolitan Chicago sponsored an exhibition titled *My Brother's Keeper* at the Museum of Science and Industry, which focused on Jewish organizational life. An exhibition titled *Continuity and Change* honored both the bicentennial and the seventy-fifth anniversary of the founding of The Federation of Jewish Agencies of Greater Philadelphia. Installed at the Philadelphia Civic Center, *Continuity and Change* presented a history of the Jewish community of Philadelphia as seen through the prism of the Talmudic dictum "all Jews are responsible each for the other."[13]

In 1977, the National Foundation for Jewish Culture convened a meeting of the seven professionally staffed Jewish museums—The Jewish Museum (New York City), the HUC Skirball Museum (Los Angeles), B'nai B'rith National Museum (Washington, District of Columbia), Yeshiva University Museum (New York City), Spertus Museum of Judaica (Chicago), Magnes Museum (Berkeley), and the Museum of American Jewish

History (Philadelphia).[14] The participating museums established the Council of American Jewish Museums as a program of the National Foundation for Jewish Culture. The Council of American Jewish Museums has since grown to more than seventy member institutions in North America and is now an independent organization.[15]

Toward the 350th Anniversary of Jewish Life in America

The last two decades of the twentieth century saw an efflorescence of Jewish museums. One notable feature was the proliferation of local and regional projects, many of which focused on historic synagogues. The most ambitious program was that of the Museum of the Southern Jewish Experience (1986), based in Jackson, Mississippi, which has carried out research, programs, and preservation projects in twelve states. The Touro Synagogue (1763) in Newport, Rhode Island, the only surviving colonial synagogue; the Eldridge Street Synagogue (1887), the only purpose-built synagogue on the Lower East Side; the Lloyd Street Synagogue (1845), the first synagogue erected in Maryland, and the B'nai Israel Synagogue (1876), both in Baltimore; K.K. Beth Elohim (1841) in Charleston, South Carolina; the Vilna Shul (1919) in Boston; and the Adas Israel Synagogue (1876) in Washington, DC, have all been restored as historic landmarks. So was the Luis Moses Gomez Mill House (1714), the oldest surviving Jewish homestead in the United States.[16]

Figure 13.2 J. L. Asher and his family on the porch of their single-family home in Portland, Oregon, 1906.

Courtesy of the Oregon Jewish Museum and Holocaust Education Center. OJM 03911.

Jewish museum projects in many locales have incorporated historic preservation projects including the Jewish Museum of Maryland (Baltimore), the Jewish Historical Society of Greater Washington (District of Columbia), and the Jewish Museum of Florida in Miami. Other local history centers include the Oregon Jewish Museum and Center for Holocaust Education (1989/2014) in Portland, the Mizel Museum (1982) in Denver, the Maltz Museum of Jewish Heritage (2005) in Cleveland, the Breman Museum (1996) in Atlanta, and the Azeez Museum of Jewish Heritage in Woodbine, New Jersey (2003). A number of Jewish communities have established archives in cooperation with secular organizations, among them The Rauh Jewish History Program & Archives (1989) at the Heinz History Center in Pittsburgh; The Jewish Archives of the Washington State Jewish Historical Society at the University of Washington in Seattle; the Berman Upper Midwest Jewish Archives (Jewish Historical Society of the Upper Midwest) at the University of Minnesota in Minneapolis; and the Jewish Historical Society of South Carolina's Jewish Heritage Collection at the College of Charleston.

The best-known development in the late twentieth century was the opening of major museums devoted to the interpretation of the Holocaust, the destruction of European Jewry. The first major American project was the Los Angeles Museum of the Holocaust (1968), followed by the Holocaust Memorial Center in West Bloomfield, Michigan, which opened in 1984. The U.S. Holocaust Memorial Museum, just off the National Mall in Washington, DC, was opened in 1993—the same year as the Simon Wiesenthal Center and Museum of Tolerance in Los Angeles. They were followed in quick succession by Holocaust Museum Houston (1996) and the Museum of Jewish Heritage–A Living Memorial to the Holocaust (1997) in New York. Other important Holocaust centers were established in Toronto, Skokie, Illinois, Dallas, Montreal, and Los Angeles. Today there are more than 150 Holocaust centers and museums in North America, and many states now mandate study of the Holocaust as part of the required curriculum.[17] Significant collections of oral and video testimonies can be found at the Visual History Archive of the University of Southern California Shoah Foundation, the Fortunoff Video Archive for Holocaust Testimonies at Yale University, and the Steven Spielberg Film and Video Archive at the U.S. Holocaust Memorial Museum.[18]

A very different process was at work in the creation in 2000 of the new Center for Jewish History in New York City. Instead of proliferation, the Center for Jewish History represented an effort at consolidation and concentration of organizations and resources. The center brought together under a single roof the American Jewish Historical Society (1892), the YIVO Institute for Jewish Research (1925), the Leo Baeck Institute (1955), the Yeshiva University Museum (1973), and the American Sephardi Federation (1973). While each of the constituent organizations retains its own corporate identity and collections, the five partners share a reading room and public spaces. The Center for Jewish History is today the most comprehensive single resource for the study of Jews in American history and culture.[19]

In 2004, the celebration of 350 years of Jewish life in America brought together the American Jewish Historical Society, the American Jewish Archives, The Library of Congress, and the National Archives in a Commission for Commemorating 350 Years of American Jewish History. A major exhibition and catalogue, both titled *From Haven to Home*, were organized by the Library of Congress. Using the prisms of "haven" and "home," "the exhibition examines the intertwined themes, and sometimes conflicting aims, of accommodation, assertion, adaptation, and acculturation that have characterized the American Jewish experience from its beginnings in 1654 to the present day." The commission distributed a poster series on *Jewish Life in America* and helped to support publication of an atlas of American Jewish history prepared by Jonathan Sarna. The Celebrate 350 committee was also able to make use of the internet to encourage participation by communities nationwide through its website www.celebrate350.org. Activities celebrating the 350th were organized in every state, among them more than sixty exhibitions, some of which traveled to several states. For American Jews, the 350th was an opportunity to learn about their heritage; for non-Jewish Americans, the observance was a reminder of core principles that promise freedom and justice for all citizens.[20]

Jewish History Organizations as Resources

As this overview suggests, there are a substantial number of Jewish history organizations whose collections and expertise can provide useful information and guidance to public history professionals interested in interpreting American Jewish history and culture. Two of many good starting points are the American Jewish Historical Society (www.ajhs.org) and the American Jewish Archives (http://americanjewish archives.org), both of which collect nationally and both of which offer reference help online. Three other partner organizations at the Center for Jewish History (www.cjh.org), the YIVO Institute for Jewish Research, the Leo Baeck Institute, and the American Sephardi Federation hold collections relating to eastern European Jews, German Jews, and Sephardi Jews, respectively. The Jewish Women's Archive (http://jwa.org) documents the history of American Jewish women and publishes an online encyclopedia.

A listing of professionally staffed Jewish museums and related organizations in North America can be found on the website of the Council of American Jewish Museums, which is also an excellent portal to exhibitions (www.cajm.net). Contact the Council of American Jewish Museums executive director at cajmexec@gmail.com. The American Jewish Historical Society (see above) maintains a list of local Jewish historical societies and archives on its website. The Jewish Museum in New York (http://thejewishmuseum .org), the National Museum of American Jewish History in Philadelphia (http://www .nmajh.org), and the Skirball Cultural Center in Los Angeles (www.skirball.org) maintain outstanding collections of American Jewish art and material culture. The U.S. Holocaust Memorial Museum (www.ushmm.org) is the best starting point for information on all matters pertaining to the Holocaust, but see also the list of American Holocaust centers at the Association of Holocaust Organizations website (www.ahoinfo.org).

The bibliography (toward the end of the book), the overview and endnotes of this chapter, and the following list provide an introduction to the subject matter of Jewish museum exhibitions and catalogs on a wide range of themes. Listings of other public interpretive programs can be found at the website of Jewish American Heritage Month (www.jewishamericanheritagemonth.us), which maintains an interactive events calendar. None of these sources is intended to be comprehensive, but they are suggestive of the many possibilities open to interpreters of American Jewish history.

Interpretive Exhibitions in American Jewish Museums

The following list is suggestive rather than comprehensive. It is limited to interpretive exhibitions organized by Jewish museums in the past twenty-five years, preferably those with related catalogs or other publications. The exhibitions cover a wide range of topics in social and cultural history and make use of many material culture forms.

A Perfect Fit: The Garment Industry and American Jewry, 1860-1960 (Yeshiva University Museum, 2012). The role of Jews in the development of the national garment industry from the Civil War forward. Publication.

A Worthy Use of Summer: Jewish Summer Camping in America (National Museum of American Jewish History, 1993). The history of Jewish camping as a reflection of evolving culture and identity in the twentieth century. Publication.

Beyond Swastika and Jim Crow: Jewish Refugee Scholars at Black Colleges (Museum of Jewish Heritage, 2009). The story of German Jewish academics who came to the United States in the 1930s and found positions at historically black colleges and universities in the Jim Crow South.

Bridges and Boundaries: African-Americans and American Jews (The Jewish Museum, 1992). A look at how African Americans and Jews have related to each other during the past century in light of each one's cultural identity and experiences of marginality and dislocation over time. Publication.

California Dreaming: Jewish Life in the Bay Area from the Gold Rush to the Present (Contemporary Jewish Museum, 2011). Explores the pioneering spirit that led to model collaborations of Jews with other ethnic and cultural groups.

Chasing Dreams: Baseball and Becoming American (National Museum of American Jewish History, 2014). A look at baseball fans and the Jewish players who served them as athletic, cultural, and ethical role models. Publication.

Chosen Food: Cuisine, Culture, and American Jewish Identity (Jewish Museum of Maryland, 2011). Exploration of the ways what we eat and how we eat it are central to identity, a means to celebrate, to maintain tradition, and to mark transition. Publication.

Emma Lazarus: Poet of Exiles (Museum of Jewish Heritage, 2011). Story of the American Jewish poet who re-cast the Statue of Liberty as the "Mother of Exiles."

Enterprising Emporiums: The Jewish Department Stores of Downtown Baltimore (Jewish Museum of Maryland, 2001). An examination of the role of department stores in the history of urban life and the culture of consumption. Publication.

Entertaining America: Jews, Movies, and Broadcasting (The Jewish Museum, 2003). The story of first- and second-generation American Jews in the development of popular entertainment and mass culture. Publication.

Facing the New World: Jewish Portraits in Colonial and Federal America (The Jewish Museum, 1997). Portraits of Jewish sitters, demonstrating how the self is portrayed by means of cultural roles and images and how imagery and other modes of representation evolved over time. Publication.

Getting Comfortable in New York: The American Jewish Home, 1880-1950 (The Jewish Museum, 1990). A study of immigrant life and acculturation as reflected in the material culture of domestic life. Publication.

Greetings from Home: 350 Years of American Jewish Life (American Jewish Historical Society in cooperation with the Yeshiva University Museum and the American Sephardi Federation, 2005). An exploration of the relationship between American Jews and the places from which they, or their forebears, came. Publication.

Helena Rubinstein: Beauty Is Power (The Jewish Museum, 2014). The story of the cosmetics entrepreneur who blurred the boundaries between commerce, art, fashion, beauty, and design. Publication.

Jews@Work: 150 Years of Commerce and Industry (Oregon Jewish Museum and Center for Holocaust Education, 2005). The progress of Oregon Jews as they integrated into the life of the state, from their days as "greenhorns" to Oregonians and Americans.

Lives Lost, Lives Found: Baltimore's German Jewish Refugees, 1933-1945 (Jewish Museum of Maryland, 2004). The story of ordinary Jews who fled Nazi Germany and made new homes for themselves in Maryland. Publication.

Monsters and Miracles: A Journey Through Jewish Picture Books (Skirball Cultural Center and Eric Carle Museum of Picture Book Art, 2010). A survey of Jewish children's books from Bible stories to graphic novels. Publication.

Ours to Fight For: American Jews in the Second World War (Museum of Jewish Heritage, 2003). The Jewish experience of military life, encountering concentration camps, and American racial and ethnic relations in the pre- and postwar periods. Publication.

People of Faith, Land of Promise (Library of the Jewish Theological Seminary, 2003). A survey of Jewish life and Judaism in America. Publication.

Project Mah Jongg (Museum of Jewish Heritage, 2010). A study of how a game excited the American Jewish imagination and became a building block of community. Publication.

Revolution of the Eye: Modern Art and the Birth of American Television (The Jewish Museum, 2015). An exploration of how the pioneers of television—many of them young Jews—adopted avant-garde art as a source of inspiration.

Seeking Justice: The Leo Frank Case Revisited (Breman Museum of Jewish Heritage, 2008). Examines antisemitism in America through the murder case and trial that captured the attention of the nation and led to the lynching of a Jewish man in Marietta, Georgia, in 1915. Publication.

Sting Like a Maccabee: The Golden Age of the American Jewish Boxer, 1910-1940 (National Museum of American Jewish History, 2000). A look at some of the great American Jewish boxers. Publication.

The New Authentics: Artists of the Post-Jewish Generation (Spertus Museum, 2007). An exploration of the unstable, multiform categories of Jewish ethnic, religious, and cultural identity. Publication.

The Other Promised Land: Vacationing, Identity, and the Jewish American Dream (Jewish Museum of Maryland, 2005). A study of how the ways Jews construct their vacations reflect their values as individuals, families, and communities. Publication.

The Snowy Day and the Art of Ezra Jack Keats (The Jewish Museum, 2011). A retrospective of Keats' work, which helped to break the color barrier in mainstream children's books. Publication.

To Bigotry No Sanction: George Washington and Religious Freedom (National Museum of American Jewish History, 2012). Explores religious freedom in early America, featuring the historic correspondence between Washington and the Jewish community of Newport, Rhode Island. Publication.

Too Jewish? Challenging Traditional Identities (The Jewish Museum, 1996). An examination, through art, of how Jewish artists are struggling with the complexity of their difference and expressing their complicated personal identities. Publication.

Vida Sephardi: A Century of Sephardic Life in Portland (Oregon Jewish Museum and Center for Holocaust Education, 2014). The dramatic story of Portland's Sephardic Jews, who trace their origins to the Isle of Rhodes and Turkey and who found a new home in the Pacific Northwest. Publication.

We Call This Place Home: Jewish Life in Maryland's Small Towns (Jewish Museum of Maryland, 2002). A look at the contours and evolution of Jewish life in small towns and villages from the nineteenth century to the present. Publication.

Notes

1. Grace Cohen Grossman, "Jewish Museums in America," in *Encyclopaedia Judaica*, second ed. (Detroit: Macmillan Reference USA, 2007), 14, 631–34; Grace Cohen Grossman, *Jewish Museums of the World* (Westport, CT: Hugh Lauter Levin Associates, Inc., 2003). See also Elisabeth Kaplan, "We Are What We Collect, We Collect What We Are: Archives and the Construction of Identity," *The American Archivist* 63 (Spring/Summer 2000): 126–51, which uses the American Jewish Historical Society as a case in point.

2. John Maass, *The Glorious Enterprise: The Centennial Exhibition of 1876 and H.J. Schwarzmann, Architect-in-Chief* (Watkins Glen, NY: American Life Foundation, for the Institute for the Study of Universal History through Arts and Artifacts, 1973), 81, as cited in Barbara Kirshenblatt-Gimblett, *Destination Culture: Tourism, Museum, and Heritage* (Berkeley and Los Angeles: University of California Press, 1998), 88. Descriptions of some of the sculptures, all of which focused on patriotism, are to be found in J.S. Ingram, *The Centennial Exposition Described and Illustrated* (Philadelphia: Hubbard Bros., 1876). *Religious Liberty* is described on page 711. The history of the "Religious Liberty" sculpture is discussed more fully in Grace Cohen Grossman with Richard Eighme Ahlborn, *Judaica at the Smithsonian: Cultural Politics as Cultural Model* (Washington, DC: Smithsonian Institution Press, 1993), 8–9.

3. Cyrus Adler's long history at the Smithsonian and his involvement with the World's Columbian Exposition is to be found in *Judaica at the Smithsonian.*

4. "A Treasure Comes Home," *The JHU Gazette*, January 4, 2010, accessed January 10, 2016, http://archive.gazette.jhu.edu/2010/01/04/a-treasure-comes-home/.

5. Barbara Kischenblatt-Gimblett, *Destination Culture*, 111–17.

6. "History of YIVO," YIVO Institute for Jewish Research, accessed January 7, 2016, https://www.yivo.org/History-of-YIVO.

7. Grace Cohen Grossman, "Jewish Museums in America," 632f. See also American Jewish Archives website, accessed January 10, 2016, http://americanjewisharchives.org/about/; Leo Baeck Institute website, accessed January 10, 2016, https://www.lbi.org/about/about-lbi/.

8. *Under Freedom* (exhibition catalog) (The Jewish Museum, New York, 1954).

9. Tercentenary Archives, Yeshiva University Museum.

10. Stephen S. Kayser, editor, and Guido Schoenberger, associate editor, *Jewish Ceremonial Art* (The Jewish Publication Society of America, Philadelphia, 1955). Stephen S. Kayser (1900–1988) was an emigre German scholar who became the curator (and de facto director) of The Jewish Museum in 1947. He organized the "Under Freedom" exhibition with his wife, Louise Kayser, and also co-curated the exhibition at the Met with Guido Schoenberger (1891–1974), another emigre, formerly a curator at the Frankfurt Historical Museum.

11. Information on the Brooklyn and Philadelphia exhibitions is found in the archives of the Jewish Theological Seminary of America Communications Department, Box 62, Folder 25. Ellen Smith discusses the importance of this group in the context of other portraits of Jews in the period. Ellen Smith, "Portraits of a Community: The Image and Experience of Early American Jews," in Richard Brilliant, *Facing the New World: Jewish Portraits in Colonial and Federal America* (Munich and New York: Prestel, 1997), 9–13.

12. Grace Cohen Grossman, "WHO KNEW? The American Jewish Experience—Creating Our Own Image," unpublished conference paper originally presented at "Jewish LA—Then and Now," November 12, 2005, at the UCLA Center for Jewish Studies, 18f.

13. Gerald Bernstein and Gary Tinterow, *Two Hundred Years of American Synagogue Architecture* (Waltham, MA: the American Jewish Historical Society, 1976); Lauren Weingarden Rader, *Faith and Form: Synagogue Architecture in Illinois* (Chicago: Spertus College Press, 1976); *Continuity and Change* (Philadelphia: Federation of Jewish Agencies of Greater Philadelphia, 1976).

14. The Magnes Museum Collection has since been absorbed into the Library of the University of California, Berkeley, and the B'nai B'rith National Museum collection has been transferred to the Hebrew Union College in Cincinnati.

15. Council of American Jewish Museums website, accessed January 10, 2016, http://www.cajm.net/about-us/.

16. On the Institute for Southern Jewish Life, see http://www.isjl.org/; on the Touro Synagogue, see http://www.tourosynagogue.org/history-learning/synagogue-history; on the Eldridge Street Synagogue, see http://www.eldridgestreet.org/history/; on the Lloyd Street and B'nai Israel Synagogues, see http://jewishmuseummd.org/; on Beth Elohim, see http://www.kkbe.org/index.php?page=history; on the Vilna Shul, see http://www.vilnashul.org/about/our_history; on the Adas Israel Synagogue, see https://www.jhsgw.org/history/synagogue; on the Gomez Mill House, see http://www.gomez.org/about.html, all accessed January 10, 2016.

17. Association of Holocaust Organizations website, accessed January 12, 2016, http://www.ahoinfo.org/membersdirectory.html.

18. University of Southern California Shoah Foundation website, "Visual History Archive," accessed January 12, 2016, https://sfi.usc.edu/vha/about; Fortunoff Video Archive website, accessed January 12, 2016, http://web.library.yale.edu/testimonies/about; Steven Spielberg Film and Video Archive website, accessed January 12, 2016, http://www.ushmm.org/online/film/search/simple.php.

19. Center for Jewish History website, accessed January 12, 2016, http://www.cjh.org/p/2.

20. Alice Herman and Steven Bayme, "Celebrating the 350th" in D. Singer and L. Grossman, eds., *American Jewish Yearbook, 2006* (New York: American Jewish Committee, 2006), 115–32. The companion volume to *From Haven to Home* is Michael W. Grunberger, ed. *From Haven to Home: 350 Years of Jewish Life in America* (New York: Braziller, Inc. in association with the Library

of Congress, 2004). A complete listing of the events and exhibitions appears in *Celebrate350 Jewish Life in America 1654-2004: A Final Report*. Some of the exhibitions developed regionally include: *Stories Untold: Jewish Pioneer Women 1850-1910*, New Mexico; *U.S. Postage Stamps with a Jewish Twist*, Arizona; *Jewish Freemasons of the West*, Judah L. Magnes Museum, California; *Milch & Herring—Jewish Foodshops in New York*, Copia –the American Center for Winde Food & the Arts, California; *Driven Into Paradise: LA's European Jewish Emigres of the 1930s and 1940s*, Skirball Cultural Center; *Pioneering Jews of Colorado*, Rocky Mountain Jewish Historical Society and Beck Archives, Colorado; *The Story of Jewish Life in America*, Jewish Historical Society of Lower Fairfield County, Connecticut; *Half a Chance: Stories of Jewish Delawareans*, the Jewish Historical Society of Delaware; *Jewish Washington: Scrapbook of an American Jewish Community*, Jewish Historical Society of Greater Washington, DC (on view at the national Building Museum); *Jewish Mothers: Strength, Wisdom, Compassion*, Florida; *Florida's Pioneer Jewish Families* and *Treasures of Florida's Jews*, Jewish Museum of Florida; *Shalom Y'All: Images of Jewish Life in the American South* (photographs by Bill Aron), organized by the Museum of the Southern Jewish Experience, Goldring/Woldenberg Institute for Jewish Life, Mississippi; *My Kind of Town: Immigration to Chicago in the Twentieth Century*, Spertus Institute, Chicago; *Lives Lost, Lives Found: Baltimore's German Jewish Refugees, 1933-1945* and *Weaving Women's Words: Baltimore Stories*, The Jewish Museum of Maryland; *We Call This Place Home: Jewish Life in Maryland's Small Towns*, Maryland; *The Art of the Game: Jewish Athletes in America*, Starr Gallery at the Levnthal-Siman Jewish Community Center, Boston; *Jews @ Work: 150 Years of Commerce & Industry in Oregon,* Oregon Jewish Museum*; History of Jews in Tennessee*, Tennessee State Library and Archives; and *A Homeland in the West: Utah Jews Remembered*, Museum of Utah Art and History.

CHAPTER 14

TOWARD NEXT PRACTICE

Interpretation is not information; it is provocation. —Freeman Tilden

[I want] to construct a story as a space of exchange and invite the reader in. —Aleksander Hemon

W HY "NEXT PRACTICE" and not "Best Practice"? This book appears at a time of rapid cultural, demographic, communal, and technological change in America. The proliferation of digital media, new forms of learning, engagement with a multiplicity of voices, and generational shifts are having profound effects on our history organizations—and on our interpretations. Even the historiography of America, the bedrock of our narratives, is being re-thought amid changing circumstances. The history of Jews in America is no exception: like the histories of other communities and movements covered in this American Association for State and Local History series, American Jewish history is in play. We therefore need to re-consider our priorities in interpretation. We cannot stay with what is supposedly safe, agreed-upon, or "best," but instead need to work on a "next" iteration of practice that looks to the future.

At present, history organizations are increasingly faced by what Ronald Heifetz distinguishes as "adaptive challenges"—those for which there is no established solution, no clear path forward, and no external consultant who can offer tried-and-true remedies. Adaptive challenges are hard to address, "because they demand of organizational leaders that they question their own ingrained assumptions, admit contrary evidence, and deviate from established behavioral comfort zones." Moreover, embracing an adaptive approach entails new risks with unknown outcomes.[1]

Our history organizations will need to adapt to novelty. Anything less is likely to lead to short-term frustration and long-term failure. As has been observed, "Repeating the same behavior under changing circumstances leads to a muddle." We therefore need to move beyond "best practice," which however important will bring us to a muddle, and instead venture into "next practice"—the development of new ways of interpreting our shared histories with new methods and strategies that go beyond our comfort zones. Many of the ideas and suggestions that follow apply broadly to historical interpretation, but they also apply to the interpretation of American Jewish history. Conversely, what is proposed specifically about the interpretation of American Jewish history may apply also to historical interpretation more broadly.

Our Challenge: Key Indicators

Let's start with demography. Anyone working in a history organization is (or should be) aware of generational transition, historically one of the most powerful drivers of social, intellectual, and cultural change. The rapidity of generational change in our own time, however, appears to be forcing a revision in our definition of "generation." What was once a matter of twenty years or more seems to be getting shorter as successive youth cultures, each with its distinctive aspirations and behaviors, pile one on top of another. Moreover, many of the life events and relationships—independence, marriage, and so on—that in the past have shaped each generation's life trajectory and allowed us to identify the characteristics of that generation have been radically challenged or disrupted.

Meanwhile longer-term trends like the "browning" of America are having broad and often challenging effects on our society, culture, and polity. So-called white Americans (which ostensibly includes American Jews) will soon become a minority in America, though remaining the largest minority in a plurality of minorities. Demographic changes, augmented by recent trends in the distribution of income and wealth, are making it harder and harder to speak of "mainstream" or even middle-class America. And all these changes are having an impact on American Jews. A growing number of Jews intermarry, increasing the population of multicultural families within the Jewish community, while also growing the number of non-Jewish Americans who have Jewish relatives and their own forms of Jew-ish identity.

The 2013 Pew Research Center study of American Jewry, "Portrait of Jewish Americans," confirmed that the Jewish community is today more plural and more fragmented than in any other decade of the postwar period.[2] Established organizations—synagogues, Jewish federations, and Jewish community centers—are pressing to reinvent themselves. Meanwhile, a variety of alternative organizations are springing up to engage cultural Jews, the unaffiliated, young adults, and other segments of the community. Jewish philanthropy is also going through a generational change, and giving priorities as they relate to cultural organizations are very much in flux at both the national and local levels. The sheer volume of new Jewish start-ups and pop-ups across North America is ample testimony to the significance of generational change.

Generational change directly affects our history organizations and our narratives. A recent study by Humanities Indictors shows that visits to historic sites declines by generation and by age, and while some or even many of the younger generation surveyed may expand their interest in history over time, we have to be aware of the need to address what may well be a growing problem and to cultivate our audiences just as any business attends to its current and future markets.[3] In a broader context, the number of liberal arts degrees has long been in decline, whereas the number of vocational degrees has risen among recent college graduates. The number of courses and majors in history and the humanities dropped rapidly in the 1970s and have stayed depressed since then. Future visitors to our museums and sites are likely to bring narrow contexts and a diminished base of information to our institutions and to our historical narratives, presenting a serious interpretive challenge. These cautions, of course, apply with special force to the interpretation of American Jewish history, about which most Americans (including many American Jews) are lamentably ignorant, despite a growing number of Jewish Studies courses on American college campuses.

And then there is the matter of the interpretive revolution. As Rick Beard notes, for at least two generations, from the 1960s into the 1990s, public history professionals were energized by the findings of the New Social History (augmented by postmodernist cultural history). Some expressions of the interpretive revolution generated controversy, including brouhahas over *Mining the Museum* (Maryland Historical Society, 1992) and *The Last Act: The Atomic Bomb and the End of World War II* (National Air and Space Museum, 1994/1995).[4] However, writes Beard, "by the end of the 1990s, attention and energy within the history museum community began to shift, from focusing on interpretive content to enhancing the visitor experience and reexamining the balance of power between institutions and their audiences." This shift in focus has had profound effects on our field. History organizations, accustomed to listening to scholars and funders such as the National Endowment for Humanities, are now faced with the challenge of listening to users, many of whom have come of age in a time of pervasive digital media. These new audiences arrive at our museums and sites with very different expectations than did their predecessors: they are seeking experiences that draw on all their senses, that are highly interactive, and that are authentic to *them* as well as to the historical narrative. Finding new ways to facilitate meaning-making *with* our users grows ever more complex.[5]

The Need for Adaptive Leadership

We have entered what Janet Carding has termed "a perpetual beta world." In the next generation of interpretation, museums and sites will need to embrace both "public curation," a process that invites visitors to help shape the content of our narratives, and inclusivity, which implies a multiplicity of voices and stories. Indeed, these challenges may be at odds with each other: one is about going deeper, the other about going broader. To address either or both successfully, argues Benjamin Filene, requires a broader range of skills than in the past: "Museum professionals will need to supplement command of historical content with expertise at interpreting, facilitating, engaging, listening, and learning with their visitors."[6] However, many museums and sites are unprepared to reexamine their missions, challenge their assumptions, or even reflect on their practice. Even those public history professionals who would like to do so are lacking in support, training, and tools. Responding to the complex challenges of ongoing change requires skill sets and attitudes that are not part of conventional training nor of on-the-job experience. What our museums and sites will need are adaptive leaders, capable not only of doing things better, but of doing things *differently*.[7]

As public history professionals, we will need to discover and learn new ways. If we want our organizations to be responsive and resilient, we are going to have to become more open and more nimble, enablers and not just providers. Our practice and our perspectives will have to change—at a time when financial constraints and risk-aversion tend to limit our options. Still, our organizations and our leaders will need to seek out adaptive responses rather than merely technical solutions. We may need to let go of some of the very things that drew us to our professions in the first place, including assumptions about our authority and the utility of "treasures" as interpretive devices. To meet the challenges of shared authority and diverse constituencies will require us to experiment relentlessly and to reflect rapidly on what we are learning, devising new kinds of metrics to measure our effectiveness. The Levine Museum of the New South in Charlotte, North Carolina, for example, counts how many organizations it has partnered with each year and how many other organizations in the community have invited the museum to collaborate.[8]

Let's take the interpretation of American Jewish community life as a case in point. If we want to reach a new or underserved community, its members will have to be in the room. This means not only familiarizing ourselves with the scholarly literature, but inviting members of Jewish communities to participate in the planning, development, and marketing of programs. Diversifying our staff and our board will help to ensure that our interpretive activities are relevant and accessible to Jewish and other constituents. But even if we cannot add a Jewishly knowledgeable colleague to our staff or elect a Jewish scholar or communal leader to our organization's board, we can find ways to engage relevant human resources. Creating inclusive ethnic, religious, and cultural advisory bodies, working groups, and collaborations will take time and effort. But these efforts are likely to pay off in terms of community engagement and alliances that can transcend an immediate project and inform our practice over the long run, as evidenced by many of the case studies presented previously. Taking on new partnerships, however complicated, can take our narratives to new levels of meaning.[9]

Next Narratives:
The Stories We Tell Ourselves and Others

Richard Rabinowitz, founder-president of American History Workshop, has remarked that over the past forty years the interpretive emphasis in history museums and historic sites has shifted—broadly speaking—from displays of stuff, to stories of place, community, and identity. These trends suggest that in our perceptions and in our practices, public history professionals are responding to a pervasive search, not only for meaning, but also a sense of belonging—to a tradition, to a culture, or to a people. Object and place will remain key resources in our interpretive repertoire, but they are likely to be harnessed to narratives about community. Objects and places are often assumed to "speak for themselves," and their physicality is often evocative. But our new narratives will probably center more on the stories we and our communities use to give meaning and value to our things and our places, not to speak of other, unfamiliar places and things.[10]

The historiography of American Jewry over the next generation is likely to open some interesting opportunities for narratives set in larger, transnational contexts. Much work is already underway on Jews in the context of the Atlantic world, and we can expect new studies of Jews in the global context as well. In the Colonial period, we find mercantile and kin networks that criss-cross the Atlantic, linking North America, Europe, the Caribbean, and Africa. In the nineteenth century, we find dense ethnic neighborhoods crowded with first-generation Jewish immigrants that range from East Coast cities to London, Buenos Aires, and Johannesburg. And in the most recent century, cultural currents sweep across the ocean, engaging Jewish intellectual and artistic leaders in a series of dynamic conversations. By adopting wider perspectives and a comparative approach—as Adam Mendelsohn does in *The Rag Race: How Jews Sewed Their Way to Success in America and the British Empire*—we can see more clearly commonalities that are obscured by use of national categories and distinctions that are hidden by masses of detail or ungrounded generalizations. Transnational perspectives will also help us to shed geographic determinism and other assumptions that have long held ethnic assumptions in place.[11]

New historical studies are also like to extend and deepen a trend toward the comparative within American society. Hasia Diner's book on Italian, Irish, and Jewish foodways in the age of migration, *Hungering for America*, is one model of how we can proceed. In the past generation, a spate of books on Jews and race has appeared, including Eric Goldstein's *The Price of Whiteness: Jews, Race, and American Identity*, Karen Brodkin's *How Jews Became White Folks and What That Says About Race in America*, Victoria Hattam's *In the Shadow of Race: Jews, Latinos, and Immigrant Politics in the United States*, and Matthew Frye Jacobson's *Whiteness of a Different Color: European Immigrants and the Alchemy of Race*. As we focus more on the cultural, social, and commercial interactions between Jews and other American minorities, our stories are likely to get denser, more interesting, and more meaningful both for Jews and for other communities (as well as more contested).[12]

We still have much to learn about the micro-histories of American Jews. Several new studies of the Jewish ethnic economy have appeared just recently (as described in chapter 8), but there are many dimensions of the ethnic experience still waiting for substantial research. The process of continual Jewish renewal in America, described by Jonathan Sarna and others, will be worth exploring, in part because it is such a marked feature of American Jewish history and in part because it parallels renewal movements among other American religious, ethnic, and racial groups. The subject of Jewish power, long neglected, is ripe for new consideration. The complex world of Jewish philanthropy and communal welfare is only now beginning to receive sustained critical attention, although both have long been cited as models for other communities. Jewish engagement and leadership in a variety of postwar efforts to "repair the world" will be fruitful areas of interrogation, especially because so many Americans are active in local, regional, and national movements to reform or recast our attitudes and behaviors toward everything from local issues like curbing our dogs to global warming.[13]

Choice, Context, and Causality

Historians and public history professionals have long cited a plethora of reasons as to why it is important and useful to study history. Mantras like "Knowing where we come from," "Learning the lessons of the past," and "Understanding the people and movements that have shaped our world" are commonplace in our field. Most of these maxims, however, seem to be facile and incorrect—what does it even mean to "learn the lessons of the past," for example—as well as self-serving. We should also be more skeptical about our "educational" function, at least in the narrow sense of imparting to visitors a lot of information (let alone ideas). Museum modalities—particularly exhibitions—tend to be exceptionally inefficient (and often costly) transmitters of information. And we all know how rarely we hear about museum visits as transformative events in people's lives. Some visitors may come to us looking for a way to make peace with the past, which, as Ken Yellis has observed, is a very different need and a very different process from making sense of the past.

For the most part, visitors come to our museums and sites looking for confirmation not provocation, nostalgia not new understanding, reassurance not challenges. We will want to consider a somewhat different view of what engaging history is about. Encountering people in historical circumstances—talking and thinking about where historical characters were and how they reacted to their situations—is a humanistic endeavor. As we understand more about the diversity of human experiences, we generally (though not always) develop a degree of empathy for others (or even the Other). As we learn about the choices that people have made in history, we begin to understand contingency and agency. And as we encounter the welter of circumstances in which all people, then and now, function, we begin to develop an appreciation for the complex challenges of our own time and place. This is not easy knowledge, but it can be affirming, liberating, and empowering.[14]

In short, our history organizations are likely to be important to the degree that they help our users to understand that *they (and we) are actors in history*—with all that this entails. As David Hackett Fischer writes, contingency is about "people making choices, and choices making a difference in the world." It is therefore our primary responsibility to construct interpretive narratives that tell "a story of real choices that living people actually made . . . [within] a dense web of contingency . . . [and] a structure of relationships."[15] Encouraging our users to confront the dense web of contingency and to take personal responsibility for their choices comports well with our growing sense of civic engagement and our missions as community institutions. One leading indicator of this idea in action is the burgeoning number of history museums and historic sites in the International Coalition of Sites of Conscience and their efforts to engage audiences in issues of truth, justice, and reconciliation. The Sites of Conscience motto might well serve as a mantra for many of our museums and sites: "Memory to Action."[16]

Ideas about contingency, choice, and agency are especially germane, as it happens, to the interpretation of American Jewish history. In America, from the very start of Jewish settlement, Jews were confronted by an unprecedented liberty, including the freedom to opt out as Jews. In a sense, all American Jews have been and are today "Jews by choice."

Figure 14.1 Boston Jews demonstrate for fair labor practices in the food industry, one manifestation of the "New Jewish Food Movement."

Photograph by Carole Counihan. Courtesy of Carole Counihan and the Jewish Museum of Maryland. JMM CP 84.2011.1.

That American Jews have chosen to express their Jewish identity in varied and sometimes radically different ways underscores the agency of American Jews—and by implication, of other Americans as well. And, despite conventional narratives of helpless Jews driven from their age-old homes in Europe, arriving ignorant and impoverished on these shores, and struggling desperately to adjust, most Jewish arrivals in America—like many contemporary immigrants—made conscious (and often informed) decisions to emigrate, arrived with skills and networks of support, and chose for themselves the degrees and ways that they would adapt and acculturate. Like all newcomers, immigrant Jews have faced challenges; like all minorities, they have suffered a share of prejudice and discrimination. But Jewish grumbling and rumbles of dissatisfaction—many of which have become classics of American shtick—should not hide from view the fact that Jews *decided* to come, *decided* to stay, and *decided* how to shape their lives as Jews and as Americans.

Of course, the historical story is complicated. Each wave of Jewish newcomers, each generation of immigrants, faced different circumstances and had to choose among different alternatives. Jews coming to South Carolina in the 1750s confronted a society, economy, polity, and culture different from that met by Jews from the former Soviet Union coming in the 1990s. Even as people arrived or moved to new places, America itself was in motion, so the range of circumstance and choices was itself evolving—sometimes slowly and imperceptibly and sometimes with extraordinary rapidity.

Giving visitors a sense of circumstance and choice is challenging work, but it can be done. Certainly it can be done suggestively, if not exhaustively. At the Tenement

Museum, for example, educators provide visitors just enough context to engage their minds and imaginations. But visitors do not need to understand the nuances of Shabbat observance or the intricate details of kashrut to begin considering how challenge and choice might have played out in real time among the members of an actual household. What the Tenement Museum can do and does so well—inspiring an awareness of contingency and choice—others can do also.

We come, then, to causality. People seem always to want to know the "why" of things. How did Jews become so prominent in mass culture, marketing, and the media? Conspiracy theorists and bigots have their explanations, but most people would just as soon have narratives that deal in real-life terms. The correlation of Jews as the largest minority in New York at the very moment that the metropolis was becoming the world center of culture and communication makes for a more realistic, accurate, and satisfying story. It is also a more human and therefore accessible story. Even the story of Jews and the making of Hollywood is more engaging when one considers the business outlook and sometimes philistinism of the early movie moguls. And, then, there is the matter of unintended consequences—choices that led to unanticipated outcomes or set off a chain of tangentially related events.

We live in a time when human agency has an increasingly important role in shaping our world. In fact, Edward O. Wilson and others argue that we are now living in the Anthropocene, "a new geological epoch in which the entire global environment has been altered by humanity."[17] Occasionally, natural forces, and particularly natural disasters, bring home to us the limits of our ability to control the world around us. But now, more than in any earlier epoch of human history, we must come to grips with our role as decision-makers and as agents of change. Some of our contemporaries have launched concrete initiatives to address environmental issues—reducing their carbon footprint or re-thinking their patterns of personal consumption. Jews across the country, for example, are transforming their foodways by cultivating their own foodstuffs, avoiding processed foods, and promoting new standards for ethical eating.[18] If there is one thing to be learned from the 2016 election cycle, it is that in the United States today we have activists of many stripes and colors working to encourage changes in our culture, society, economy, and polity—that is, in how humanity perceives and shapes the world today and tomorrow. It is our task and our privilege to embrace American activism, past and present, on small scales and large, and to encourage our constituents to reflect on contingency, choice, and consequences.

Interpretive Concepts and Strategies

Having focused on the rapid pace of contemporary change, it would be foolhardy to prescribe specific templates for the next generation of narratives and interpretive programs. However, there are some promising ideas and practice already out in the world that can serve as springboards for "next practice" projects in our museums and historic sites. The strategies described here will not be universally applicable, needless to say. But these projects emphasize choice and human agency in history. They exemplify the spirit of next practice in user-centered, experiential institutions. While these strategies are suggestive, not comprehensive, they illustrate approaches that history museums and historic sites can emulate and adapt, with appropriate, site-specific variations.

Interpret American Activism: A little more than a year ago, the Museum of the City of New York opened a gallery devoted to "Activist New York." The idea is simple: tell the stories of New Yorkers who chose to advocate or agitate on behalf of some cause of local import. The gallery comprises fourteen distinct issues ranging from the abolition of slavery to biker's rights and covers a period from the early nineteenth century to the present. Each of the fourteen sections includes a statement of the issue and the contending forces, provides a timeline of activists, identifies individuals and organizations who were involved, and displays a variety of objects, images, texts, and media that reflect the debates. Touch-screens in each section enable users to learn more about organizations involved in that particular issue and to nominate other organizations for inclusion in an accessible database. This project is civic engagement by example.

"Activist New York" neither takes sides nor encourages visitors to adopt a preferred point of view. Instead, the museum makes it clear that New York (and by implication, other communities) has a long history of continual agitation over public affairs. The project also informs visitors that a variety of people, some rich and powerful, some not, were active campaigners in their time and place. Without ever using words like "contingency" or even "choice," the exhibition invites viewers to reflect on both the merits of different issues and the value of civic engagement. Jewish Americans, incidentally, have a long history of engagement in civic affairs (and arguments), as well as a significant involvement in radical politics, so this is a good way into American Jewish history.

Since every community has its public issues and a history of civic debates, not to speak of its gadflies, agitators, cranks, mavericks, and rebels, the concept of a dedicated space or ongoing program that interprets local activism could have wide application. The issues might differ substantially from one community to another and so might the mode of presentation. An institution strapped for space or money could feature one civic issue at a time, rotating in new instances of community activism as resources become available. Also, the treatment of each example of public debate could be more or less elaborate: a few items from the collection (or borrowed from community bulletin boards) could suffice, if the interpretive framework were made clear; a mock debate using speeches or sermons drawn from local newspapers and similar sources offers another variant. Developing interpretive programs devoted to local activism creates opportunities to partner with local organizations who are engaged in the public discourse to draw in area residents who have a stake in the outcome. If we want to be seen as authentic and relevant to our communities while underlining the theme of widespread agency, activism provides a direct route to those ends.

Making Story a Space of Exchange: The Lower East Side Tenement Museum, as described in chapter 3, has long experience in situation-setting and inviting visitors to share in the storytelling. Each restored apartment at 97 Orchard Street and each of the three new apartments to be opened at 103 Orchard Street is arranged and furnished to a specific moment in time and in the life of a particular family. A museum educator leads each group into the space, where they outline a concrete social situation. Typically, the historical family is confronted with a complex decision to which they must respond. It is here that visitors are invited to speculate on how the family would react and encouraged to share stories of their own families' responses in similar or analogous circumstances.

The Tenement Museum approach rests on the bedrock of decades of research and planning. At this point, the museum has identified more than seven thousand former residents of 97 Orchard Street, studied surviving records, gathered oral histories, and brought into play leading experts on everything from immigration policy to immigrant foodways. All of this prep work is premised on ownership of an actual tenement building in its original configuration, a resource few other organizations will command or have the means to document so thoroughly. But many history organizations do have one or more period rooms at their disposal—and use of sophisticated projection systems can turn an ordinary gallery or public space into a simulated period room, as is done at the Cooper Hewitt Museum's Immersion Room Installation in New York. It might even be possible to set a stage in minimalist fashion rather than literally, as is done in many theatrical productions, which convey an impression of archaeologically correct detail rather than reconstructing it. Whatever space is staged, it can be used, with minimal alterations, to tell the stories of multiple people—Jews one moment and Irish the next, Scandinavians today and Italians tomorrow.

Stagecraft aside, the key is bringing the audience into the storytelling. This requires both skilled situation-setting, grounded in historical research, and skilled facilitation. The latter is a matter of intensive training. The results can be rewarding—visitors engaged in animated conversation, based on their own family stories and their personal histories. The writer Aleksander Hemon says that he wants "to construct a *story as a space of exchange* [italics added] and invite the reader in, rather than saying to the reader, 'Now shut up, because I have a story to tell.' I am saying—at least I like to think I am—'Come on, join in, we are telling stories here.'"[19] This is a kind of storytelling practice to which we might aspire.

Practicing Audacious Hospitality: Like most peoples, Jews have a long-enduring and elaborate tradition of hospitality. The ancient rabbis regarded the patriarch Abraham "as the paragon of hospitality, because of his reception of wayfarers in Genesis 18. His position at the entrance of his tent in the midday heat is interpreted as a proactive seeking out of passing travelers."[20] Similarly, Christians have found an analogous model in the Rule of St. Benedict, which guided medieval monks to welcome people with needs and to create a safe space for them to express those needs. Building on this idea, both Christian and Jewish religious bodies have begun to promote the idea of "audacious hospitality" or "radical hospitality." And in a 2015 paper, Juliana Ochs Dweck, curator of academic engagement at the Princeton Art Museum, proposed that museums, too, might engage in audacious hospitality.

Describing her own practice within her primary community—in this instance, Princeton University—Dweck writes:

Figure 14.2 Visitors at the Lower East Side Tenement Museum, in the kitchen of an apartment at 97 Orchard Street, conversing with a museum educator.

Courtesy of the Lower East Side Tenement Museum.

In Princeton, hospitality sometimes comes in the form of interdisciplinarity: the inclusion, crossing, or melding of multiple academic fields. Four years ago, I began convening something called the Museum Voices Colloquium to bring together faculty and students from a range of academic departments to develop strategies for interpreting objects in the collections. Sometimes, the gatherings are formal, meeting multiple times to work towards a future exhibition through visits to art storage, honing of exhibition checklists, and analysis of object and themes. . . .

I often turn to a more informal and maybe preferred format. I invite a handful of faculty and graduate students from a range of disciplines (art history, philosophy, neuroscience) to come to the museum for an informal, one hour-long conversation about a single work of art. . . . I generally need to assure participants multiple times that there are no preparations, no presentations, no strings attached; just conversation. Sitting together on folding chairs in front of a single object, this community gains direct access to the Museum's collections. We tend to meet on a Monday when the museum is closed to the public; this ensures we'll have quiet, but it also—incidentally and fortuitously—makes for a particularly intimate experience. And I think this intimacy really has been the crux of this program's success. Intimacy both with unfamiliar colleagues and intimacy with museum objects.[21]

Hospitality can take many forms, of course. The Minneapolis Institute of Art, for example, invites visitors to participate in its "Living Rooms" project, including a Period Room Initiative. The Minneapolis Institute of Art restyled its Queen Anne Room as a Jane Austen–themed reading room and invited guests to sit and enjoy some of the books Austen read, wrote, or inspired.[22] At the Jewish Museum of Maryland, we invited six to ten guests in for a monthly luncheon conversation, during which we welcomed their ideas about future exhibitions, took them on a guided tour of our collections areas, and asked them for the names of other people we might want to invite to lunch. Another variant: invite visitors to bring in an object, image, or text that is important to them and set up a series of talking circles, in which people can tell stories about the objects that are meaningful to them.

Audacious hospitality requires effort, but the engagement, intimacy, and immediacy of the experience can produce a host of new narratives and ideas, deep connections, and a corps of community ambassadors. Equally important, audacious hospitality gives us a chance to get feedback on the stories we tell ourselves (as well as those we relate to our communities). Thinking about our purpose and mission, our value to the community, is becoming daily a more important and energizing activity.

Bringing Historians into Our Spaces: By now, many public history professionals know a good deal about the 1992/1993 project *Mining the Museum* at the Maryland Historical Society. This is just one among many projects where artists have been invited into a museum and given the opportunity to organize an exhibition, using the host institution's collections, which offers a new or different interpretation. In recent years, the Metropolitan Museum of Art has created a variant on this theme, which they describe as follows:

> Ever since it was founded in 1870, The Metropolitan Museum of Art has been a place where artists come to gain inspiration from works of art from their own time and place, and also from across time and cultures. *The Artist Project* is an online series in which we give artists an opportunity to respond to our encyclopedic collection. From March 2015 to June 2016, we will invite 120 artists—local, national, and global—to choose individual works of art or galleries that spark their imaginations. In this online series, artists reflect on what art is, what inspires them from across [five thousand] years of art, and in so doing, they reveal the power of a museum and The Met. Their unique and passionate ways of seeing and experiencing art encourage all museum visitors to look in a personal way. Over the course of six seasons, *The Artist Project* will share the perspectives of one hundred and twenty artists with the public, telling us what they see when they look at The Met.[23]

The Met Artist Project seems to offer a simple, but effective, way to introduce new narratives into our history organizations. But instead of inviting artists to comment on our collections, it might be productive to create a historian project. All we need to do is invite in a few historians—from area colleges and universities, from the local high school, or from among the many community and family historians—and ask them to ruminate on our collections. It would be fun—and perhaps surprising—to learn what is meaningful or enjoyable to them and why. An obvious variant would be to invite them to select an object from stored collections. The Met employs online modalities to share the artists' interpretations, and this could work also for our history organizations. But we could also post their comments on exhibition texts beside or beneath object labels, on audio guides, on bulletin boards, or on printed guidesheets. And, for best effect, it would be fun to post multiple comments on individual objects or assemblages, giving our visitors an insight into the construction of our interpretations.

Seeking the Macrocosm in the Microcosm: There is a lot of talk today about community curation of interpretive projects. The best-known of these is probably the exhibition development process developed by the Wing Luke Museum in Seattle. In that institution, staff act as facilitators of the planning, research, and design process, and the resulting exhibitions are closely linked to the interests and concerns of the community depicted. Their process is well-documented or codified and is being replicated to one degree or another by other organizations such as the Asian Arts Initiative in Philadelphia.[24]

A very different way to approach new practice and next narratives is to focus in on a small number of people, usually a group linked in some fashion such as a family, a class of students, or one block in a neighborhood. This kind of approach is especially useful with regard to small Jewish communities or small communities where only a few Jews live (or have lived). Benjamin Filene, director of public history at the University of North Carolina Greensboro, argues that "the closely observed story" can lead to "new ways of understanding the past, handling source limitation, building partnerships, and reaching audiences." Instead of speaking in generalities, a micro-history project can empower audiences "to identify personally with our historical subjects, to connect with history's humanity."[25]

Filene describes several projects he carried out with his students at University of North Carolina Greeensboro. One project tracked down students at an African American private school who were photographed in 1963. With intensive effort, the research team identified thirty-five of the forty-six students and conducted interviews with eighteen of them. Their first-person stories became the basis for an exhibition about the school—and about a critical period in desegregation. A second project concentrated on local segregated mill villages built by the Cone family of prominent Jewish industrialists. The project team conducted forty oral interviews and created a community "Memory Map." Then the project team visited a dozen sites in Greensboro inviting people to add their comments and anecdotes to the map. With these rich resources, the students created a van tour of the neighborhood narrated by the students and former mill village residents. A third project, which also resulted in an exhibition, concentrated on local mill villages built by the Pomona Terra Cotta Manufacturing Company in the 1880s.[26]

Quite aside from their modest scale and low cost, micro-projects can lead to new narratives and fresh insights. In Filene's case studies, for example, the project team discovered a surprising degree of nostalgia for life during segregation. This may reflect the interconnectedness and mutual dependence of life in small, segregated communities, where everyone relied on family, neighbors, and friends to deal with the vicissitudes of everyday life. A close look, in high focus, reveals greater complexity, "allowing room for contradictions, surprises, and challenges to received opinions," as Filene puts it. The micro-history approach also makes use of new sources and "allows room for other people to be recognized as experts." Ultimately, small-scale, tightly focused projects can help our history organizations to build new relationships, "making one's institution visible and present in the lives of its constituents."[27]

In Conclusion

Just as the past overflows with myriad events, experiences, and stories, so, too, does our tool kit of ways to share those stories with our communities. Despite a plethora of distractions and a dearth of formal education in history, most people remain fascinated with the past. More, they are interested in how people recover and relate the stories of past events.[28] Over the next generation, new models and tools will continue to proliferate. Many of these will be technical innovations like the Digital Pen project that is being piloted by a number of leading museums. Efforts to augment reality using new digital technologies will become more readily available, and as the costs of new technology declines, these new modalities will become more common and more useful to history organizations. Meanwhile, the amount of historical information accessible via the Internet will continue to grow at very high rates. In fact, our history organizations may discover an important new role in helping users to sort out accurate, reality-based digital information and ideas from that which is false.[29]

Story will continue to trump all our other modes of interpretation, as it always has in the past. Our challenge in telling the stories of American Jews, or of any other religious, ethnic, cultural, or racial group, will be twofold. First, we ourselves are going to need to deepen our understanding of what makes a compelling story—whether it is the story of our institution or the story of one interesting person—and what is the best and most engaging way of telling that story. Our second challenge will be, in an age of visitor-centered experiences, how to leave enough room in our storytelling so that our users and constituents can share their narratives as well. Facilitating a multiplicity of next narratives while negotiating the boundaries of our authority will be very challenging. But if we elect to adapt to novelty, the history of our plural communities will continue to engage, inform, and inspire.

Notes

1. Ronald A. Heifetz, *Leadership without Easy Answers* (Cambridge, MA: Belknap Press of Harvard University Press, 1994). See also Karen Whitehair, "We are All in This Together: Twenty-First-Century Museum Leadership," *History News* 71, no.1 (Winter 2016), 18–23.

2. Pew Research Center website, "Portrait of Jewish Americans," October 1, 2013, accessed March 8, 2016, http://www.pewforum.org/2013/10/01/jewish-american-beliefs-attitudes-culture-survey/.

3. Humanities Indicators website, "Historic Site Visits," February 2016, accessed March 8, 2016; http://www.humanitiesindicators.org/content/indicatordoc.aspx?i=101. "With each birth cohort, Americans of all ages have been less likely to visit historic sites. . . . As people aged they

were less likely to visit a historic site." See also Heidi Tworek, "The Real Reason the Humanities are 'in Crisis,'" *The Atlantic*, December 18, 2012, accessed March 28, 2016; Michael Berube, "The Humanities, Declining: Not According to the Numbers," *The Chronicle of Higher Education*, July 13, 2013, accessed March 28, 2016.

4. Ken Yellis, "Fred Wilson, PTSD, and Me: Reflections on the History Wars," *Curator* 52, no. 4 (October 2009), 333–48; Edward Linenthal, "Anatomy of a Controversy," in Edward Linenthal and Tom Engelhardt, eds., *History Wars: The Enola Gay and Other Battles for the American Past* (New York: Metropolitan, 1996), 9–62.

5. Rick Beard, "Is It Time for Another Revolution?" *History News* 70, no. 2 (Spring 2015), 22–27. See also Bill Adair, et al., eds., *Letting Go? Sharing Historical Authority in a User-Generated World* (Philadelphia: Pew Center for Arts & Heritage, 2011); Nina Simon, *The Participatory Museum* (Santa Cruz, CA: Museum 2.0, 2010).

6. Benjamin Filene, "Letting Go? Sharing Historical Authority in a User-Generated World," *History News* 66, no. 4 (Autumn 2011), 12.

7. Grantsmakers in the Arts website, Richard Evans, "Adapting to Novelty," *Gia Reader* 21, no. 3 (Fall 2010), accessed March 29, 2016, http://www.giarts.org/article/entering-upon-novelty; Richard Evans, "Building a Resilient Sector," *GIA Reader* 24, no.3 (Fall 2013), accessed March 29, 2016, http://www.giarts.org/article/building-resilient-sector. See also Janet Carding, "Changing Museums," CODE/WORDS: Technology and Theory in the Museum, September 8, 2015. https://medium.com/code-words-technology-and-theory-in-the-museum/changing-museums -f82c98f33f92#.ts8iksvd1.

8. Benjamin Filene, "Passionate Histories: 'Outsider' History-Makers and What They Teach Us," *The Public Historian* 34, no. 1 (February 2012), 11–33.

9. American Association of Museums, *Mastering Civic Engagement: A Challenge to Museums*, (Washington, DC: American Association of Museums, 2002); Doug Borwick, ed,. *Building Communities, Not Audiences: The Future of the Arts in the United States* (Winston-Salem, NC: ArtsEngaged, 2012).

10. See Richard Rabinowitz, *Curating America: Journeys Through Storyscapes of the American Past* (Chapel Hill: University of North Carolina Press, 2016).

11. Adam D. Mendelsohn, *The Rag Race: How Jews Sewed Their Way to Success in America and the British Empire* (New York: New York University Press, 2015). See also Hasia Diner, "The Local and the Global: Lombard Street and the Modern Jewish Diaspora," in Deborah R. Weiner, et al., eds., *Voices of Lombard Street: A Century of Change in East Baltimore*, (Baltimore: Jewish Museum of Maryland, 2007), 10–21.

12. Hasia R. Diner, *A Hungering for America: Italian,* Irish, *and Jewish Foodways in the Age of Migration* (Cambridge, MA: Harvard University Press, 2001). See also Matthew Frye Jacobson, *Special Sorrows: The Diasporic Imagination of Irish, Polish, and Jewish Immigrants to the United States* (Cambridge, MA: Harvard University Press, 1995); Christopher M. Sterba, *Good Americans: Italian and Jewish Immigrants during the First World War* (New York: Oxford University Press, 2003).

13. See, for example, Pam Korza, et al., *Civic Dialogue, Arts & Culture: Findings from Animating Democracy* (Washington, DC: Americans for the Arts, 2005); and also the International Coalition of Sites of Conscience training program, "Essential Engagement: Dialogic Interpretation."

14. Rebecca Herz, Adam Nilsen, and Miriam Bader, "Exploring Empathy: Research on a Hot (But Tricky) Topic," Museum Questions website, May 4, 2015, https://museumquestions. com/2015/05/04/exploring-empathy-research-on-a-hot-but-tricky-topic/.

15. David Hackett Fischer, *Washington's Crossing* (New York: Oxford University Press, 2004), 364.

16. Sites of Conscience website, accessed March 29, 2016, http://www.sitesofconscience.org/.

17. See, for example, Edward O. Wilson, *Half Earth: Our Planet's Fight for Life* (New York: Liveright Publishing, 2016).

18. Mary L. Zamore, "Ethical Eating: The New Jewish Food Movement," in Avi Y. Decter and Juliana Ochs Dweck, eds., *Chosen Food: Cuisine, Culture, and American Jewish Identity* (Baltimore: Jewish Museum of Maryland, 2011), 84–97.

19. Quoted in Ayana Mathis, "Bookends," *New York Times Book Review*, June 29, 2015, 39.

20. My Jewish Learning website, "Jewish Hospitality," accessed March 30, 2016, http://www.myjewishlearning.com/article/jewish-hospitality/.

21. Juliana Ochs Dweck, "Audacious Hospitality and the Museum Object: Connecting Collections and Communities," paper presented at the Council of American Jewish Museums Idea Lab, May 21, 2015.

22. Minneapolis Institute of Art website, "Living Rooms," accessed March 8, 2016, http://new.artsmia.org/living-rooms/jane-austen-reading-room/.

23. The Metropolitan Museum of Art website, "The Artist Project," accessed March 30, 2016, http://artistproject.metmuseum.org/about/.

24. Wing Luke Asian Museum, *Community-Based Exhibition Model Handbook* (Seattle: Wing Luke Museum, n.d.).

25. Benjamin Filene, "Power in Limits: Narrow Frames Open Up African American Public History," in Max van Balgooey, ed., *Interpreting African American History and Culture at Museums and Historic Sites* (Lanham, MD: Rowman & Littlefield, 2015), 135.

26. Ibid., 136–39.

27. Ibid., 140–43.

28. Filene, "Passionate Histories," 14–19.

29. Lee C. McIntyre, *Respecting Truth: Willful Ignorance and Standards of Evidence in the Internet Age* (New York: Routledge, 2015).

BIBLIOGRAPHY

Adair, Bill, Benjamin Filene, and Laura Koloski, eds. *Letting Go? Sharing Historical Authority in a User-Generated World*. Philadelphia: Pew Center for Arts & Heritage, 2011.

Alexander, Edward P., and Mary Alexander. *Museums in Motion: An Introduction to the History and Functions of Museums*. Second ed. Nashville: AltaMira Press, 2007.

American Association of Museums. *Mastering Civic Engagement: A Challenge to Museums*. Washington, DC: American Association of Museums, 2002.

Anderson, Gail, ed. *Reinventing the Museum: The Evolving Conversation on the Paradigm Shift*. Second ed. Nashville: AltaMira Press, 2012.

Ariel, Yaakov. *Evangelizing the Chosen People: Missions to the Jews in America, 1880-2000*. Chapel Hill: University of North Carolina Press, 2000.

Baldwin, Neil. *Henry Ford and the Jews: The Mass Production of Hate*. New York: Public Affairs.

Barkai, Avraham. *Branching Out: German-Jewish Immigration to the United States, 1820-1914*. New York: Holmes and London, 1994.

Bergeron, Anne, and Beth Tuttle. *Magnetic: The Art and Science of Engagement*. Washington, DC: The AAM Press, 2013.

Berman, Lila Corwin. *Metropolitan Jews: Politics, Race, and Religion in Postwar Detroit*. Chicago: University of Chicago Press, 2015.

Boris, Staci. *The New Authentics: Artists of the Post-Jewish Generation*. Chicago: Spertus Press, 2007.

Borwick, Doug, ed. *Building Communities, Not Audiences: The Future of the Arts in the United States*. Winston-Salem, NC: ArtsEngaged, 2012.

Braunstein, Susan L., and Jenna Weissman Joselit, eds. *Getting Comfortable in New York: The American Jewish Home, 1880-1950*. Bloomington: Indiana University Press, 1991.

Cohen, Naomi W. *Encounter with Emancipation: The German Jews in the United States, 1830-1914*. Philadelphia: Jewish Publication Society, 1984.

Cohen, Naomi Wiener. *Jews in Christian America: The Pursuit of Religious Equality*. New York: Oxford University Press, 1992.

Cohen, Steven M., and Paula E. Hyman, eds. *The Jewish Family: Myths and Reality*. New York: Holmes and Meier, 1986.

Cutler, Irving. *The Jews of Chicago: From Shtetl to Suburb*. Urbana: University of Illinois Press, 1996.

Decter, Avi Y., and Juliana Ochs Dweck, eds. *Chosen Food: Cuisine, Culture, and American Jewish Identity*. Baltimore: Jewish Museum of Maryland, 2011.

Decter, Avi Y., and Melissa Martens, eds. *The Other Promised Land: Vacationing, Identity, and the Jewish American Dream*. Baltimore: Jewish Museum of Maryland, 2005.

Diner, Hasia R. *A Hungering for America: Italian, Irish, and Jewish Foodways in the Age of Migration.* Cambridge, MA: Harvard University Press, 2001.

———. *A Time for Gathering: The Second Migration, 1820-1880.* Baltimore: Johns Hopkins University Press, 1992.

———. *Her Works Praise Her: A History of Jewish Women in America from Colonial Times to the Present.* New York: Basic Books, 2002.

———. *Roads Taken: The Great Jewish Migrations to the New World and the Peddlers Who Forged the Way.* New Haven: Yale University Press, 2015.

———. *The Jews of the United States, 1654 to 2000.* Berkeley: University of California Press, 2004.

Dinnerstein, Leonard. *Antisemitism in America.* New York: Oxford University Press, 1994.

Donim, Hayim Halevy. *To Be A Jew: A Guide to Jewish Observance in Contemporary Life.* New York: Basic Books, 1972.

Dreams of Freedom. Philadelphia: National Museum of American Jewish History, 2011.

Eisen, Arnold M. *The Chosen People in America: A Study in Jewish Religious Ideology.* Bloomington: Indiana University Press, 1983.

Encyclopaedia Judaica. Second ed. (22 vols). Detroit: Macmillan Reference USA, 2007.

Erdman, Harley. *Staging the Jew: The Performance of an American Identity.* New Brunswick: Rutgers University Press, 1997.

Faber, Eli. *A Time for Planting: The First Migration, 1654-1820.* Baltimore: Johns Hopkins University Press, 1992.

———. *Jews, Slaves, and the Slave Trade: Setting the Record Straight.* New York: New York University Press, 1998.

Falk, John H. *Identity and the Museum Visitor Experience.* Walnut Creek, CA: Left Coast Press, 2009.

Falk, John H., and Lynn D. Dierking, *Learning from Museums: Visitor Experiences and the Making of Meaning.* Nashville: AltaMira Press, 2000.

Falk, Karen, and Avi Y. Decter. *We Call This Place Home: Jewish Life in Maryland's Small Towns.* Baltimore: Jewish Museum of Maryland, 2002.

Farber, Roberta Rosenberg, and Chaim I. Waxman, eds. *Jews in America: A Contemporary Reader.* Hanover, NH: University Press of New England, 1999.

Feingold, Henry L. *A Time for Searching: Entering the Mainstream, 1920-1945.* Baltimore: Johns Hopkins University Press, 1992.

Ferris, Marcie Cohen, and Mark I. Greenberg, eds. *Jewish Roots in Southern Soil: A New History.* Hanover, NH: University Press of New England, 2006.

Ferris, Marcie Cohen. *Matzoh Ball Gumbo: Culinary Tales of the Jewish South.* Chapel Hill: University of North Carolina Press, 2005.

Friedman, Reena Sigmund. *These Are Our Children: Jewish Orphanages in the United States, 1880-1925.* Hanover, NH: University of New England Press, 1994.

Gamm, Gerald. *Urban Exodus: Why the Jews Left Boston and the Catholics Stayed.* Cambridge: Harvard University Press, 1999.

Garland, Libby. *After They Closed the Gates: Jewish Illegal Immigration to the United States, 1921-1965.* Chicago: University of Chicago Press, 2014.

Geffen, Rela M., ed. *Celebration and Renewal: Rites of Passage in Judaism.* Philadelphia: Jewish Publication Society, 1993.

Gerber, David, ed. *Anti-Semitism in American History.* Urbana: University of Illinois Press, 1986.

Glazier, Jack. *Dispersing the Ghetto: The Relocation of Jewish Immigrants across America.* Ithaca: Cornell University Press, 1989.

Glenn, Susan A. *Daughters of the Shtetl: Life and Labor in the Immigrant Generation*. Ithaca: Cornell University Press, 1990.

Goldman, Karla. *Beyond the Synagogue Gallery: Finding a Place for Women in American Judaism*. Cambridge: Harvard University Press, 2000.

Goldstein, Eric L. *The Price of Whiteness: Jews, Race, and American Identity*. Princeton: Princeton University Press, 2006.

Grunberger, Michael W., ed. *From Haven to Home: 350 Years f Jewish Life in America*. Washington, DC: Library of Congress, 2004.

Gurock, Jeffrey S., ed. *American Jewish History* (8 vols.). New York: Routledge, 1998.

———. *From Fluidity to Rigidity: The Religious Worlds of Conservative and Orthodox Jews in Twentieth Century America*. Ann Arbor, MI: Frankel Center for Judaic Studies, 1998.

———. *Orthodox Jews in America*. Bloomington: Indiana University Press, 2009.

Hoberman, J., and Jeffrey Shandler, eds. *Entertaining America: Jews, Movies, and Broadcasting*. New York: The Jewish Museum, 2003.

Hyman, Paula E., and Deborah Dash Moore, eds. *Jewish Women in America: An Historical Encyclopedia* (2 vols.). New York: Routledge, 1998.

Jacobson, Matthew Frye. *Special Sorrows: The Diasporic Imagination of Irish, Polish, and Jewish Immigrants to the United States*. Cambridge: Harvard University Press, 1995.

———. *Whiteness of a Different Color: European Immigrants and the Alchemy of Race*. Cambridge: Harvard University Press, 1998.

Jewish Women's Archive Encyclopedia.

Joselit, Jenna Weissman. *A Perfect Fit: Clothes, Character, and the Promise of America*. New York: Metropolitan Books, 2001.

———. *The Wonders of America: Reinventing Jewish Culture, 1880-1950*. New York: Hill and Wang, 1994.

Joselit, Jenna Weissman, with Karen S. Mittelman, eds. *A Worthy Use of Summer: Jewish Summer Camping in America*. Philadelphia: National Museum of American Jewish History, 1993.

Kahn, Ava Fran, ed. *Jewish Life in the American West: Perspectives on Migration, Settlement, and Community*. Los Angeles: Autry Museum of Western Heritage; Seattle: University of Washington Press, 2002.

Kahn, Ava F., and Adam Mendelsohn, eds. *Transnational Traditions: New Perspectives on American Jewish History*. Detroit: Wayne State University Press, 2014.

Kassof, Anita, Avi Y. Decter, and Deborah R. Weiner, eds. *Lives Lost, Lives Found: Baltimore's German Jewish Refugees, 1933-1945*. Baltimore: Jewish Museum of Maryland, 2004.

Katz, Steven T., ed., *Why Is America Different? American Jewry on Its 350th Anniversary*. Lanham, MD: University Press of America, 2010.

Kaufman, David. *Shul with a Pool: The "Synagogue-Center" in American Jewish History*. Hanover, NH: University Press of New England, 1999.

Klapper, Melissa R. *Jewish Girls Coming of Age in America, 1860-1920*. New York: New York University Press, 2005.

Kleeblatt, Norman L., ed. *Too Jewish? Challenging Traditional Identities*. New York: The Jewish Museum, 1996.

Korza, Pam, and Barbara Schaffer Bacon. *History as Catalyst for Civic Dialogue: Case Studies from Animating Democracy*. Washington, DC: Americans for the Arts, 2005.

Korza, Pam, and Barbara Schaffer Bacon. *Museums and Civic Dialogue: Case Studies from Animating Democracy*. Washington, DC: Americans for the Arts, 2005.

Kraemer, David C. *Jewish Eating and Identity through the Ages*. New York: Routledge, 2007.

————, ed. *The Jewish Family: Metaphor and Memory*. New York: Oxford University Press, 1989.

Kugelmass, Jack, ed. *Key Texts in American Jewish Culture*. New Brunswick: Rutgers University Press, 2003.

Lambert, Joshua N. *American Jewish Fiction*. Philadelphia, Jewish Publication Society, 2009.

Lehman, David. *A Fine Romance: Jewish Songwriters, American Songs*. New York: Nextbook, 2009.

Linzer, Norman, et al., eds. *Crisis and Continuity: The Jewish Family in the 21st Century*. Hoboken, NJ: Ktav Publishing House, 1995.

Martens, Melissa, and Avi Y. Decter, eds. *Enterprising Emporiums: The Jewish Department Stores of Downtown Baltimore*. Baltimore: Jewish Museum of Maryland, 2001.

Mayo, Louise A. *The Ambivalent Image: Nineteenth-Century America's Perception of the Jew*. Rutherford, NJ: Fairleigh Dickinson University Press, 1988.

Melnick, Jeffery. *A Right to Sing the Blues: African Americans, Jews, and American Popular Song*. Cambridge: Harvard University Press, 1999.

Mendelsohn, Adam D. *The Rag Race: How Jews Sewed Their Way to Success in America and the British Empire*. New York: New York University Press, 2015.

Moore Deborah Dash. *To the Golden Cities: Pursuing the American Jewish Dream in Miami and L.A.* New York: Free Press, 1994.

————. *Urban Origins of American Judaism*. Athens, GA: University of Georgia Press, 2014.

Morawska, Ewa. *Insecure Prosperity: Small-Town Jews in Industrial America, 1890-1940*. Princeton: Princeton University Press, 1996.

Nadell, Pamela S., and Jonathan D. Sarna, eds. *Women and American Judaism: Historical Perspectives*. Hanover, NH: University Press of New England, 2001.

————. *Women Who Would Be Rabbis: A History of Women's Ordination, 1889-1985*. Boston: Beacon Press, 1998.

Ochs, Vanessa L. *Inventing Jewish Ritual*. Philadelphia: Jewish Publication Society, 2007.

People of Faith, Land of Promise: 350 Years of Jewish Life in America. New York: Library of the Jewish Theological Seminary, 2003.

Perlmann, Joel. *Ethnic Differences: Schooling and Social Structure among the Irish, Italians, Jews, and Blacks in an American City, 1880-1935*. New York: Columbia University Press, 1988.

Pew Research Center. "Portrait of Jewish Americans."

Postal, Bernard, and Lionel Koppman. *A Jewish Tourist's Guide to the U.S.* Philadelphia: Jewish Publication Society of America, 1954.

Prell, Riv-Ellen. *Fighting to Become Americans: Jews, Gender, and the Anxiety of Assimilation*. Boston: Beacon, 1999.

————. *Prayer and Community: The Havurah in American Judaism*. Detroit: Wayne State University Press, 1989.

————, ed. *Women Remaking American Judaism*. Detroit: Wayne State University Press, 2007.

Rabinowitz, Richard. *Curating America: Journeys Through Storyscapes of the American Past*. Chapel Hill: University of North Carolina Press, 2016.

Raphael, Marc Lee, ed. *The Columbia History of Jews and Judaism in America*. New York: Columbia University Press, 2008.

————. *Profiles in American Judaism: The Reform, Conservative, Orthodox, and Reconstructionist Traditions in Historical Perspectives*. New York: Harper and Row, 1988.

Rogin, Michael, *Blackface, White Noise: Jewish Immigrants in the Hollywood Melting Pot*. Berkeley: University of California Press, 1996.

Rogoff, Leonard. *Down Home: Jewish Life in North Carolina*. Chapel Hill: University of North Carolina Press, 2010.

———. *Homelands: Southern Jewish Identity in Durham and Chapel Hill, North Carolina*. Tuscaloosa: University of Alabama Press, 2001.

Rogow, Faith. *Gone to Another Meeting: The National Council of Jewish Women, 1893-1993*. Tuscaloosa: University of Alabama Press, 1993.

Rosenzweig, Roy, and David Thelen. *The Presence of the Past: Popular Uses of History in the American Past*. New York: Columbia University Press, 2000.

Sachar, Howard M. *Diaspora: An Inquiry into the Contemporary Jewish World*. New York: Harper & Row, 1985.

———. *A History of the Jews in America*. New York: Random House, 1992.

Sarna, Jonathan D. *American Judaism: A History*. New Haven: Yale University Press, 2004.

———. *When General Grant Expelled the Jews*. New York: Nextbook, 2012.

Schrerer, Barbara A. *Becoming American Women: Clothing and the Jewish Immigrant Experience, 1880-1920*. Chicago: Chicago Historical Society, 1994.

Schultz, Kevin M. *Tri-Faith America: How Catholics and Jews Held Postwar America to Its Protestant Promise*. Oxford: Oxford University Press, 2011.

Seltzer, Robert M., and Norman J. Cohen, eds. *The Americanization of the Jews*. New York: New York University Press, 1995.

Shapiro, Edward S. *A Time for Healing: American Jewry Since World War II*. Baltimore: Johns Hopkins University Press, 1992.

Simon, Nina. *The Participatory Museum*. Santa Cruz, CA: Museum 2.0, 2010.

Sorin, Gerald. *A Time for Building: The Third Migration*. Baltimore: Johns Hopkins University Press, 1992.

Soyer, Daniel. *Jewish Immigrant Associations and American Identity in New York, 1880-1939*. Cambridge: Harvard University Press, 1997.

Spieler, Marlena. *Jewish Festival Food: Eating for Special Occasions*. London: Lorenz Books, 2015.

Sterba, Christopher M. *Good Americans: Italian and Jewish Immigrants during the First World War*. New York: Oxford University Press, 2003.

Strassfeld, Michael. *The Jewish Holidays: A Guide and Commentary*. New York: Harper & Row, 1985.

Svonkin, Stuart. *Jews against Prejudice: American Jews and the Fight for Civil Liberties*. New York: Columbia University Press, 1997.

Tenenbaum, Shelly. *A Credit to Their Community: Jewish Loan Societies in the United States, 1880-1945*. Detroit: Wayne State University Press, 1993.

Toll, William. *The Making of an Ethnic Middle Class: Portland Jewry over Four Generations*. Albany: State University of New York Press, 1982.

Wechsler, Harold S. *The Qualified Student: A History of Selective College Admissions in America*. New York: Wiley, 1977.

Weiner, Deborah R. *Coalfield Jews: An Appalachian History*. Urbana: University of Illinois Press, 2006.

Weiner, Deborah R., Anita Kassof, and Avi Y. Decter, eds. *Voices of Lombard Street: A Century of Change in East Baltimore*. Baltimore: Jewish Museum of Maryland, 2007.

Weissbach, Lee Shai. *Jewish Life in Small-Town America*. New Haven: Yale University Press, 2003.

Wenger, Beth S. *History Lessons: The Creation of American Jewish Heritage*. Princeton: Princeton University Press, 2010.

———. *The Jewish Americans: Three Centuries of Jewish Voices in America*. New York: Doubleday, 2007.

Wertheimer, Jack. *A People Divided: Judaism in Contemporary America*. New York: Basic Books, 1993.

Whitfield, Stephen J. *American Space, Jewish Time*. Hamden, CT: Archon Books, 1988.

———. *In Search of American Jewish Culture*. Hanover, NH: University Press of New England, 1999.

———. *Voices of Jacob, Hands of Esau: Jews in American Life and Thought*. Hamden, CT: Archon Books, 1984.

Zurawik, David. *The Jews of Prime Time*. Hanover, NH: University Press of New England, 2003.

INDEX

Page references for figures are *italicized*.

CONTRIBUTORS

Avi Decter (principal author) is the managing partner of History Now, a consulting firm that specializes in interpretive planning and program development. He has been active in public history for more than forty years and has had major roles in developing new museums including the U.S. Holocaust Memorial Museum, National Civil War Museum, Jewish Museum of Maryland, Louisville Slugger Museum and Visitor Center, Liberty Hall Museum, Boott Cotton Mill Museum at Lowell National Historical Park, and the Liberty Bell Pavilion at Independence National Historical Park. He is a graduate of the Seminar for Historical Administration and a past board chair of the Council of American Jewish Museums.

Zev Eleff, PhD ("The Jewish Encounter with Discrimination, Tolerance, and Pluralism") is chief academic officer of Hebrew Theological College in Skokie, Illinois. He is also assistant professor of Jewish history at Touro College and University System. Eleff has written a number of books and scholarly articles in the field of American Jewish history. His most recent books, *Who Rules the Synagogue: Religious Authority and the Formation of American Judaism* (Oxford University Press) and *Modern Orthodox Judaism: A Documentary History* (Jewish Publication Society) both appeared in 2016.

Joshua J. Furman ("Across the Ocean and Across Town") is the Stanford and Joan Alexander Postdoctoral Fellow in Jewish Studies at Rice University. He received his PhD in modern Jewish history from the University of Maryland in 2015. Furman is a specialist in American Jewish history, with research interests in family life and Jewish education since World War II. His work has been supported by research fellowships from the Center for Jewish History and the American Jewish Archives.

Grace Cohen Grossman, PhD ("Jewish Museums as Interpretive Resources") began her career as an archivist at the American Jewish Historical Society. She then served as curator at the Spertus Museum for a decade and curator for Judaica and Americana at the Skirball Museum for thirty years. She has also had an ongoing association with the Smithsonian Institution's National Museum of American History, where she was most recently a Goldman Sachs Fellow. Currently she is a contract acquisitions curator at the U.S. Holocaust Memorial Museum. Her publications include *Jewish Art*; *Judaica at the Smithsonian: Cultural Politics as Cultural Model*; and *Jewish Museums of the World.*